Gender & Nation

Nira Yuval-Davis

SAGE Publications
London • Thousand Oaks • New Delhi

© Nira Yuval-Davis 1997

First Published 1997. Reprinted 1998, 2000

SAGE Publications Ltd
6 Bonhill Street
London EC2A 4PU

SAGE Publications Inc
2455 Teller Road
Thousand Oaks, California 91320

SAGE Publications India Pvt Ltd
32, M-Block Market
Greater Kailash – I
New Delhi 110 048

British Library Cataloguing in Publication data

A catalogue record for this book is
available from the British Library

    ISBN 0 8039 8663 7
    ISBN 0 8039 8664 5 (pbk)

Library of Congress catalog record available

Typeset by M Rules
Printed in Great Britain by The Cromwell Press Ltd,
Trowbridge, Wiltshire

This book is dedicated to Gul, Alain, Ora and to my wonderful friends who've enabled me to go on, and sometimes to even dance

Politics and Culture

A Theory, Culture & Society series

Politics and Culture analyses the complex relationships between civil society, identities and contemporary states. Individual books will draw on the major theoretical paradigms in politics, international relations, history and philosophy within which citizenship, rights and social justice can be understood. The series will focus attention on the implications of globalization, the information revolution and postmodernism for the study of politics and society. It will relate these advanced theoretical issues to conventional approaches to welfare, participation and democracy.

SERIES EDITOR: Bryan S. Turner, *Deakin University*

EDITORIAL BOARD

J.M. Barbalet, *Australian National University*
Mike Featherstone, *University of Teeside*
Stephen Kalberg, *Boston University*
Carole Pateman, *University of California, Los Angeles*

Also in this series

Welfare and Citizenship
Beyond the Crisis of the Welfare State?
Ian Culpitt

Citizenship and Social Theory
edited by Bryan S. Turner

Citizenship and Social Rights
The Interdependence of Self and Society
Fred Twine

The Condition of Citizenship
edited by Bart van Steenbergen

National Formation
Towards a Theory of Abstract Community
Paul James

Gender & Nation

CONTENTS

PREFACE

Writing this book has been, in some ways, a culmination of many years of work – both academically and politically – in the areas of gender and ethnic studies. The original impetus arose from studying gender relations in Israel and the ways they have related to the Zionist settlement project and the Israeli–Arab conflict. I then moved on to study gender and ethnic divisions in South East London and later turned to examine them in other settler societies as well as in Europe. A particularly significant landmark quite early on in the journey has been the international workshop I organized in 1984 on *Women and National Reproduction* in which I had, for the first time, the opportunity to share with 'significant others' from other parts of the globe my ideas on women as 'bearers of collectivities' (Yuval-Davis, 1980) and out of which eventually came the volume *Woman–Nation–State* (Yuval-Davis and Anthias, 1989). Just before the present book went to press, another important signpost emerged. In a much larger conference on *Women, Citizenship and Difference*, also organized at the University of Greenwich in July 1996 (see the special issue of *Feminist Review* (autumn 1997) based on this conference and the volume co-edited by Pnina Werbner and myself for Zed Books (1988)), we celebrated the growth of consciousness and insight in this arena of study, at a time when so many new and urgent questions, both political and theoretical, continue to emerge.

As is already clear from the above, my journey, which has involved personal travel, displacement, shifting and 'anchoring' (rather than 'rerooting'), would not have been possible without the many companions I have had for shorter or longer stretches. I can't possibly name them all here, but in particular I want to mention the other members of the Khamsin collective, especially Avishai Ehrlich; my friend and colleague Floya Anthias with whom I've worked on the Gender and Ethnic Divisions project and on several books; the members of Women Against Fundamentalism, especially Gita Sahgal and Pragna Patel; as well as other friends and colleagues from near and far without whom the ideas and narratives in this book could never have been constructed in the ways they have been. To mention some of them in alphabetical order: Martha Ackelsberg; Alison Assiter; Gill Bottomley; Avtar Brah; Stephen Castles; Amrita Chhachhi; Cynthia Cockburn; Phil Cohen; Clara Connolly; Cynthia Enloe; Robert Fine; Marieme Helie-Lucas; Deniz Kandiyoti; Helma Lutz; Helen Meekosha; Maxine Molineux; Ephraim Nimni; Ruth Pearson; Jindi Pettman; Annie Phizaclea; Ann Phoenix; Shula Ramon; Nora Rätzel; Paula Rayman; Israel Shahak; Max

Silverman; Elaine Unterhalter; Gina Vargas; Peter Waterman; and Pnina Werbner.

Special thanks are due to Daiva Stasiulis (of the Lithuanian connection) with whom I worked on the book *Unsettling Settler Societies* (Stasiulis and Yuval-Davis, 1995) and who went over the present text in its raw state. Her many useful comments, as well as those of Bryan Turner, the series editor, and the Sage editors, Karen Phillips and Kiren Shoman, have vastly improved the book. I also want to thank my students in the MA in Gender and Ethnic Studies at the University of Greenwich and of the short course Gender and Nation I taught in 1994 at the Institute of Social Studies in The Hague, with whom I have used various drafts of the book for teaching purposes, and who, in response, generously shared with me experiences and insights from their own standpoints. The responsibility for the way it is, however, is of course all mine.

Given everything else which needs to be done, the writing of this book would not have been possible were it not for the breathing space given to me for a few months as a Morris Ginsburg Fellow at the London School of Economics in 1991; as a Visiting Research Fellow at the Institute of Social Studies in The Hague (in 1992); and as a result of the QR allowance which released me from some weekly teaching hours at the School of Social Sciences (under the benevolent headship of Mike Kelly) at the University of Greenwich (1993–6). I am indebted to all these institutions. Most of the inspiration, however, whenever I got 'stuck' in the writing, came while gazing at the sea waves from 'Romani' in Happisburgh, Norfolk.

The last, or probably first, thanks are due of course to Alain, who has constantly been there for me. And to Gul – who did his best – but my English never could come up to his standards.

Although this book was written as a coherent whole, parts of the various chapters were published as separate papers elsewhere ('Gender and nation', *Ethnic and Racial Studies*, 1993, 16(4): 621–32; 'Women as biological reproducers of "the nation"', *Women's Studies International Forum*, 19(12): 17–24; 'Women, citizenship and difference', *Feminist Review*, 1997 (Autumn); 'Women, ethnicity and empowerment', *Feminism and Psychology*, 1994, 4(1): 179–98).

1

THEORIZING GENDER AND NATION

If the Woman does not want to be Mother, Nation is on its way to die.[1]

The mothers of the nation, the womenfolk as a whole, are the titans of our struggle.[2]

This book is about gender relations and the ways they affect and are affected by national projects and processes. The main focus of the book is on the positions and positionings of women, but men and masculinity are correspondingly central to the book's focus. As one of my sociology teachers at the Hebrew University, Eric Cohen, used to say, 'Talking about women without talking about men, is like clapping hands with one hand only.' Although I have come to reject much of what I was taught during my studies there all those years ago, I still agree with the sentiment of this statement. 'Womanhood' is a relational category and has to be understood and analysed as such. Moreover, one of the main arguments of the book is that constructions of nationhood usually involve specific notions of both 'manhood' and 'womanhood'.

The epistemological framework of the book is based on the recognition that knowledge is situated (Haraway, 1990), and that knowledge emanating from one standpoint cannot be 'finished' (Hill-Collins, 1990). Although I have read – before and during the writing of this book – many books and articles written by scholars and activists from different standpoints, I am aware, of course, that the perspective of the book is unavoidably affected by my own specific positioning, and that a high percentage of the concrete examples with which I have chosen to illustrate many of the theoretical points are based on events which took place in the societies in which I have lived (mainly Israel and Britain) or in those of my close colleagues and friends (mentioned in the preface). I do believe, however, that 'unfinished' is not the same as 'invalid', and this has given me the courage to actually write this book.

Most of the hegemonic theorizations about nations and nationalism (for example, Gellner, 1983; Hobsbawm, 1990; Kedourie, 1993; Smith, 1986; 1995), even including, sometimes, those written by women (for example, Greenfeld, 1992), have ignored gender relations as irrelevant. This is most remarkable because a major school of nationalism scholars, the 'primordialists' (Geertz, 1963; Shils, 1957; van den Berghe, 1979), have seen in nations a natural and universal phenomenon which is an 'automatic' extension of kinship relations.

And yet, when discussing issues of national 'production' or 'reproduction', the literature on nationalism does not usually relate to women. Instead, it relates to state bureaucrats or intellectuals. Materialist analyses, such as those by Amin (1978) and Zubaida (1989), have given primary importance to state bureaucracy and other state apparatuses in establishing and reproducing national (as well as ethnic) ideologies and boundaries. Although national and ethnic divisions also operate within the civil society, it is the differential access of different collectivities to the state which dictates the nature of the hegemonic national ethos in the society.

Other theorists of nationalism and the sociology of knowledge, such as Gellner (1983) and Smith (1986), have stressed the particular importance intellectuals have had in the creation and reproduction of nationalist ideologies, especially those of oppressed collectivities. Being excluded from the hegemonic intelligentsia and from open access to the state apparatus, these intellectuals 'rediscover' 'collective memories', transform popular oral traditions and languages into written ones, and portray a 'national golden age' in the distant mythical or historical past, whose reconstitution becomes the basis for nationalist aspirations.

However, as this book elaborates, it is women – and not (just?) the bureaucracy and the intelligentsia – who reproduce nations, biologically, culturally and symbolically. Why, then, are women usually 'hidden' in the various theorizations of the nationalist phenomenon?

Pateman (1988) and Grant (1991) offer explanations which might be relevant here. Carole Pateman studied the classical theories of 'the social contract' which are widely influential and have laid the foundation for common sense understanding of western social and political order. These theories divide the sphere of civil society into the public and private domains. Women (and the family) are located in the private domain, which is not seen as politically relevant. Pateman and other feminists have challenged the validity of this model and the public/private divide even within its own assumptions, and Pateman claims that

> the public realm cannot be fully understood in the absence of the private sphere, and, similarly, the meaning of the original contract is misinterpreted without both, mutually dependent halves of the story. Civil freedom depends on patriarchal right. (1988: 4)

As nationalism and nations have usually been discussed as part of the public political sphere, the exclusion of women from that arena has affected their exclusion from that discourse as well.

Following Pateman, Rebecca Grant (1991) has an interesting explanation of why women were located outside the relevant political domain. She claims that the foundation theories of both Hobbes and Rousseau portray the transition from the imagined state of nature into orderly society exclusively in terms of what they both assume to be natural male characteristics – the aggressive nature of men (in Hobbes) and the capacity for reason in men (in Rousseau). Women are not part of this process and are therefore excluded from the social and remain close to 'nature'. Later theories followed these assumptions as given.

Some notable exceptions to the gender-blind theorizations of nationalism have been Balibar (1990a), Chatterjee (1990) and Mosse (1985). Their insights were influenced and nurtured by a small but growing group of feminist scholars who have been working in this area (for example, Enloe, 1989; Jayawardena, 1986; Kandiyoti, 1991a; Parker et al., 1992; Pateman, 1988; Yuval-Davis, 1980; 1993; Yuval-Davis and Anthias, 1989). Nevertheless I think it is indicative that in the Oxford University Press reader *Nationalism* (edited by John Hutchinson and Anthony D. Smith, 1994), the editors placed the only extract in the book which relates to nationalism and gender relations in the last section, 'Beyond Nationalism'. They introduced that extract (which was taken from the introduction to the book *Woman–Nation–State*: Yuval-Davis and Anthias, 1989) in the following words:

> The entry of women into the national arena, as cultural and biological reproducers of the nation and as transmitters of its values, has also redefined the content and boundaries of ethnicity and the nation. (1994: 287)

But, of course, women did not just 'enter' the national arena: they were always there, and central to its constructions and reproductions! However, it is true that including women explicitly in the analytical discourse around nations and nationalisms is only a very recent and partial endeavour.

The aim of this book is to promote this analytical project of a gendered understanding of nations and nationalisms, by examining systematically the crucial contribution of gender relations into several major dimensions of nationalist projects: national reproduction, national culture and national citizenship, as well as national conflicts and wars.

Nationalist projects are sharply differentiated in the book from 'nation-states', and it is emphasized that membership of 'nations' can be sub-, super- and cross-states, as the boundaries of nations virtually never coincide with those of the so-called 'nation-states'. As becomes clear when reading the book, my analysis is deconstructionist. At the same time, however, I reject the extreme postmodernist construction of contemporary citizens as disembedded 'free floating signifiers' (Wexler, 1990). On the contrary, I highlight the crucial importance of social and economic power relations and the cross-cutting social divisions in which any concrete historical social categorization is enmeshed. These social divisions have organizational, experiential and representational forms, which can have implications for the ways they are linked to other social relations and actions (Anthias, 1991; Brah, 1992). They are not reducible to each other and have different ontological bases (Anthias and Yuval-Davis, 1983; 1992).

Nor do I accept unproblematically that we are all indeed in the 'postmodern era'. Postmodernism includes the uncritical assumption that we have all gone through the 'modern' era. In spite of the acceleration of the processes of globalization, this is a very westocentric[3] assumption (see more discussion of this in Chapter 3). Moreover, as Rattansi admits – while at the same time promoting 'the postmodern frame' (1994: 16–17) – various features which have been promoted by him and others as characteristic of the postmodern era have been features of other forms of society. His insistence on the need 'to decentre and de-essentialize both "subjects" and "the social"', to analyse temporality and spatiality as 'constitutive features of the social, of subjectivity and of processes of identification' and – what would be a cornerstone of any feminist analysis of any society at any time – to seek 'an engagement with questions of sexuality and sexual difference', are all part of, as I and many others would argue, what good sociological·analysis should always be. Moreover, at a time when religious fundamentalist movements are growing in all religions, in the North as well as in the South, to describe contemporary society as one in which the grand narratives have ended is absurd. On the other hand, even the most hegemonic naturalized grand narratives in historical societies have never had homogeneous unified control over the differentially positioned members of those societies.

Given these observations, the project of the book is to introduce a framework for discussing and analysing the different ways in which the discourse on gender and that on nation tend to intersect and to be constructed by each other. Before embarking on this, however, there is a need to look at each discourse separately; this will be done in the next two sections of this chapter. The focus of the discussion on 'gender' is on the theoretical debates around the category of 'woman' as well as on the relationship between the notions of 'sex' and 'gender'. Understanding these debates is crucial to any attempt to analyse the ways the relations between women and men affect and are affected by various nationalist projects and processes, as well as the ways notions of femininity and masculinity are constructed within nationalist discourses.

The notion of 'the nation' has to be analysed and related to nationalist ideologies and movements on the one hand and the institutions of the state on the other. Nations are situated in specific historical moments and are constructed by shifting nationalist discourses promoted by different groupings competing for hegemony. Their gendered character should be understood only within such a contextualization.

Following these two sections, the last section of this chapter outlines the main dimensions of the intersections between gender and nation which are examined in the following chapters of the book, moving from the more 'naturalized' roles of women as biological reproducers of the nation, through their roles in the cultural constructions of nations, to the ways civil constructions of nationhood, via rights and duties of citizenship, are gendered. The penultimate chapter looks at the gendered nature of militaries and wars. The book concludes with an examination of the complex relationship between feminism and nationalism and points towards transversal politics as a model of feminist politics, which takes account of national as well as other forms of difference among women, without falling into the trap of identity politics.

Analysing Women and Gender Relations

In spite of their great quantity and variety, one may crudely reduce the pre-occupations of feminist literature into three major questions. The first question was an attempt to analyse the causes of a common concern of feminists: why/how are women oppressed? There has been a search for the organizing principles which determine the power differences between men and women. Theories concerning 'patriarchy' (Eisenstein, 1979; Walby, 1990), or – as others prefer to call it – the sex/gender system (Rubin, 1975) or 'gender regimes' (Connell, 1987), have been at the centre of feminist theory since its inception. Dichotomous constructions of social spheres such as the public/private domains or nature/civilization have been central to these analyses.

The second question relates to the ontological basis of the differences between men and women: are these differences determined biologically, socially, or by a combination of the two? The discussion about this issue is generally known as 'the sex and gender debate' (Assiter, 1996; Butler, 1990; Delphy, 1993; Hood-Williams, 1996; Oakley, 1985). Enquiries about the basis and the boundaries of the categories 'woman' and 'man' became more problematic with the rise of poststructuralist and postmodernist frameworks of analysis (Barrett and Phillips, 1992).

The third question arose to a large extent as a reaction to some of the more simplistic – as well as ethnocentric and westocentric – perspectives of early feminist literature. It concerns the differences among women and among men and their effects upon generalized notions of gender relations. This question was first pursued by mostly black and ethnic minority women (hooks, 1981) and then became incorporated into feminist deconstructive postmodernist analyses (Barrett, 1987).

Given the limitations of space and scope of this chapter, I cannot even attempt to give a systematic review of all the debates on these three questions. However, any discussion on the issues raised in this book implies and is informed by certain positions on these questions which thus need to be referred to here, even briefly.

Much of the explanation of women's oppression has been related to their location in a different social sphere from that of men. Two such binary divides have been the public/private and the natural/civilized domains. Much of the feminist literature, while pointing out and objecting to the fact that women have been 'hidden from history' (Rowbotham, 1973), accepts the naturalized locations of men in the public sphere and women in the private sphere.

In the chapter on citizenship (Chapter 4), some of the problems of the dichotomy of the private/public domains and the ways these relate to the positioning of women as citizens will be discussed. It will be argued that this division is fictional to a great extent as well as both gender and ethnic specific, and that often this division has been used to exclude women from freedom and rights (Phillips, 1993: 63). Moreover, there have been claims (Chatterjee, 1990) that the line between the public and the private is a completely inadequate tool for analysing constructions of civil societies in post-colonial nations and that a non-westocentric analysis of gender relations cannot assume the boundary between the public and the private as a given.

The private/public dichotomy, however, is only one of the dichotomies in which women have been positioned at an opposite pole to that of men in the social sciences literature, including the feminist one. Another is that of the nature/civilization divide. The identification of women with 'nature' has been seen not only as the cause for their exclusion from the 'civilized' public polit-ical domain (Grant, 1991), but also as the explanation of the fact that in all cultures women are less valued socially than men. Simone de Beauvoir argued that

> It is not in giving life but in risking life that man is raised above the animal: that is why superiority has been accorded in humanity not to the sex that brings forth but to that which kills. (quoted in Harding, 1986: 148)

Sherry Ortner (1974) has argued more generally that women tend to be iden-tified with 'nature' while men tend to be identified with 'culture'. This is so because in bearing children women create new 'things' naturally, while men are free/forced to create culturally. Women are also, as a result, more confined to the domestic sphere and rear children who are 'pre-social' beings. Since human beings everywhere rank their own cultural products above the realm of the physical world, as every culture is aimed at controlling and/or tran-scending nature, women end up with an inferior symbolic position. Henrietta Moore (1988) adds, after Goodale (1980), the concept of pollution as rein-forcing women's symbolic devaluation and their connection to 'nature', as women are often constructed as 'polluting' when they are bleeding during menstruation or after child-birth. However, she also points out some of the problems that such generalized notions about women's position can raise. Such generalizations homogenize and discard the diversity of the different societies. They also assume specific western cultural values of 'nature' as inferior to 'culture' to be universal and shared by all societies. Last but not least, they assume that there is no difference among different members of the society, including between men and women, as to how they value themselves and the other gender. In this way, notions of social conflict, domination, resistance and, most importantly, of social change seem to be defined away. Moreover, the search for a universal, 'original' reason for the subordination of women can detract attention from historically specific ways in which gender relations are constructed in different societies and the ways they are reproduced.

This critique of generalized notions of women's position holds also in rela-tion to the notion of 'patriarchy' which has been widely used by feminist theorists to describe the autonomous system of women's subordination in society.

In the 1970s and 1980s feminist politics were neatly divided into separate schools of liberal, socialist, radical and sometimes dual-system feminisms (Walby, 1990). The difference among these schools of thought was primarily focused on the question of what they considered to be 'the' cause of women's oppression – whether it was the law, capitalism or just men holding on to their privileges. There was also a lot of discussion about the 'unhappy marriage' between Marxism and feminism (Hartman, 1981) and the ways one should theorize patriarchal oppression in relation to class exploitation.

The notion of 'patriarchy' in itself is highly problematic. Although it was often acknowledged that the rule of the 'pater', the father, has been traditionally applied to younger men, not only to women, this did not usually play a significant theoretical role in these generalized feminist usages of the term. This remained so even when these usages were developed in more sophisticated theoretical models, such as in Sylvia Walby's (1990) work (see also the special issue of *Sociology*, 1989), which differentiated between different forms of patriarchy operating in the different social domains of employment, household production, culture, sexuality, violence and the state.

Exceptions to this rule of generalized use can be found when patriarchy is consigned to a specific historical period or geographical region. For example, in the works of Carole Pateman (1988) patriarchy is specific to the premodern historical period. In the modern liberal state, according to her, the system is transformed from patriarchy into fraternity. While in patriarchy the father (or the king as a father figure) ruled over both other men and the women, in a fraternity the men get the right to rule over their women in the private domestic sphere, but agree on a contract of a social order of equality among themselves within the public, political sphere.

Val Moghadam (1994), on the other hand, follows the demographer John Caldwel and locates patriarchy in a specific geographical zone, 'the patriarchal belt', which stretches from Northern Africa across the Middle East to the northern plains of the Indian subcontinent and parts of rural China. In this 'belt' of 'classical patriarchy' (Kandiyoti, 1988) the patriarchal extended family is the central social unit, in which the senior man rules everyone else and family honour is closely linked to women's controlled 'virtue'.

Although limiting patriarchy to specific social institutions, historical periods or geographical regions does go somewhat in the direction of differentiating between diverse forms of social relations in different societies, it is still a much too crude analytical instrument. It does not allow, for instance, for the fact that in most societies some women have power at least over some men as well as over other women. Nor does it take into account the fact that in concrete situations women's oppression is intermeshed in and articulated by other forms of social oppression and social divisions.

This is the reason why elsewhere Floya Anthias and I have rejected the notion of patriarchy as a distinct social system which is autonomous of other types of social systems such as capitalism and racism (Anthias and Yuval-Davis, 1992: 106–9). Rather, we argued that women's oppression is endemic and integral to social relations with regard to the distribution of power and material resources in the society. Gender, ethnicity and class, although with different ontological bases and separate discourses, are intermeshed in each other and articulated by each other in concrete social relations. They cannot be seen as additive and no one of them can be prioritized abstractly. As Avtar Brah (1992: 144) has suggested, it is imperative that we do not compartmentalize oppressions. In the theorizations of patriarchy – even the more sophisticated among them (Ramazanoglu, 1989; Walby, 1990) – gender relations end up, at least implicitly, reduced and isolated into necessary effects of biological sexual difference, which is obviously not the case. Contrary to what the notion of patriarchy suggests, women are not usually just passive recipients and non-participants in the determination of gender relations. Probably most importantly, not all women are oppressed and/or subjugated in the same way or to the same extent, even within the same society at any specific moment.

This is not to suggest, however, that there are no hegemonic social discourses and practices in different societies and in different locations within these societies which relate to the organization of sexual difference and biological reproduction and establish forms of representation around these. Gayle Rubin (1975) called these 'the sex/gender systems'. R.W. Connell (1987), writing about twelve years later, has dropped the naturalized biological 'sex' from his similar notion of 'gender regimes'. Given the state of the contemporary sex/gender debate, some argue that there might be a need to say 'goodbye' to them both (Hood-Williams, 1996) and to just concentrate on the notion of difference.

The question of the fixity of difference between women and men has been central to the feminist debate on the ontological basis of that difference. From its inception, feminist politics has depended on the differentiation between sex and gender. Claims that sexual divisions of labour, power and dispositions are not biological ('sex') but are socially constructed ('gender') have enabled feminists of various schools to argue that women's social position can/should be transformed towards sexual equality. It is 'a central explanatory and organizing category of their accounts of the social and familial and/or discursive construction of subjectivity' (Gatens, 1991: 139) and is defended against the 'danger of biological reductionism'.

Christine Delphy (1993) has outlined the development of the debate about sex and gender as stretching through the work of Margaret Mead, the Parsonian theories of sex roles, and finally the ground breaking work of Ann Oakley's *Sex, Gender and Society* (1985). There is a progressive denaturalization of the divisions of labour and psychological differences between men and women and a stress on cultural variation. According to Delphy, however, none of these works, nor later feminist work, has questioned the assumption that gender is based on a natural, sexual dichotomy. Judith Butler adds that when 'gender' is understood to be constructed by 'culture' in the same way that 'sex' is constructed by 'nature', then 'not biology but culture becomes destiny' (1990: 8).

This last point is of crucial importance and will be discussed in more detail in the chapter on culture (Chapter 3). However, of most relevance here is the fact that in spite of the great theoretical differences between them, both Delphy and Butler point out that 'gender precedes sex' and that the cultural construction of the social division of labour (Delphy) and of meaning (Butler) is the very means by which sexual differences are constructed (and used) as natural and pre-social. So-called 'objective' 'scientific' tests have looked for the presence or absence of chromosome Y to determine if a specific person is male or female, or, more recently, in view of empirical ambiguity in some people, for a specific gene – such as the SRY, isolated in 1991 by Goodfellow and his team. However, as Hood-Williams points out, this scientific project is tautological and has a circular logic: the scientists 'must already know what it is to be a man [socially], before they can confirm it genetically' (1996: 11). As Foucault (1980a) and Laqueur (1990) have pointed out, the mere need to construct every human being as either male or female is historically – and therefore culturally – specific.

As Floya Anthias and I have argued (Anthias and Yuval-Davis, 1983: 66), there are no necessary 'natural' social effects of sexual differences or biological reproduction, and thus they are not an equivalent material basis for gender as production is for class. In analyses which attempted to discover a feminist materialism in the social relations of reproduction we saw a superimposition of a materialist project onto a different object, inappropriately reproducing its terms of reference.

Gender should be understood not as a 'real' social difference between men and women, but as a mode of discourse which relates to groups of subjects whose social roles are defined by their sexual/biological difference as opposed to their economic positions or their membership in ethnic and racial collectivities. Sexual differences should also be understood as a mode of discourse, one in which groups of social subjects are defined as having different sexual/biological constitutions. In other words, both 'gender' and 'sex' can be analysed as modes of discourse, but with different agendas.

The insistence on the discursive construction of meaning and the insistence on the non-natural non-essentialist nature of both 'sex' and 'gender' have brought about a blurring of the boundaries between these two constructions. Anyone who has been involved in feminist politics in non-English-speaking countries would know, however, that one of the first and most urgent tasks of feminists there is to 'invent' a word in the local language for 'gender'. Unless there is a separation between the discourse of 'sex' and that of 'gender', biology would be constructed as destiny in the moral and political discourse of that society.

However, the objection to the blurring of the boundaries can be theoretical as well as political. Gatens points out that a non-essentialist theoretical approach to sex and gender might involve

> the unreasoned, unargued assumption that both the body and psyche are a post-natally passive *tabula rasa*. That is, for theorists of gender, the mind of either sex is a neutral, passive entity, a blank state on which is inscribed various social 'lessons'. The body, on their account, is the passive mediator of these inscriptions. (1991: 140)

From here to 'political correctness' the path can be short and direct. If only an appropriate 'Skinner box' could be constructed to supply the right social environmental conditions in socializing the young and in 're-educating' the old, all men and women could become equal – because they could all become, in principle, the same.

Gatens' critique of this line of thinking is that it is based on a simplistic dichotomy of social theory into either environmental or essentialist, and points out that at least the body is never passive. It is always a sexed body, and therefore the same behaviour would have quite a different personal and social significance according to whether it is carried out by a man or by a woman. In other words, the self is always situated.

Gatens' insistence on the last point, following Donna Haraway's (1990) 'situated knowledge' and others, is of utmost importance in analysing gender relations. However, the crucial importance of the insistence that 'the self is always situated' concerns the analysis not only of gender relations but of *all* social relations. The situation of the body is not constructed only around sex differences (biological or discursive), nor is the situation of the self affected only – or even always primarily – by the body. For Gatens, and other feminist theorists like her, the sexual difference is crucial because they observe society via the gaze of middle class westocentric psychoanalytic theory, especially that of Lacan (1982). However, macro social divisions of class, ethnicity, 'race' and nation, as well as more subjective body-related differences of particular physical 'type', age and ability, are crucial in this process. In the same way that the boy or the girl looking at the mirror would not know that they are male or female unless they have had access to those who are different from them, subjective identities are always situated in relation to others according to all these dimensions, not only the sexual. Otherness, in the concrete social world of the children, whether micro or macro, is very rarely dichotomous and/or confined to sex alone.

The category 'woman' can be perceived as a unified category only if all these other differences are suppressed, as was the situation in feminist white middle class 'consciousness-raising groups' in the 1970s which aimed at their participants' 'discovering' that the condition of all women is essentially the same (Yuval-Davis, 1984).

If women are different from each other, the question that has been asked by many postmodernist feminists has been to what extent there is any meaning to the term 'women' at all. Denise Riley sees 'women' as a fluctuating identity and has argued that the category '"women" is historically and discursively constructed, always in relation to other categories which themselves change' (1987: 35). Elizabeth Weed argues, however, that

> the lack of a reliable positive identity does not mean an endless proliferation of differences. It means, rather, that the very categories of difference are displaced and denaturalized through the articulation of those categories with the structures of domination in which they were historically produced. (1989: xix)

These historical structures of domination, therefore, determine which differences are considered socially and politically relevant and which are not. However, as Elizabeth Spelman has argued, the similarities between women exist within the context of the differences between them, and 'there is ongoing debate about what effect such differences have on those similarities . . . not all participants in that debate get equal air time or are invested with equal authority' (1988: 159).

The concern should not be, therefore, with differences among women *per se*, as it is not just with what is common to women in different social positionings. The concern is how to construct feminist political mobilization which would take on board all of the above. Some attempt to tackle this issue will be made in the last chapter of the book (Chapter 6).

One of the most important differences among women is their membership in ethnic and national collectivities, which is the subject matter of this book. Like other differences among women, their membership in the different collectivities should be understood within structures of domination and as articulated by other social relations. These can affect not only the status and power of some women versus others, within and between the collectivities they belong to, but also the extent to which their membership in the collectivity constitutes a 'forced identity' (to use Amrita Chhachhi's 1991 terminology) or can become little more than a postmodernist 'free floating signifier' of identity (Wexler, 1990). Relations between nations and states in specific historical circumstances play a central role in these constructions.

Theorizing Nations and States

The concept of the 'nation-state' assumes a complete correspondence between the boundaries of the nation and the boundaries of those who live in a specific state. This, of course, is virtually everywhere a fiction. There are always people living in particular societies and states who are not considered to be (and often do not consider themselves to be) members of the hegemonic nation, there are members of national collectivities who live in other countries, and there are nations which never had a state (like the Palestinians) or which are divided across several states (like the Kurds). However, this fiction has been at the basis of nationalist ideologies. Gellner has actually defined nationalism as a

> theory of political legitimacy which requires that ethnic boundaries should not cut across political ones, and in particular, that ethnic boundaries within a given state . . . should not separate the power holders from the rest . . . and therefore state and culture must now be linked (1983: 1, 36).

The effect of this fiction is to naturalize the hegemony of one collectivity and its access to the ideological apparatuses of both state and civil society. This naturalization is at the roots of the inherent connection that exists between nationalism and racism. It constructs minorities into assumed deviants from the 'normal', and excludes them from important power resources. It can also lead the way to an eventual 'ethnic cleansing'. Deconstructing this is crucial to tackling racism on the one hand and to understanding the state itself on the other hand.

The discussion in this section of the introductory chapter turns first to the notion of modern states and to debates concerning their specificity and heterogeneity as well as to the need to theorize states as an analytical sphere separate from society. The chapter argues that it is necessary to differentiate analytically between the state, the civil society and the family, treating them as three separate if interrelated social and political spheres. It then turns to define the specificity of national projects and how these relate to the state. This section of the chapter ends with a brief discussion of different dimensions of nationalist projects, those relating to the mythical notions of common origin (*Volknation*), those relating to the myth of common culture (*Kulturnation*) and those relating to nations as based on the myth of equal citizenship in states (*Staatnation*).

State and Society

Theorizing the state as a sphere separate from both 'the nation' and 'the civil society' is vital for any adequate analysis of the relationships between gender relations and national projects, in which the state often plays crucial roles.

Stuart Hall defines the 'modern state' as one which includes the following features:

> power is shared; rights to participate in government are legally or constitutionally defined; representation is wide, state power is fully secular and boundaries of national sovereignty are clearly defined. (1984: 9–10)

This definition, of course, is highly idealistic and inaccurate even in relation to the European context in which he describes it. Hall looks at the variants of later European states of both liberal and collective tendencies (of both the Bolshevist and fascist types) as well as at the welfare state. However, he does not take account of the imperial state which has become part of most modern European states, and which positioned different civil societies and nations in very different relations to the same state. One cannot understand, for instance, the ways in which contemporary nationalisms interrelate with racism without looking at this, both in Europe itself and in Third World post-colonial states.

The state has been analysed in very different ways from different theoretical perspectives (for some overviews see, for example, Held, 1984; Peterson, 1992; Yuval-Davis and Anthias, 1989). It is interesting, for instance, that in international relations, states are usually considered as single, individual identities. On the other hand when dealing with relations between state and society, states become much more heterogeneous if not all-encompassing creatures. The classical theories of 'the social contract' which are widely influential and have laid the foundation for a common sense understanding of state and society have been examined by Carole Pateman (1988). These theories divide the sphere of civil society into the public and private domains. Women (and the family) are located in the private domain, which is not seen as politically relevant. As nationalism and nations have usually been discussed as part of the public political sphere, the exclusion of women from that arena has affected their exclusion from that discourse as well.

A welcome exception in this respect has been the work of George L. Mosse (1985; see also the discussion in the introduction to Parker et al., 1992). He linked the rise of bourgeois family morality to the rise of nationalism in Europe at the end of the eighteenth century. In a sense Mosse follows the anthropological tradition of Lévi-Strauss (1969) which has been more aware of the central links between gender relations and social cohesion. Lévi-Strauss has seen the exchange of women as the original mechanism for creating social solidarity among men of different kinship units and thus as the basis of constructing larger collectivities. It is not the exchange of women but the control of them (or their subordination, to use Pateman's terminology) which is so often at the base of the social order (Yuval-Davis, 1980). Nevertheless it would have been greatly beneficial for political theory to have been more open to anthropological literature rather than continuing to count, even unintentionally, on 'man's pre-contractual natural state' that has never been more than a convenient fiction. It would have also helped to locate the phenomenon of nationalism beyond narrow westocentric boundaries (Yuval-Davis, 1991b).

One of the main issues debated about the state is the extent to which it should be seen as independent of society. Positions have varied from crude Marxist approaches which have seen the state as purely reflecting the interests of the 'ruling class', to approaches which have seen it as an independent institution which mediates between contending pluralist interest groups à la Dahl's *Polyarchy* (1971). The division between these two approaches is not as extreme as one might think, however, because even Lenin (1977) saw the rise of the modern state as a 'product and manifestation of the irreconcilability of class antagonisms' which has acquired a relative autonomy. He quotes Engels expressing the Marxist view on the nature of the state as

> a power, seemingly standing above society, that would alleviate the conflict and keep it within the bounds of order; and this power, arisen out of society but placing itself above it, and alienating itself more and more from it, is the state. (1977: 10)

Although Lenin warns against concluding from the above that the state can become the organ for the reconciliation of the differing classes, this kind of explanation has been most often used in relation to the rise of the welfare state (Marshall, 1950).

Another debate is the extent to which the state should be seen as a purely coercive instrument which imposes law and order in a variety of ways (via legal, constitutional and executive powers), or as incorporating a variety of other institutions, such as education and the media as well as economy and welfare (Althusser, 1971; Balibar, 1990a). Directly related to this, however, is the question to what extent we can see the state as a homogeneous and coherent 'being' as opposed to one in which different parts operate in different directions and with different ideological orientations which might even sometimes conflict. The coexistence of anti-racist legislation and racist immigration laws are a case in point.

With the rising hegemony of Foucauldian and postmodernist paradigms, the above point has led many to reject the idea of a unitary state altogether, and instead to focus on social policies, the law, institutional arrangements and discourses as heterogeneous elements which are not reducible to the state. Foucault's (1980b) perspective has been that horizontal power grids exist on all levels in society and come into action when resisted.

However, theoretical perspectives which have altogether dispensed with the state as a meaningful analytical category cannot explain the centrality of struggles in civil society to gain further access to the state and state power, or the extent to which the different positionings of men and women, kinship units and various ethnic collectivities (as well as of other groupings in civil society) is determined by their differential access to the state. Analytically, as well as politically, therefore, the state has to be differentiated from civil society. However, the state is not unitary in its practices, its projects or its effects. As Floya Anthias and myself have expanded elsewhere, the state can be defined as:

> a body of institutions which are centrally organized around the intentionality of control with a given apparatus of enforcement (juridical and repressive) at its command and basis . . . Different forms of the state will involve different relationships between the control/coercion twin which is the residing characteristic of the state. (Anthias and Yuval-Davis, 1989: 5)

Different social institutions, primarily those of schooling and the media, can be used for ideological production in the modern liberal democratic state. However, they are not inherently part of the state as such, and often are not even owned by it.

As will be argued in Chapter 4, there has been a conflation between the dichotomy of state and civil society and that of public and private domains. In order to avoid a westocentric reading of states and societies, there is a need to differentiate between state institutions, as mentioned above, civil society institutions, and the domain of family and kinship relations. Civil society includes those institutions, collectivities, groupings and social agencies which lie outside the formal rubric of state parameters outlined but which both inform and are informed by them. This may include voluntary associations and institutions controlling the production of signs and symbols as well as the economic market (Cohen, 1982; Keane, 1988; Melucci, 1989). The domain of the family includes social, economic and political networks and households which are organized around kinship or friendship relations.

All three domains (the state, civil society and the familial domain) produce their own ideological contents and in different states would have differential access to economic and political resources. Ideology does not reside (in a priv-ileged sense), therefore, in any of these spheres. None of these spheres is ever homogeneous, and different parts of the state can act in contradictory ways to others – and their effects on different ethnic, class, gender and other groupings in the society could be different. Different states (and the same state in different historical circumstances) also differ in the extent to which their powers of control are concentrated in the central state government or in local state governments. Furthermore, they differ in their tolerance towards different political projects which are in conflict with those that are hegemonic within central government. These questions of the correspondence, in political projects, of the different components and levels of the state, involve also the questions of what are the mechanisms by which these projects are being reproduced and/or changed; of how state control can be delegated from one level to another; and, probably most importantly, of how sections and groupings from the domains of civil society and the family gain access to the state's coercive and controlling powers. It is within this context that the relationship between 'nations' and 'states', as well as between other forms of ethnic groupings and the state, has to be analysed – a precondition to understanding the ways women affect and are affected by these processes. We shall turn, therefore, to examine the notion of the 'nation' as an ideological and political construct separate from that of the 'nation-state'.

The Notion of Nations

There is a rumour (I never actually managed to find the exact reference) that Enoch Powell, the first theoretician of the British 'new right', once defined 'the nation' as 'two males plus defending a territory with the women and children'. This definition is based on a naturalized image of the nation (or actually an ethologist image clearly based on the behaviour of a pack of wolves) which other 'primordialist' theoreticians of the nation also share (for example, Van den Berghe, 1979). According to these theories, nations not only are eternal and universal but also constitute a natural extension of family and kinship relations. The family and kinship units in these constructions are based on natural sexual divisions of labour, in which the men protect the 'womenandchildren'(to use Cynthia Enloe's 1990 term).

Against this naturalized image, Ben Anderson (1983) has presented his, by now classic, construction of 'the nation' as an 'imagined community'. According to Anderson and other 'modernists' (for example, Gellner, 1983; Hobsbawm, 1990), nations are not an eternal and universal phenomenon but specifically modern and a direct result of particular developments in European history. Nations could arise, according to Anderson, only when technological innovations established 'print capitalism', when reading spread from the elites into other classes and people started to read mass publications in their own languages rather than in classical religious languages, thus establishing linguistic national 'imagined communities'. However, Anderson emphasizes the importance of the fact that people feel that their membership in the nation is 'natural' and not chosen: 'Precisely because such ties are not chosen, they have about them a halo of disinterestedness' (1991: 143). For that reason, claims Anderson, the nation, like the family, can ask for sacrifices – including the ultimate sacrifice of killing and being killed. Kitching

(1985) has pointed out that Anderson's approach to nationalism begins to explain the passions (to differentiate from just interests) which are involved in the attachment of people to their nations.[4]

Gellner (1983) explains the nationalist passions somewhat differently. He traces the development of nationalism to the need of modern societies for cultural homogeneity in order to function smoothly. This need, when satisfied, is sponsored by the modern nation-state; but when it is unfulfilled, it stimulates the growth of ideological movements among the excluded groupings (those who have not been absorbed into the hegemonic culture), which call for the establishment of alternative nation-states.

Another influential approach to the study of nations is that of Anthony Smith (1986) who looks at the 'ethnic origins of nations'. While agreeing with the 'modernists' that nationalism, both as an ideology and as a movement, is a wholly modern phenomenon, Smith argues that

> the 'modern nation' in practice incorporates several features of pre-modern ethne and owes much to a general model of ethnicity which has survived in many areas until the dawn of the 'modern era'. (1986: 18)

Smith claims that the specificity of ethnic collectivities is to be found in its 'myth-symbol complex' which is very durable over time (although the specific meaning of the myths and symbols can change), rather than in any other social, economic or political features of the collectivity. He warns against oversimplistic notions of imagined communities and 'invented traditions' (Hobsbawm and Ranger, 1983; Smith, 1995).

Sami Zubaida (1989), in criticizing this approach, has anchored the durability of ethnicities in certain socio-economic and political processes. He claims (by using examples from the histories of both Europe and the Middle East) that ethnic homogeneity is not a cause but rather a result of a long history of centralized governments which created a 'national unity' in the premodern era. It 'was not given – but was achieved precisely by the political processes which facilitated centralization' (1989: 13).

Whether it is the state which homogenizes ethnicity or whether it is other socio-economic and political processes (Balibar, 1990a), it is important to recognize, as both Smith and Zubaida have done, that there is an inherent connection between the ethnic and national projects. While it is important to look at the historical specificity of the construction of collectivities, there is no inherent difference (although sometimes there is a difference in scale) between ethnic and national collectivities: they are both the Andersonian 'imagined communities'.

What is specific to the nationalist project and discourse is the claim for a separate political representation for the collective. This often – but not always – takes the form of a claim for a separate state and/or territory, although some states are based on bi- or multi-national principles (like Belgium or Lebanon) and some supra-state political projects like the European Union can, at specific historical moments, develop state characteristics. Nationalist demands can also be aimed at establishing a regional autonomy rather than a separate state, as in the case of Scotland or Catalonia; or they can be irredentist, advocating joining a neighbouring state rather than establishing one of their own, such as the republican movement in Northern Ireland or the Kashmiri movement for unification with Pakistan. Although state and territory have been closely bound together, there have been cases of nationalist movements which called for the state to be established in a different territory than that where they were active. Both the Jewish Zionist movement (which established the state of Israel) and the black Zionist movement (which established Liberia) called for the mass emigration of their members from the countries where they lived. Others have not articulated any specific territorial boundaries for their national independence. It is the demand for political sovereignty which separates the 'Black Nation' from other 'black community activists', or those who call for the 'Khalipha', the global nation of Islam, from other committed Muslims. The Austrian Marxist Otto Bauer (1940; see Nimni, 1991; Yuval-Davis, 1987a) called for the separation of nationalism and the state as the only viable solution to the hopeless mix of collectivities in the territories which constituted the Austro-Hungarian empire, and a very similar situation is emerging today with the fall of the Soviet empire and in many other places in the post-colonial world (such as Rwanda).

The separation of nationality and the state also exists, however, in many other cases. In many parts of the world there exist immigrant communities which are culturally and politically committed to continue to 'belong' to their 'mother country' – or more specifically to the national collectivity from where they, their parents or their forebears have come. The rise of these 'committed diasporas' has been co-determined by several factors. Firstly, technological advances both in means of international travel and in media and communications, have made the preservation of links with the 'homeland' much easier, as they have enabled intergenerational cultural and linguistic reproduction. 'Ethnic videos', for example, constitute one of the largest video markets and have been consumed by people who have little or no access to the mass media of the countries where they live. And cable systems or satellite dishes have given many people direct access to their own national and ethnic media, as well as establishing new diffuse ethnic collectivities (such as the international South Asian community). Deutch (1966) and Schlesinger (1987) have pointed out that

> Membership in a people consists in wide complementarity of social communication. It consists in the ability to communicate more effectively, and over a wider range of subjects, with members of one large group than with outsiders. (Deutch, 1966: 97)

It is now easier than ever for diasporic communities to keep communicating within the boundaries of their collectivities and thus to reproduce them.

At the same time, as a result of certain successes of the anti-racist and civil rights movements, there has been a certain shift in national ideologies in many western countries and multi-culturalism has become a hegemonic ideology

which, with all its problematics (see discussion in Chapter 3), has eased somewhat the pressures on immigrants to assimilate. This was aided by the fact that
in the post-colonial world there are many ongoing nationalist struggles where
different collectivities compete not just for access to their states' powers and
resources, but also on the constitutive nature of these states. One cannot imagine the continued nationalist struggles of the Irish Republican Army, for
instance, without the financial, political and other help of the diaspora Irish
communities, especially in the USA. In the case of the Jewish diaspora – the
oldest 'established' diaspora – the hegemony of zionism has meant that many
have transformed Israel into an *ex post facto* 'homeland' even if they have
never been there, let alone lived there, and international Jewish support has
played a crucial role in the establishment and development of Israel (Yuval-
Davis, 1987b). As Anderson (1995) commented, not enough recognition is
given to the role of diaspora communities in contemporary nationalist struggles.

One has to distinguish, however, between 'diaspora communities' (Brah,
1996; Lavie and Swedenburg, 1996; Lemelle and Kelly, 1994) and political
exiles. The latter are usually individuals or families who have been part of
political struggles in the homeland; their identity and collectivity membership
continue to be directed singularly, or at least primarily, towards there, and
they aim to 'go back' the moment the political situation changes. For diaspora communities, on the other hand, participation in the national struggles
in the homeland, including sending ammunition to Ireland or 'gold bricks' to
build the Hindu temple in place of the Muslim mosque in Ayodhya which was
burned in December 1992, can be done primarily within an ethnic rather
than a nationalist discourse, as an act of affirmation of their collectivity
membership. Their destiny is primarily bound up with the country where
they live and where their children grow up, rather than with their country of
origin – although as hybrids they at the same time belong to and are outside
of both national collectivities. Their ambivalences are sharper, however, the
more racialized is their ethnic collectivity in their country of immigration.

Bhabha (1990) has talked about the specific role people on the national
margins like hybrids have in the continuous reconstruction of nations by pro-
ducing their counter-narratives. Nora Rätzel (1994) has found that
immigrants tend to imagine *Heimat* (home) as a much less physical place
than do the 'natives' and more as the place where they feel comfortable and
where their nearest and dearest live as well. Attachments of political exiles to
their homelands, on the other hand, often concentrate on the climate, the
smells and other physical characteristics of the country, and there are much
more ambivalent feelings towards the people, let alone the state.

If 'nations' are not to be identified with 'nation-states', one must ask if
there are any 'objective' characteristics according to which nations can be recognized. This question is not purely theoretical, given the wide consensus,
affirmed by the United Nations, regarding 'the right of nations to self-determination'.

There have been many definitions of 'the nation'. Some of them sound like a shopping list, as, for example, this influential 'formula definition' of 'the nation' by Stalin, which he developed as 'the expert on the national question' among the Bolsheviks before the October Revolution. According to Stalin,

> A nation is a historically evolved, stable community of language, territory, economic life and psychological make-up manifested in a community of culture. (1972: 13)

Other definitions dispense with this shopping list altogether. Greenfeld, for example, argues persuasively that

> common territory or common language, statehood or shared traditions, history or race – none of these relationships has proved inevitable . . . National identity . . . is an identity which derives from membership in a 'people', the fundamental characteristic of which is that it is defined as a 'nation'. Every member of the 'nation' thus interpreted partakes in its superior, elite, quality, and it is in consequence that a stratified national population is perceived as essentially homogeneous, and the lines of status and class are superficial. This principle lies at the basis of all nationalisms . . . Apart from it, different nationalisms share little. (1992: 7)

Greenfeld sees a historical affinity between the notion of *natio* and that of *ethne*, which originally, in both Latin and Greek respectively, meant 'a group of foreigners'. However, following the transformation of the idea of the nation in European history she argues forcefully that 'nationalism is not necessarily a form of particularism' and that 'a nation coextensive with humanity is in no way a contradiction in terms' (1992: 7). This perspective differs sharply from that of Anthony Smith who insists on the 'ethnic origin of nations' (1986) and their intrinsic particularisms:

> Its [nationalism's] success depends on specific cultural and historical contexts, and this means that the nations it helps to create are in turn derived from pre-existing and highly particularized cultural heritages and ethnic formulations. (1995: viii)

The ingredient missing from all of these definitions, however, is the element emphasized by Otto Bauer (1940; Yuval-Davis, 1987a) – that of 'common destiny', which is of crucial importance for the construction of nations. It is oriented towards the future, rather than just the past, and can explain more than individual and communal assimilations within particular nations. On the one hand, it can explain a subjective sense of commitment of people to collectivities and nations, such as in settler societies or in post-colonial states, in which there is no shared myth of common origin (Stasiulis and Yuval-Davis, 1995). At the same time it can also explain the dynamic nature of any national collectivity and the perpetual processes of reconstruction of boundaries which take place within them, via immigration, naturalization, conversion and other similar social and political processes.

'The United States of the World' which Greenfeld sees as a possible nation would have to gain this sense of shared destiny which would differ from other (intergalactic?) collective destinies before it could evolve into a national collectivity, as collectivities are organized around boundaries which divide the world into 'us' and 'them'.

The Multi-Dimensionality of Nationalist Projects

There have been many attempts to classify the different kinds of nationalist movements and nationalist ideologies which have arisen in the world during the last 200 years (for example, Smith, 1971: Chapter 8; Snyder, 1968: Chapter 4). Some classifications have tried to maintain scientific 'neutralism', and developed either historical taxonomies (which focus virtually exclusively on Europe) or sociological taxonomies (which focus on the various social locations and specific goals of the national movements, aimed at secession, pan-national liberation and so on). An influential classification has been developed by Anthony Smith (1971; 1986) based on the specific character of the nationalist project, including both the 'ethnic-genealogical' movement and the 'civic-territorial' movement. In this he is continuing a German tradition which tends to differentiate between nation-states and state-nations, or, to use the German terminology *Kulturnation* and *Staatnation* (see Neuberger, 1986; Stolcke, 1987).

Recent books on nationalism by Michael Ignatieff (1993) and Julia Kristeva (1993) basically maintain this dichotomous classification, but give it a much more explicit moralistic tone of 'good' and 'bad' nationalism than Smith. Ignatieff promotes 'civic nationalism' as one which enables individuals to 'reconcile their rights to shape their own lives with the need to belong to a community' (1993: 4). He sees the promotion of 'civic nationalism' as a way to reduce pressures for the rise of 'ethnic nationalism' which is exclusive, authoritarian and consumed by racial hatred. Such pressures usually increase in crisis and transition times such as after the collapse of the Soviet empire.

Similarly, Kristeva sees ethnic nationalism and the cult of origins as a hate reaction triggered by deep crises of national identity. For her, democratic nationalism is good not in itself, but as the best available option, given the reality of the modern world where people without a nationality are usually deprived of citizenship and rights. Robert Fine (1994) has made a critique of these approaches and of Habermas (1992) which he also includes in the 'new nationalism' paradigm. (Fine argues that Habermas' concept of 'post-nationalist' patriotism is, ultimately, not that different from the 'new nationalism' of Ignatieff and Kristeva.) He points out (using some of the insights of Hannah Arendt, 1975, who discussed political shifts in Europe during the inter-war years) that there can be no simplistic mutually exclusive separation between these two types of nationalism. Hannah Arendt has argued that the antinomies of the modern democratic nation-state exist already in its constitution, as representative governments are themselves built upon the exclusion from political life of the majority of citizens. As will be discussed further in Chapter 4, citizenship itself has been exclusionary and therefore cannot be the polar negation of ethnic exclusion. As Fine puts it: 'It [the 'new nationalism'] presents itself as the antidote to ethnic consciousness, but there is no sphere nor moment of innocence within modern political life' (1994: 441).

The realization that a theory of nationalism must embrace both 'good' and 'bad' nationalisms and that there can be no easy separation of specific nationalist movements into one or the other is what brought Thomas Nairn (1977) to call nationalism 'the modern Janus'. Janus, the Roman god who stood at the gates of people's homes, had two faces: he looked backwards and forwards at the same time.

Moreover, nationalist projects are usually multiplex, although often one version is much more hegemonic than others at different historical moments. Different members of the collectivity tend to promote contesting constructions which tend to be more or less exclusionary, more or less linked to other ideologies such as socialism and/or religion. Attempts to classify all different states and societies according to these different types of nationalist projects would constitute an ahistorical, impossible and misleading mission, as are all such classifications of social phenomena. Rather, we need to treat these 'types' as different major dimensions of nationalist ideologies and projects which are combined in different ways in specific historical cases.

Rather than using the dichotomous classifications put forward by the above writers, I would like to differentiate between three major dimensions of nationalist projects (Yuval-Davis, 1993). In my view it is very important not to conflate concerns emanating from constructions of nations based on notions of origin and those based on culture. Both of them need also to be analytically distinguished from constructions of nations based on citizenship of states. Different aspects of gender relations play an important role in each of these dimensions of nationalist projects and are crucial for any valid theorization of them, as will be elaborated throughout the book. One major dimension of nationalist projects to be related to gender relations in the book is the genealogical dimension which is constructed around the specific origin of the people (or their race) (*Volknation*). The myth of common origin or shared blood/genes tends to construct the most exclusionary/homogeneous visions of 'the nation' (see Chapter 2). Another major dimension of nationalist projects is the cultural dimension in which the symbolic heritage provided by language and/or religion and/or other customs and traditions is constructed as the 'essence' of 'the nation' (*Kulturnation*). Although such a construction allows for assimilation, it tends to have little tolerance of 'non-organic' diversity (see Chapter 3). The civic dimension of nationalist projects focuses on citizenship (*Staatnation*) (see Chapter 4) as determining the boundaries of the nation, and thus relates it directly to notions of state sovereignty and specific territoriality.

Nationed Gender and Gendered Nations

In the previous sections of the chapter we looked at issues concerning gender and nation as they have been theorized and debated as separate social phenomena. The aim of this book, however, as mentioned above, is to show that a proper understanding of either cannot afford to ignore the ways they are informed and constructed by each other. In this last section of the introductory chapter, I would like to point out some of these intersections as they construct both individuals' subjectivities and social lives, and the social and political projects of nations and states. Each of these intersections will be further developed in the following chapters of the book.

Women and the Biological Reproduction of the Nation

The struggle of women for reproductive rights has been at the heart of feminist struggles since the inception of the movement. The right of women to choose whether to have children, as well as how many to have and when, has been seen by many feminists as the basic 'touchstone' of feminist politics.

Most of the discussions on women's reproductive rights, however, until the last decade at least, have been concentrated on the effects of the existence or absence of these rights on women as individuals. There were discussions, for instance, on how these rights affect women's health; how they affect their working lives and opportunities for upward mobility; and how they affect their family life.

However, often the pressures on women to have or not to have children relate to them not as individuals, workers and/or wives, but as members of specific national collectivities. According to different national projects, under specific historical circumstances, some or all women of childbearing age groups would be called on, sometimes bribed, and sometimes even forced, to have more, or fewer, children. The three main discourses discussed in Chapter 2 which are applied in these cases are: the 'people as power' discourse, which sees maintaining and enlarging the population of the national collectivity as vital for the national interest; the Malthusian discourse, which, in contrast to the first discourse, sees the reduction of the number of children as the way to prevent future national disaster; and the eugenicist discourse, which aims at improving the 'quality of the national stock' by encouraging those who are 'suitable' in terms of origin and class to have more children and discouraging the others from doing so.

These policies, as the heated debates before and during the 1994 UN Cairo Conference on Population and Development Policies demonstrated, are at the heart of most contemporary politics, both in the North and in the South. Any discussions of women's reproductive rights which do not take into account this national dimension can be held to be seriously wanting. At the same time, any discussion of national (and international) policies concerning development, the economy, welfare, etc., would be wanting if the gendered character of their population policies were not taken into account.

A central dimension of these policies would usually be, to a greater or lesser extent, a concern about the 'genetic pool' of the nation. Nationalist projects which focus on genealogy and origin as the major organizing principles of the national collectivity would tend to be more exclusionary than other nationalist projects. Only by being born into a certain collectivity could one be a full member in it. Control of marriage, procreation and therefore sexuality would thus tend to be high on the nationalist agenda. When constructions of 'race' are added to the notion of the common genetic pool, fear of miscegenation becomes central to the nationalist discourse. In its extremity this includes the 'one-drop rule' (Davis, 1993) which dictates that even if 'one drop of blood' of members of the 'inferior race' is present, it could 'contaminate' and 'pollute' that of the 'superior race'.

Cultural Reproduction and Gender Relations

The notion of 'genetic pools', however, is but one mode of imagining nations. People's 'culture and tradition', which is usually partly composed of a specific version of a specific religion and/or a specific language, is another essential-izing dimension, which in different national projects acquires a significance higher or lower than that of genealogy and blood. The mythical unity of national 'imagined communities' which divides the world between 'us' and 'them' is maintained and ideologically reproduced by a whole system of what Armstrong (1982) calls symbolic 'border guards'. These 'border guards' can identify people as members or non-members of a specific collectivity. They are closely linked to specific cultural codes of style of dress and behaviour as well as to more elaborate bodies of customs, religion, literary and artistic modes of production, and, of course, language.

Gender symbols play a particularly significant role in this, and thus con-structions of manhood and womanhood, as well as sexuality and gendered relations of power, need to be explored in relation to these processes. Chapter 3 discusses women's roles as symbolic border guards and as embodiments of the collectivity, while at the same time being its cultural reproducers. This dimension of women's lives is crucial to understanding their subjectivities as well as their relations with each other, with children and with men. At the same time, discourse and struggles around the issues of 'women's emancipa-tion' or 'women following tradition' (as have been expressed in various campaigns for and against women's veiling, voting, education and employ-ment) have been at the centre of most modernist and anti-modernist nationalist struggles.

In order to understand this centrality of gender relations to nationalist projects, one needs to analyse culture as a dynamic contested resource which can be used differently in different projects and by people who are differen-tially positioned in the collectivity. Chapter 3 explores issues pertaining to projects of multi-culturalism on the one hand and cultural and religious fun-damentalism on the other hand within contemporary globalization processes. It also discusses the particular effects these have on gender relations and on notions of cultural identities and social difference.

Citizenship and Difference

As mentioned in the previous section of this chapter, a third major dimension of nationalist projects, in addition to *Volknation* and *Kulturnation*, is that of *Staatnation*, or state-related citizenship. In Chapter 4 the book explores issues relating to gender relations, citizenship and difference. In some ways, state cit-izenship as a criterion for membership in the national collectivity is the most inclusive mode of joining a collectivity, because in principle anybody – of whatever origin or culture – might be able to join. In practice this inclusiveness is usually dependent not only on the socio-economic resources of those who are applying, but on a myriad of rules and regulations concerning immigration and naturalization, which generally ensure easier access for some categories of people than for others. Women have tended to be differentially regulated to men in nationality, immigration and refugee legislation, often being constructed as dependent on their family men and expected to follow them and live where they do. Although equal opportunity legislation in the west has weakened this sharp differentiation over the last fifteen years, it is by no means obliterated (Bhabha and Shutter, 1994).

However, citizenship in this book is treated in a much wider sense than just the formal right to carry a passport or even to reside in a specific country. It follows T.H. Marshall's definition (1950; 1975; 1981) of citizenship as 'full membership in the community' which encompasses civil, political, and social rights and responsibilities. Thus citizenship is perceived to be multi-layered and often diverse, relating to local, ethnic, state and often trans-state communities. Women's citizenship in these communities is usually of a dual nature: on the one hand they are included in the general body of citizens; on the other hand there are always rules, regulations and policies which are specific to them.

Of course, gender is not the only factor which affects people's citizenship. Ethnicity, class, sexuality, ability, place of residence and so on, affect it as well. The extent to which citizenship should be seen as an individual or a collective attribute, and how this affects constructions and distributions of citizenship rights, are issues which are explored in Chapter 4.

The chapter also examines the classical location of women in the private domain and that of men in the public domain and how this has affected constructions of citizenship. Similarly it explores the notions of passive and active citizenship which, like the private/public dichotomy, have been a base for a comparative typology of citizenship (Turner, 1990).

Gendered Militaries, Gendered Wars

Active citizenship involves not only rights but also duties and responsibilities. The ultimate citizenship responsibility used to be that of being prepared to die for one's country. Chapter 5 examines the constructions of manhood and womanhood which have been linked to participation in militaries and in wars, and how those have been linked to citizenship rights and other social divisions such as ethnicity and class. The chapter examines the effects of modern technology and the professionalization of militaries on the participation of women in the military and their constructions as soldiers. It also looks at the effects these might have on nationalist ideologies which mobilize men to fight for the sake of 'womenandchildren' (Enloe, 1990).

The chapter moves then to examine the gendered character of wars and the sexual divisions which take place not only among the fighters but also among the war victims – the murdered, the raped, the interned and the refugees. The symbolic character of systematic rapes in war is discussed within this context. The chapter ends with a discussion of the relationship between 'womanhood', feminism and 'peace'.

Women, Ethnicity and Empowerment: Towards Transversal Politics

The final chapter of the book (Chapter 6) looks at questions of gender, nation, and the politics of women's empowerment. Within this frame, the chapter examines women's co-operation with and resistance to nationalist struggles on the one hand and international feminist politics on the other. As a way of dealing with some of the difficult issues involved, the chapter starts to develop a model of transversal politics, a mode of coalition politics in which the differential positionings of the individuals and collectives involved will be recognized, as well as the value systems which underlie their struggles. As such, the transversal politics model adheres to Elizabeth Spelman's warning:

> The notion of the generic 'woman' functions in feminist thought much the way the notion of generic 'man' [or 'person'] has functioned in Western philosophy: it obscures the heterogeneity of women and cuts off examination of the significance of such heterogeneity for feminist theory and political activity. (1988: ix)

Notes

1 Msg. Karaman, in *Narod* (Zagreb, Croatia), no. 10, 9 September 1995, p. 14, quoted in Meznaric (1995: 12).

2 Address of the National Executive Committee of the African National Congress (1987: 8), quoted in Gaitskell and Unterhalter (1989: 71).

3 I am using in the book the term 'westocentric' rather than 'Eurocentric' because I want to highlight the fact that 'the western front' expands far beyond Europe.

4 Going over the text of this chapter during the collective madness of Euro '96, one cannot but relate this passion to the playing field and the 'tribal identities' of competitive sport (see Mangan, 1996).

2

WOMEN AND THE BIOLOGICAL REPRODUCTION OF THE NATION

Women affect and are affected by national and ethnic processes in several different ways. This chapter focuses on the dimension of this relationship which corresponds most closely to the so-called 'natural' role of women – to bear children – and on its implications for both the constructions of nations and women's social positionings. As Paola Tabet (1996) argues, one cannot dichotomize between 'natural' and 'controlled' reproduction: all so-called natural biological reproduction takes place in the specific social, political and economic contexts which construct it. A variety of cultural, legal and political discourses are used in constructing boundaries of nations, as will be discussed in the following chapters. However, these boundaries are constructed in order to sort people into 'us' and 'them' and stretch from generation to generation. As the biological 'producers' of children/people, women are also, therefore, 'bearers of the collective' within these boundaries (Yuval-Davis, 1980).

This is something which is often ignored in feminist literature. For example, the editorial of the special issue on population and reproductive rights of the Oxfam journal *Focus on Gender*, published ahead of the UN conference on this question in Cairo, states that 'biology, conjugal relations and kinship obligations can override women's freedom to decide their own fertility' (1994: 4). The argument in this chapter is that women's positionings in and obligations to their ethnic and national collectivities, as well as in and to the states they reside in and/or are citizens of, also affect and can sometimes override their reproductive rights.

Before discussing, however, the specific ways which are usually used in various nationalist discourses to construct women as 'bearers of the collective', the chapter examines the intersections between women's reproductive roles and the constructions of nations.

Blood and Belonging

The central importance of women's reproductive roles in ethnic and national discourses becomes apparent when one considers that, given the central role that the myth (or reality) of 'common origin' plays in the construction of most ethnic and national collectivities, one usually joins the collectivity by being born into it. In some cases, especially when nationalist and racist ideologies are very closely interwoven, this might be the only way to join the collectivity, as those who are not born into it are excluded. The only way 'outsiders' can conceivably join the national collectivity in such cases might be by intermarriage. But even then, as for example was the case in Nazi law, the 'pure blood' can be 'contaminated' even if one-eighth or one-sixteenth is the blood of the others (Jews, blacks). And James Davis, in his book *Who Is Black? One Nation's Definition* (1993), describes the 'one-drop rule' which has operated in the construction of the definition of 'who is black' in the USA.

It is not incidental, therefore, that those who are preoccupied with the 'purity' of the race would also be preoccupied with the sexual relationships between members of different collectivities. Typically, the first (and only) legislative proposal that Rabbi Kahana, the leader of the Israeli fascist party Kach, raised when he was a member of the Israeli Parliament was to forbid sexual relationships between Jews and Arabs. Legal permission for people from different 'races' to have sex and to marry was one of the first significant steps that the South African government took in its journey towards the abolition of apartheid.

The inclusion of a new baby in a national collectivity is far from being, of course, purely a biological issue. In different religious and customary laws, the membership of a child might depend exclusively on the father's membership (as in Islam) or the mother's membership (as in Judaism), or it might be open for a dual or voluntary choice membership. A variety of rules and regulations govern when children born to 'mixed parenthood' become part of the collectivity and when they do not. They can be considered a separate social category, as was the case in South Africa; part of the 'inferior' collectivity, as during slavery; or – although this is rarer – part of the 'superior' collectivity, as was the case in marriages between Spanish settlers and aristocratic Indians in Mexico (Gutierrez, 1995). Social as well as legal conventions are of crucial importance here. A man from Ghana tried in the 1970s to claim his British origin, stating the patriality clause in the British Immigration Act, and arguing that his African grandmother was legally married to his British grandfather. The judge rejected his claim, arguing that at that period no British man would have genuinely married an African woman (WING, 1985).

The importance of 'common origin' as an organizing principle of nations varies. There are some nations, like Switzerland and Belgium, where several specific ethnic groupings constitute the 'nation'. In settler societies, such as the USA or Australia, 'common destiny' rather than 'common origin' might be the crucial factor in the constitution of 'the nation', but nevertheless there would be an implicit, if not explicit, hierarchy of desirability of 'origin' and culture which would underlie the nation building processes, including immigration and natal policies (Stasiulis and Yuval-Davis, 1995). While the position of women as migrants, immigrants and refugees can be deeply affected by nationalist constructions of boundaries, differential natal national policies can affect the lives of all women in 'the nation'.

Even when 'common origin' is not the most important dimension of specific nationalist projects, the knowledge of one's 'true' origin can deeply affect
one's identity and identification with particular ethnic and national collectivities. Marilyn Strathern (1996a; 1996b) claims that this is a specific
Euro-American cultural configuration, as is the notion that conception of a
child is an outcome of a single sexual act (rather than of a continuous process
of involvement). The fashionable search by adopted children and those born
through artificial insemination for their 'true' parents – rather than acceptance of the parents who continuously cared for and nurtured them while they
were growing up – needs to be viewed in the light of this western mode of
identity construction. An extreme case reported in the British press in 1995
was of a man who was adopted as a baby by a Jewish family and who claimed
that he discovered, when papers related to his adoption were made accessible
to him, that he was not 'Jewish' at all but an 'Arab' – born as a result of an
affair between an English woman and a Kuwaiti man when they were both
students in London. Although the man realized that his 'biological' father did
not want to have anything to do with him, he became engaged in a (most
probably futile) legal battle to be given Kuwaiti citizenship. Membership in an
ethnic and national collectivity, as well as in a particular family, was the goal
in this search for origin. In order not to allow any ambiguity in this respect,
the law in Israel concerning surrogate motherhood declares that the surrogate
mother and the 'real' mother have to be of the same religious origin (*Ma'ariv*,
10 July 1996). The attempt in many local authorities in Britain during the
1980s not to allow inter-racial fostering and adoption also assumed an essentialist linear relationship between individual identity, family membership and
uncrossable collectivity boundaries.

New developments in genetic engineering, and the identification of a mul-
titude of genes which supposedly determine our moral and social aptitude as
well as our chances of becoming ill in specific ways, bring to the fore new,
medical reasons for the need for knowledge of biological origin. However, the
renewed interest in genetic theories of intelligence (Herrnstein and Murray,
1994) again shows the close interrelationship between such so-called scientific
interests and racialized constructions of collectivities.

Funnily enough, people's need for discovery of their 'true' biological origin,
and the direct implications this has on their constructions of identities of
selves, is happening at the same time that other medical and genetic engineering developments enable transplantations of human – and recently
animal (pig) – body parts. This latter development does not seem to affect
people's perceptions about who they – and others – are, even when vital and
symbolically significant organs, such as the heart, are involved. It seems that
in this discourse of biology/identity some parts of the body are more directly
linked with identity than others. The moral and legal debates around issues of
in vitro fertilization and 'surrogate motherhood' prove the centrality in this
debate of 'women as wombs' and the commodification of women's reproductive powers, especially those women from lower economic and ethnic
positions (Raymond, 1993).

This commodification also has an international dimension in the trafficking of women and of babies for adoption and the horrific trade in foetal and children's organs for research and transplantations (1993: 187). As such, the relationship here is not only between individual people, desperate for economic resources or for children, selling and buying reproductive 'products', but also between less and more powerful national collectivities, with higher and lower national reproductive rates.

Surrogacy and adoption notwithstanding, whether women are encouraged, discouraged or sometimes forced to have or not to have children, or – especially since the development of the appropriate antenatal tests – to have children of a particular sex, depends on the hegemonic discourses which construct nationalist projects at specific historical moments. One or more of three major discourses tend to dominate nationalist policies of population control. They are the discourse I call 'people as power'; the eugenicist discourse; and the Malthusian discourse. In the following sections of the chapter these discourses will be described, although it is beyond the scope of this book to examine closely the actual processes of implementation of these policies and women's responses to them.

People as Power

In this discourse, the future of 'the nation' is seen to depend on its continuous growth. Sometimes this growth can be based also on immigration. At other times, it depends almost exclusively on the reproductive powers of women who are called upon to have more children. The need for people – often primarily for men – can be for a variety of nationalist purposes, civil and military. They can be needed as workers, as settlers, as soldiers. For example, in Japan the government is currently offering a reward of 5000 yen ($38) a month for each child under school age and twice as much for third children. They are worried as the birth rate in Japan is now the lowest in its history. (There is talk about Japanese women having gone on a 'birth strike' because conditions for raising children are so bad.) TV advertisements exhort people to 'Get a brother (or sister) [*sic*] for your child.' The official reason for this campaign is the welfare of 'the nation': if Japan's population declines it will cause 'labour shortages, sluggish economic growth and higher tax burdens to support social services for the elderly'. This campaign, however, has raised echoes of the coercive 1930s campaign to 'breed and multiply' for the good of the Japanese empire (WGNRR, 1991).

In settler societies, such as Australia, the call has been to 'populate or perish' (deLepervanche, 1989). A certain 'critical mass' of people was seen as crucial for the viability of the 'nation building' process there. Although immigration was encouraged as a quick way to achieve this goal, measures were originally taken to keep 'undesirable elements' out, such as the construed Asian 'yellow peril'. In Israel, also, immigration was highly encouraged to provide people to settle the country. In this case, however, the desired immigration was even more exclusive – namely Jewish, although it included more or less 'desirable' Jewish communities, Ashkenazi (western) and Mizrakhi (oriental). However, unlike the sparse Aboriginal population in Australia, the indigenous Palestinian population has been fiercely resisting the Zionist Jewish settlement project, and the military aspect of the 'nation building' process has been predominant (Abdo and Yuval-Davis, 1995; Ehrlich, 1987). In order to encourage Jewish women to have more children, a variety of policies have been developed, including child allowances, maternity leave and, for some years after the establishment of the state (following a similar policy in the Soviet Union), declaring an award for 'heroine mothers' who had ten children or more.

The 'demographic race' with the Palestinians has been prominent in Israel's history (Portuguese, 1996; Yuval-Davis, 1989). Shimon Peres, in his role as the Israeli Foreign Minister, was reported in the Israeli press (October 1993) to have said that 'Politics is a matter of demography, not geography' when explaining his readiness for Israeli (very partial) withdrawal from the Occupied Territories (those occupied since the 1967 war). In other societies in which national conflict exists between two national groupings which compete on the same territory, similar importance has been given to the 'demographic balance' – as in Lebanon, Cyprus and former Yugoslavia. In Slovenia, for example, in 1991, the platform of the major party Demos explicitly stated that 'women should not have the right to abort future defenders of the nation.' In Poland, one of the arguments for criminalizing abortion in 1989 referred to Poland's 1920 victory over the Red Army as proof of the need for a large population (Fuszara, 1993). There are also claims that the pressure for finding a solution to the Northern Ireland problem is currently mounting owing, to a great extent, to the fact that Catholics are going to become, before too long, the majority of the population there.

The 'demographic race' can take place not only where there is a national conflict on a contested territory but also where an ethnic majority is seen as crucial in order to retain the hegemony of the hegemonic collectivity. Angela Davis describes how in 1906 President Roosevelt 'admonished the well-born white women who engaged in wilful sterility – the one sin for which the penalty is national death, race suicide' (1993: 351, quoted in Portuguese, 1996: 33–4). Recently in Bulgaria, with similar concerns, the government has implemented measures to encourage ethnic Bulgarian women to have more children in their 'demographic race' with the Turkish and Romani minorities who have a higher birth rate (Petrova, 1993).

The pressure on women to bear more children can also be a national strategy to overcome a national disaster. In Russia, for instance, pro-natalist policies were a direct response to the depletion of the population following the revolution and the civil war (Riley, 1981b: 193, in Portuguese, 1996: 48). Similarly in Israel, pro-natalist ideologies have been connected not only to the Zionist settlement project but also to the aftermath of the Nazi Holocaust in which 6 million Jews died. Not having children – or even marrying and having children 'out' of the Jewish community – has been seen as contributing to a 'demographic Holocaust'. In the early 1980s a senior Internal Affairs Ministry civil servant attempted (but luckily failed) to force Jewish women who contemplated legal abortions to watch a video in which appeared not only the usual 'pro-life' movement images of foetuses as murdered babies, but also images of Jewish children in the Nazi concentration camps (Yuval-Davis, 1989: 99).

Of course the height of coercion of women to breed children for the sake of the nation took place in Nazi Germany with the *Lebensborn* programme when SS men were encouraged to father as many children as possible with Aryan women of 'pure stock'. The men were not expected to marry the women and the children would be brought up by the state (Koontz, 1986: 398–402). The Nazis, however, not only forced certain German women to have children, they forced others not to have them. This has been part of their eugenistic discourse on national reproduction: 'The struggle of the males for the female grants the right or opportunity to propagate only to the healthiest' (Hitler, *Mein Kampf*, quoted in Koontz, 1986: 402).

The Eugenicist Discourse

Eugenics, a pseudo-science, concerned itself not with the size of the nation but with its 'quality'. Concerns about the 'quality' of 'the nation' have been shared, of course, by much wider circles than self-declared eugenicists. It was concern for the 'British race' which Beveridge describes in his famous report as the motivation for establishing the British welfare state system (Beveridge, 1942). Better health, education and housing for the poor have been promoted as necessary for improving the quality of the welfare nations. Eugenics, however, did not concern itself with better nurturing of children, but attempted to predetermine the quality of the nation via 'nature' in the way of selective breeding.

> Genetic laws, said racial scientists, would determine the future of the human race; policymakers' only option was whether to use genetic knowledge to advance humankind or to refuse to allow racial degeneration to destroy the *Volk*. (Koontz, 1986: 150)

While 'pure Aryans' were made to breed through a variety of economic and social incentives, a programme of forced sterilization was carried out (until successfully resisted) for the 'feeble minded' and other kinds of *Lebensunwurdiges* ('life unworthy of life'). This type of programme, however, was not a Nazi invention. In 1927, for instance, the US Supreme Court upheld the constitutionality of Virginia's similar involuntary sterilization law, and such programmes were practised in some of the Southern states in the USA formally until the 1970s. Testimonies at the NGO Forum of the UN Conference on Population and Development Policies in September 1994 in Cairo have described contemporary practices (though not official policies) of a similar nature aimed at disabled people in many countries in both the North and the South, and it is probable that genetic engineering will encourage this trend even more in the future.

But eugenistic constructions of national reproduction concern much more than the physical 'health' of the next generation: they concern notions of 'national stock' and the biologization of cultural traits. The Royal Commission on Population in Britain declared in its 1949 report :

> British traditions, manners, and ideas in the world have to be borne in mind. Immigration is thus not a desirable means of keeping the population at a replacement level as it would in effect reduce the proportion of home-bred stock in the population. (quoted in Riley, 1981a)

One can see here the origins of the Powellian/Thatcherite 'new racism' (Barker, 1981) in which 'culture' and 'tradition' become essentialized and biologized into notions of genealogical 'difference' and which were at the heart of the 'fear of being swamped by immigrants' with which Margaret Thatcher won her first election campaign in the UK (see discussion in Chapter 3).

The country in which today population policies are formulated in the strongest eugenistic terms is Singapore, where Prime Minister Lee Kuan Yew demanded that highly educated women as their patriotic duty should produce children who would be genetically superior, while poor uneducated mothers were given a cash award of $10,000 if they agreed to be sterilized rather than continue to produce their genetically inferior children (Heng and Devan, 1992). Although not always evident and not seen everywhere to the same extent, differential policies of encouragement and discouragement of child-bearing towards different segments of the population (based on class, ethnicity, 'race' and often all of these) exist in many countries.

Tamar Lewin, for example (WGNRR, 1991), cites a plan in Kansas to pay welfare mothers (many of whom are black) $500 plus $50 a year for having Norplant patches (containing long term slow release chemical contraceptives) implanted in them. The programme, which was suggested by a right-wing 'right to life' representative, was supported by an editorial in the local paper 'because of the growing poverty among black welfare mothers'. The USA was the only country in the North to have participated in the full scale experiments on Norplant – but the groups of women to whom it was given were carefully targeted. It is widely known that in many western countries, from Britain to Australia, unsafe contraceptive devices such as the notorious Depo-Pravera injection (long term contraceptive with life threatening side-effects banned in many countries) and sterilizations (including unapproved non-surgical sterilization methods like Quinacrine: Berer, 1995) were given almost exclusively to poor and minority women (*Reproductive Rights Campaign* newsletters, 1981–3).

The Malthusian Discourse

The story is somewhat different in many developing countries (or, as they are sometimes called, the countries of LACAAP: Latin America, the Caribbean, Africa, Asia and the Pacific) where there is a fear that the unchecked continuous growth ('explosion') of the population might bring a national (or international) disaster (Hartman, 1987). There the population control policies are primarily aimed at reducing the rate of growth overall. Women are often the 'captive' target population for such policies. In Brazil, for instance, it has been reported that 45 per cent of women who undergo Caesarean operation end up being sterilized (Bradiotti et al., 1994: 144) and such stories are common elsewhere. In India, during the 'emergency period' in the 1970s, sterilization policies were primarily aimed at men. This is considered to be one of the main reasons for the consequent defeat of the Congress Party in its strongholds in the next election, and as a result women became virtually the only targets of population control policies. While there are specific annual target numbers for women's sterilizations, especially while they are in hospitals giving birth, male vasectomy has virtually disappeared (oral report at the 1994 UN Cairo conference).

Thomas Malthus, the British clergyman turned economist, predicted before 1800 that the planet would not be able to support for long the human population, which grows much faster than global food resources. His explanation for this was that human population grows each generation at a geometrical rate, while the food supply grows only at an arithmetic rate. Only human misery – caused by poverty, famine and pestilence as well as wars and slaughters – would keep the human population size under control. As Hartman (1987: 13–14) comments, however, Malthus was wrong on two basic counts. Firstly, population growth can be slowed down and eventually stabilized by the voluntary choices of individuals and not just by 'natural' disasters. Secondly, Malthus greatly underestimated the capacity of the planet to feed its growing human population and the consequent very different relations between human production and reproduction rates.

However, Malthusian-type prophesies continued to be heard periodically, although they became increasingly more focused on Third World countries. A very influential book in that respect was *The Population Bomb* which came out in 1968, written by the Stanford University biologist Paul Ehrlich. Focusing on the rate of population growth in the Third World combined a racist fear of being 'swamped' by the non-western 'others' with an easy let-out explanation for guilty western liberal consciences for the persistence of poverty and a low standard of life in Third World countries in the post-colonial period. Most importantly, however, Malthusian discourse has not just been an ideological discourse but has become a cornerstone of population policies in many Third World countries themselves, as a major strategy to try and solve those countries' economic and social problems. There is a fear of the destabilization of the economic and political system if the balance between the supply and demand for labour power is seriously threatened as a result of 'uncontrollable' growth in the population.

The country which has gone furthest in this respect is China. While during the 1950s Mao saw the people as part of national power and resources, a total reversal of policies took place in the 1970s. Severe measures were taken so that most Chinese families would not have more than one baby (some minority and rural families were allowed two children if the first child was a girl). In their extreme form, punishments for evading these measures have involved unemployment for the parents and exclusion from education of the child. The effects of these policies, however, have been quite uneven, partly as a result of differential policies and partly because state control has been most effective in cities and in central areas of the country. This has produced a demographic shift, skewed towards backward rural areas and minority groups, and there are signs that as a reaction China is now turning to more eugenistic policies of population control, in which 'China will use abortions, sterilization and marriage bans to "avoid new births of inferior quality and heighten the standards of the whole population"' (quote from the official New China News Agency, *Washington Post*, 22 December 1993). There have also been reports that harsh population control measures have been taken against communities such as the Tibetans (Lentin, forthcoming).

The effect of Malthusian policies is often highly gendered. Where there is strong pressure to limit the number of children, and where male children are more highly valued for social and economic reasons, practices of abortions and infanticide are mainly directed towards baby girls. There are rumours about villages in China and India in which certain age groups, born after Malthusian policies were enacted, are 100 per cent male. Female babies are also often the ones which are more easily available for international adoption.

The 'national interest' behind severe population control measures in the South, however, often is not the result of an internal governmental initiative but is induced from outside because of the North's (especially the USA's) perception of their own 'national interest'. A CIA report leaked a few years ago described the effects of high birth rates as leading to 'political instability in the 3rd World which in turn would create security problems to the US' (WGNRR, 1991). Thus, the Reagan administration gave $3 billion for population control as part of its 'development' aid – three times the total amount spent for this purpose under Johnson, Nixon, Ford and Carter (although, owing to the Christian right's pressures, they banned any aid which would have supported abortion services). The US Agency for International Development (USAID) has given money for family planning purposes to 95 countries – including all the 45 states in sub-Saharan Africa (all), and also notably Mexico and the Philippines, despite the fact that, as Elizabeth Sobo remarks (WGNRR, 1991), the population density of people in Africa is one-tenth that in Europe.

In the New World Order, the World Bank is playing a key role in the formation of population policy by virtue of its leverage over other forms of development finance. Thus, population control measures can become part of the 'structural adjustment' package. There is high pressure on women (and it is almost always only on women – who are an easier 'captive audience', usually after they give birth, especially by Caesarean section) to be sterilized or to use other long term contraceptives from IUDs to Depo-Pravera, Norplant and Quinacrine. Sometimes the means used are more subtle. Apparently USAID has given $350,000 to one of Nigeria's top musicians, King Sunny

Aid, to sing about family planning and having fewer children (he, of course, has twelve children himself). This is part of the $35.4 million Five Year Program of the Population Communication Services Center at Johns Hopkins University for improving response in 'culturally appropriate ways to influence family planning acceptance and use'(WGNRR, 1991). The policy makers must have understood that somehow they had been getting it wrong. This was clearly illustrated when I visited Egypt in 1980 and saw Cairo covered with huge family planning posters showing a family of a man, a woman, a boy, a girl and a transistor radio, in reaction to which my taxi driver commented: 'the poor fools – who is going to look after them when they are old?'

The Social Context

This remark of the taxi driver is important because it draws our attention to the social context in which these policies are taking place. It is important to note that often there is a serious conflict between collective national and individual interests in terms of the number of children one has. When there are no welfare structures to look after the elderly and the ill, it is crucial for people to have enough healthy children to support them. Moreover, when there are no developed public health services and the rate of infant mortality is high, there is a real interest for the women to become pregnant as many times as possible. As Hartman (1987: 8) has pointed out, there has never been a case where the rate of population growth has gone down where the rate of infant mortality has not gone down as well. This is especially important to remember in times of structural adjustment policies, because at the same time as they create pressures to cut the rate of population growth, they also cut funds for public health care and the support required for women to bear and rear healthy babies. As Sonia Correa (1994: 7) reports, a massive international campaign by the reproductive health and rights movement succeeded in shifting the political agenda for the UN Conference on Population and Development Policies in Cairo (September 1994), so that its resolutions spoke no longer just about family planning and contraceptive services but about reproductive health. This would also encompass maternal and child care and the prevention of cancer and sexually transmitted diseases. And although there is a great distance between formal UN declarations and their implementation, this shift in the public political discourse is all for the good.

The absence of public health and welfare infrastructure is not, however, the only social factor which needs to be taken into consideration, as the fierce resistance to women's reproductive rights by the Vatican/Iran fundamentalist alliance during the Cairo conference can attest. For them and other religious leaders the ability of women to control their own bodies is seen as a direct threat to their authority, and very many women would hesitate to take any action which would be interpreted as a betrayal of sacred religious and customary laws. It is important to stress in this context, however (as will be elaborated in Chapter 3), that rather than being a result of 'intrinsic' and 'essential' religious imperatives, religious authority is being invoked in order to legitimate conflicting positions concerning women and their reproductive options (Makhlouf Obermeyer, 1994).

Moreover, in social and cultural systems where the social value of women (as well as, usually, their ability to exercise some social power, especially when old) depends on whether or not they have sons, the number of children that women bear can depend on much more thorough and all-encompassing processes of social transformation, especially in relation to what Sonia Correa and Ros Petchesky (1994) have called women's social rights. Processes of globalization – economic, political and social – also create contradictory pressures on women's fertility. On the one hand, there is more pressure on women to go out to work, and often through international aid organizations there are more contraceptives available. On the other hand, rising ethnic and religious fundamentalist identity and political movements tighten control over women and increase opposition to any reproductive rights in the name of 'custom and tradition'.

In addition to the overall context, however, we need to look also, as Rani Bang and Abhay Bang (1992) point out, at the immediate effects the usage of high-tech contraceptives can have on women's lives. In societies where so many women suffer from gynaecological conditions anyway – which are not taken care of when they are sterilized or implanted with Norplant – their physical discomfort largely grows. And in cultures where women, when they are bleeding (and Norplant, for example, often causes frequent bleeding), are prevented from carrying out ritual tasks, and their husbands cannot have sex with them, this can also have serious ramifications on their lives, including being deserted or divorced by their husbands, as many testimonies at the NGO Forum of the Cairo UN conference have brought to light. These testimonies also included cases of women whose husbands left them because of the after-effects of an early menopause once the Norplant has been removed; so the physical side-effects can be long term as well as short term.

It is important to remember that it can also be non-governmental formal and informal groupings, both religious (like the Catholic Church) and national, which exert pressure and sometimes force on women to have or not to have children. For example, there has been strong pressure on Palestinian women to bear more children for the national struggle, as a Palestinian woman told me: 'We need to have one son to fight and get killed, one son to go to prison, one son to go to the oil countries to make money and one son to look after us when we are old.' Yasser Arafat is reported to have said that 'The Palestinian woman who bears yet another Palestinian every ten months . . . is a biological time bomb threatening to blow up Israel from within' (Portuguese, 1996: 311).

On the other hand, the prospect of children born out of wedlock, and even worse, outside the 'proper' religious and national boundaries, can be considered as bringing shame on the family, and women who are suspected of 'fraternizing' with 'the enemy' might be severely punished. The reports on Bosnian children born of war rapes who have been abandoned in hospitals and orphanages because of the shame to the family and the ethnic group is another case in point (see the discussion on war rapes in Chapter 5).

Concluding Remark: Reproductive Rights, National Reproduction and Feminist Politics

As discussed in the introduction, women's membership in their national and ethnic collectivities is of a double nature. On the one hand, women, like men, are members of the collectivity. On the other hand, there are always specific rules and regulations which relate to women as women. This is especially important to remember when we consider the political implications of the ways women are constructed as biological reproducers of 'the nation'. In spite of the fact that usually, if not always, in the sex/gender systems in their societies men are dominant, women are not just passive victims, or even objects, of the ideologies and policies aimed at controlling their reproduction. On the contrary, very often it is women, especially older women, who are given the roles of the cultural reproducers of 'the nation' and are empowered to rule on what is 'appropriate' behaviour and appearance and what is not and to exert control over other women who might be constructed as 'deviants'. As very often this is the main source of social power allowed to women, they might become fully engaged in it.

Most of the feminist discourse which relates to 'reproductive rights' of women tends to relate to women in individualistic terms, as does the slogan of 'women's rights as human rights'. As Correa and Petchesky (1994: 109–10) argue, critics of 'rights' discourse have pointed out that the value and meaning of rights are always contingent upon the political and social context, are indeterminate and are dependent on the social categories and collectivities to which people belong. Specifically in relation to women's reproductive rights there has been a growing concern during the last few years among 'women of colour' that the co-option of such slogans by international agencies and the Right is part of a 'demographic war' which, if not completely genocidal, is aimed at stunting the growth and power of black and Third World people (for a summary of the debates see Petchesky and Weiner, 1990). But not only them. As Roza Tsagarousianou (1995) argues, banning abortions (as well as controlling other reproductive rights of women) signals the treatment of women as state property. On the other hand, these anti-individualistic concerns can become co-opted by nationalist and religious fundamentalists who object – as was the case in the 1994 UN Human Rights Conference in Vienna – to any international constitutional guarantees for women's reproductive rights, as interference in the collective human rights of their nations which include the right to follow their own 'culture and tradition'.

The implications of some of the above concerns will be explored in more detail in later chapters. There is no space here to fully develop a framework for feminist politics on reproductive rights which might take account of the above pitfalls. However, such a framework would take account of the fact that women are not just 'individuals' but are also members of national, ethnic and racial collectivities as well as of specific class, sexuality and life cycle positionings. Women are not just individuals, nor are they just agents of their collectivities. 'Reproductive rights' campaigns should take account of the multiplexity and multi-dimensionality of identities within contemporary society, without losing sight of the differential power dimension of different collectivities and groupings within it (see Chapter 4).

Such campaigns should also recognize that 'culture' is never an essentialist and homogeneous body of traditions and customs, but a rich resource, usually full of internal contradictions, and a resource which is always used selectively in various ethnic cultural and religious projects within specific power relations and political discourse (see Chapter 3).

In sum, 'reproductive rights' should be seen as a vital part of the more general struggle for women's emancipation. This in turn should be seen as a vital part of the more general struggle for the democratization of society, which should take into account the different positioning of people in the society (see Chapter 6).

3

CULTURAL REPRODUCTION AND GENDER RELATIONS

'Culture' has come to play a central role in both analyses and ideologies of national and other collectivities. Carl-Ulrik Schierup has even claimed that

> a general 'culturization' of the political language has taken place. Here, strategies of dominance as well as those of rebellion become increasingly phrased in the culturized terms of ethnic particularity. This takes place in manners that often act to displace the articulation of more general cleavages contained in the constitution of modern society. (1995: 2)

Aleksandra Ålund in her succinct way has summed it up as 'the cultural has colonized the social' (1995: 319).

Indeed, Verena Stolcke (1995) argues that 'cultural fundamentalism' has come to replace racism as the primary discourse of the Right, and a leftist feminist like Renate Rosaldo (1991) has been looking to 'cultural citizenship' as the solution to political issues at local and national levels. In the aftermath of the Cold War, identity politics, which started to emerge as a 'means of political empowerment among marginalized groupings such as blacks and women, has merged with national and international policies of multi-culturalism to become a new hegemonic discourse.

In this culturalized discourse, gendered bodies and sexuality play pivotal roles as territories, markers and reproducers of the narratives of nations and other collectivities. As will be examined in this chapter, gender relations are at the heart of cultural constructions of social identities and collectivities as well as in most cultural conflicts and contestations. Feminism has raised our awareness of such processes taking place as well as of resistance to them.

This chapter looks at 'the location of culture' (Bhabha, 1994a), cultural diversity and cultural changes. Within that it examines the ways gendered discourse and gender relations are articulated. Although, as will be argued below, 'culture' is dynamic and includes notions of diversity and change, for presentation purposes I discuss different aspects of culture separately. In the first part of the chapter the notion of 'culture' is examined as well as its relationship to the notions of 'civilization', 'ethnicity' and 'identity'. The chapter then moves to discuss the ways cultural difference has been related to notions of 'otherness' and boundary management. Racism, assimilationism, multi-culturalism and hybridization are some of the constructs with which notions of cultural difference have been incorporated into contestations and struggles of power relations. The chapter assesses the ways notions of manhood and womanhood, as well as sexuality and gendered relations of power, constitute parts of these processes. The articulation of gender is also investigated in relation to notions of cultural change, modernity and postmodernity and the processes of globalization and essentialization of culture and religion.

The Notion of Culture

Even more than many other central concepts in the social sciences, the definition and meaning of the term 'culture' has been contested. Raymond Williams, the 'father' of 'cultural studies', has suggested three meanings for the term: one of a general process of intellectual, spiritual and aesthetic development (culture as 'civilization'); one of 'the works and practices of intellectual and artistic activity' ('high culture'); and one of 'a particular way of life, whether of people, a period or a group' (1983: 90). It is the last which, as Anthony Giddens (1989: 31) points out, sociologists tend to use. According to him this way of life is composed of 'the values the members of a given group hold, the norms they follow and the material goods they create' (1989: 31).

Jonathan Friedman, who has looked at the emergence of the culture concept in anthropology, describes its 'long and confusing history', especially in the nineteenth century when 'culture was simply what was distinctive about others' (1994: 67–77). The confusion often stems from the conflation of the above three different meanings of the concept of culture which at the time were philosophically differentiated but anthropologically fused. It also brought about a close association between 'race' in the form of *Volkgeist*, and 'culture' used as 'people's defining characteristics'. Only at the turn of century, with the work of Franz Boaz, did culture become separated from its racial and demographic basis, and start to be studied as an autonomous abstraction, a phenomenon in its own right. One should not lose sight of the fact, however, that at least until recently the cultures studied have tended to be those of the 'other'. Popular culture as opposed to 'high culture' within western society has, only relatively recently, become a legitimate subject of study. Furthermore, essentialized constructions of 'cultural difference' constitute one of the major modes of contemporary popular racisms (Modood, 1994; Stolcke, 1995).

The development of the concept of culture has been determined for a long time by the cyclical debate which Friedman describes between those who hold universalist and those who hold relativist paradigms of culture. According to the first perspective there is one generic human culture in which different people and groupings have particular rank according to their 'stage of development', which is often described in evolutionary terms. This is being rejected by those who hold the relativist perspective, according to which different civilizations have different cultures which need to be understood/judged within their own terms. Geertz, for example, has actually claimed that there is no culture in general, but only specific cultures (quoted in Friedman, 1994: 73).

In spite of the difference between these two perspectives and the perpetual debate between them, they share, as Chatterjee (1986) has pointed out, an essentialist view of 'culture' as having specific fixed 'cultural stuff' of symbols, ways of behaviour and artifacts which coherently and unproblematically constitute cultures of specific national and ethnic collectivities. Internal differentiations and differences in positionings cannot be accounted for in either of these two approaches.

A much more useful way of theorizing culture has been developed during the last few years, using discourse analyses inspired by both Gramsci and Foucault, in which cultures have been transformed from static reified homogeneous phenomena common to all members of national and ethnic collectivities, into dynamic social processes operating in contested terrains in which different voices become more or less hegemonic in their offered interpretations of the world (Bhabha, 1994a; Bottomley, 1992; Friedman, 1994). Cultural discourses often resemble more a battleground of meaning than a shared point of departure. Cultural homogeneity in this view would be a result of hegemonization, and it would always be limited and more noticeable in the centre rather than in the social margins, being affected by the social positioning of its carriers. As Gill Bottomley claims :

> 'Culture', in the sense of ideas, beliefs and practices that delineate particular ways of being in the world, also generates conscious and unconscious forms of resistance – to homogenization, to devaluation, to marginalizing by those who fear difference. (1993: 12)

This raises questions about continuity and persistence of cultures as well as about the relationships between different cultures. Anthony Smith (1986) and Armstrong (1982) both argue that cultural myths and symbols have an enduring ability which is being reproduced generation after generation, notwithstanding changing historical and material conditions. However, this seeming durability can be very misleading. Our view of it stems from a very particular temporal perspective: we can see all the cultural stuff that has endured all these historical changes and survived. We cannot be fully aware, however, of how much cultural stuff has *not* survived historical change, archaeological and historical research notwithstanding. Moreover, even with pieces of cultural stuff that have survived historical changes, their meanings can and do undergo radical changes and often they become just symbolic markers of identity (Armstrong, 1982; Gans, 1979). Similarly, while some portray the world in terms of clashes between separate and opposing civilizations (Cox, 1995; Hartman, 1995), others are much more aware of the synthetic nature of all contemporary cultures, their appropriations of symbolic artifacts and meanings from other civilizations and their own internal heterogeneity (Bhabha, 1994a).

It is important to recognize the two contradictory coexistent elements in the operation of cultures: the tendency for stabilization and continuity on the one hand, and that for perpetual resistance and change on the other. Both of these tendencies stem from the close relationship between power relations and cultural practice (Bourdieu, 1977; Bottomley, 1992). As Friedman (1994: 76) points out, cultures are not just arbitrary collections of values, artifacts and modes of behaviour. They acquire, to a greater or lesser extent, 'stabilizing properties' which are inherent in the practices of their social reproduction. These practices of social reproduction are not just processes of cloning, but processes of social interaction in which motivation and desire play their part. As a result, cultural models become resonant with subjective experience. They become the ways individuals experience themselves, their collectivities and the world.

The religious domain, therefore, bears a close relationship to that of culture, although the two cannot be reduced to each other. Religion relates to the sphere of the sacred, of the ultimate meaning (Beyer, 1994; Durkheim, 1965; Geertz, 1966; Luckman, 1967; Tillich, 1957). It supplies the individual, within specific social and historic contexts, with explicit or implicit answers to the three basic existential questions people have to grapple with: what is the meaning/purpose of one's life; what happens to people when they die; and what are good and evil? The relation between the world of everyday life and the sacred religious domain is usually indirect. Many of what Luckman calls 'graduated strata of meaning' (1967: 58) mediate between the trivial and 'profane' and the 'ultimate' significance of a biography or a social tradition. And in a pluralist society they do not all have to come from the same religious sources. Specific religious institutions and a belief in god(s) are common, but by no means a necessary ingredient of religion defined in this way. However, once these 'transcendent superordinated and integrating structures of meaning are socially objectivated', to use Luckman's (1967: 25) terminology, a paradoxical situation often develops. Because of their ultimate meaning, they can become some of the most intractable and inflexible symbolic border guards of specific collectivity boundaries and cultural traditions – so much so that Durkheim (1965) has seen in religion the most basic socially cohesive act, in which symbolically society worships its own 'collective conscience'. At the same time, as religions often present their answers as pertaining to the whole human condition, not just members of a specific collectivity, they would tend to include an expansionary missionary element in them. This might mean an engagement in voluntary or involuntary conversion of members of other collectivities, who would culturally and politically be excluded in most other ways. What usually happens is that the same religion (whether it is Christianity, Islam or Buddhism) becomes incorporated into hegemonic traditions of the different collectivities and acquires specific cultural signifiers which would associate it with those collectivities. At the same time, this definition of the religious arena also includes ideological constructions of individuals' identity as autonomous and free from subservience to any formalized religious codes and institutions. In other words, ideological constructions which have been associated with the rise of modernity and secularism are considered in this approach to be explicitly religious.

Although analytically the discourse of religion and culture is distinct from that of power relations (Assad, 1993), concretely and historically it is always embedded in them. This is true not only in relation to hierarchies of power within the religious and cultural institutions and their relations to more general structures of class and power within the society, but also in relation to the religious and cultural imaginations and their hierarchies of desirability as well as constructions of inclusions and exclusions. Sexuality and gender are central in this (King, 1995).

Also, because of the central importance of social reproduction to culture, gender relations often come to be seen as constituting the 'essence' of cultures as ways of life to be passed from generation to generation. The construction of 'home' is of particular importance here, including relations between adults and between adults and children in the family, ways of cooking and eating, domestic labour, play and bedtime stories, out of which a whole world view, ethical and aesthetic, can become naturalized and reproduced. However, as Floya Anthias and I (1989: 7–8) have pointed out, one can hold on to the problematic notion of reproduction only if processes of growth, decline and transformation are included in it.

Cultures operate within both social and spatial contexts which cannot be understood separately from the time dimension (Massey, 1994). Different positionings, both socially and geographically, would affect the ways cultures are articulated and used, both inside and outside collectivities. Gerd Bauman (1994) has pointed out that while dominant discourse assumes the congruence of culture and community, demotic (of the people) discourse tends to deny this. A clear example of such a 'demotic' discourse has been the slogan of Southall Black Sisters and Women Against Fundamentalism when they chanted in anti-domestic-violence demonstrations in Southall and in countering the Islamist anti-Rushdie demonstration: 'Our tradition – resistance, not submission!'

Rather than being a fixed and homogeneous body of tradition and custom, therefore, 'cultural stuff' needs to be described as a rich resource, usually full of internal contradictions, which is used selectively by different social agents in various social projects within specific power relations and political discourse in and outside the collectivity. Gender, class, membership in a collectivity, stage in the life cycle, ability – all affect the access and availability of these resources and the specific positionings from which they are being used.

It is important, therefore, to differentiate and avoid the conflation of cultural discourse, identity narratives and ethnic processes (Anthias and Yuval-Davis, 1992; Yuval-Davis, 1994b). Identities – individual and collective – are specific forms of cultural narratives which constitute commonalities and differences between self and others, interpreting their social positioning in more or less stable ways. These often relate to myths (which may or may not be historically valid) of common origin, and to myths of common destiny. Martin (1995: 10) mentions the following features of these narratives: strategic syncretism; invention of tradition thanks to liberating amnesia; and efforts to make changes legitimate. He points out the close relationships between identity narratives and political processes:

the identity narrative channels political emotions so that they can fuel efforts to modify the balance of power; it transforms the perception of the past and the present; it changes the organization of human groups and creates new ones; it alters cultures by emphasizing certain traits and skewing its meanings and logic. The identity narrative brings forth a new interpretation of the world in order to modify it. (1995: 13)

However, as Stuart Hall (1992) points out, cultural identities are often fluid and cross-cutting. This instability of categories can provide us with an important insight into the politics of difference.

Identity narratives often constitute major tools of ethnic projects. Ethnicity relates to the politics of collectivity boundaries, and by using identity narratives, dividing the world into 'us' and 'them'. Ethnic projects are continuously engaged in processes of struggle and negotiation aimed, from specific positionings within the collectivities, at promoting the collectivity or perpetuating its advantages, via access to state and civil society powers (Yuval-Davis, 1994b).

Ethnicity, according to this definition, is therefore primarily a political process which constructs the collectivity and 'its interest' not only as a result of the general positioning of the collectivity in relation to others in the society, but also as a result of the specific relations of those engaged in 'ethnic politics' with others within that collectivity. Gender, class, political, religious and other differences play central roles in the construction of specific ethnic politics, and different ethnic projects of the same collectivity can be engaged in intense competitive struggles for hegemonic positions. Some of these projects can involve different constructions of the actual boundaries of the collectivity (as, for example, has been the case in the debate about the boundaries of the 'black' community in Britain (Brah, 1992; Modood, 1988; 1994). Ethnicity is not specific to oppressed and minority groupings. On the contrary, one of the measures of the success of hegemonic ethnicities is the extent to which they succeed in 'naturalizing' their social and cultural constructions.

Ethnic projects mobilize all available relevant resources for their promotion. Some of these resources are political, others are economic and yet others are cultural – relating to customs, language, religion and other cultural artifacts and memories. Class, gender, political and personal differences mean that people positioned differently within the collectivity could, while pursuing specific ethnic projects, sometimes use the same cultural resources for promoting opposite political goals (for example, using various Koran surras to justify pro- and anti-birth control politics, as was the case in Egypt, or using rock music to mobilize people for and against the extreme right in Britain). In other times, different cultural resources are used to legitimize competing ethnic projects of the collectivity – such as when Bundists used Yiddish as 'the' Jewish language in an ethnic-national project whose identity boundaries were East European Jewry, and Zionists (re)invented modern Hebrew (till then used basically for religious purposes) in order to include in their project Jews all over the world. Similarly, the same people can be constructed in different ethnic-racist political projects in Britain to be 'Pakis', 'black Asians', and 'Muslim fundamentalists'.

Given the above, it is clear why ethnicity cannot be reduced to culture, and why 'culture' cannot be seen as a fixed, essentialist category. As Aleksandra Ålund comments, 'the tendency to conflate ethnicity and culture leads to inability to attend to the political dynamics of ethnic difference' (1995: 17). Moreover, defining and differentiating between culture, identity and ethnicity in this way pre-empts debates on the notion of 'authenticity'. Authenticity assumes fixed, essential and unitary constructs of cultures, identities and groupings. 'Authentic voices' are perceived as their 'true' representatives. As we shall see when discussing identity politics and multi-culturalism, 'authenticity' can become a political and economic resource in specific ethnic projects, but can also give rise to what Kubena Mercer (1990) has called 'the burden of representation' and Amrita Chhachhi (1991), in a somewhat different context, has called 'forced identities'.

Women especially are often required to carry this 'burden of representation', as they are constructed as the symbolic bearers of the collectivity's identity and honour, both personally and collectively. Claudia Koontz (1986: 196) quotes the different mottos which were given to girls and boys in the Hitler Youth movement. For girls the motto was 'Be faithful; be pure; be German.' For boys it was 'Live faithfully; fight bravely; die laughing.' The national duties of the boys were to live and die for the nation. Girls did not need to act: they had to become the national embodiment.

A figure of a woman, often a mother, symbolizes in many cultures the spirit of the collectivity, whether it is Mother Russia, Mother Ireland or Mother India. In the French Revolution its symbol was 'La Patrie', a figure of a woman giving birth to a baby; and in Cyprus, a crying woman refugee on roadside posters was the embodiment of the pain and anger of the Greek Cypriot collectivity after the Turkish invasion. In peasant societies, the dependence of the people on the fertility of 'Mother Earth' has no doubt contributed to this close association between collective territory, collective identity and womanhood. However, women symbolize the collectivity also in other ways. As Cynthia Enloe (1990) has pointed out, it is supposedly for the sake of the 'womenandchildren' that men go to war. Women are associated in the collective imagination with children and therefore with the collective, as well as the familial, future. But this does not only happen during wars. Recently, for instance, in the riots which flared among Muslim youth in Bradford, one of the participants clarified the motivation behind their actions to a reporter:

> It's not about prostitution or unemployment or about all that nonsense of the Chief Constable. It's about the way two police officers treated one of our women. (*The Guardian*, 18 June 1995)

The 'burden of representation' on women of the collectivity's identity and future destiny has also brought about the construction of women as the bearers of the collectivity's honour. Manar Hasan (1994) describes how many

Palestinian women have been murdered by their male relatives because in their behaviour they brought 'shame' on their families and community. A case that drew much public attention and public campaigning in 1994 was that of Ihlas Basam, a 38-year-old Druze woman who was murdered by her younger brother, a soldier in the Israeli army. Her 'sin' was to appear in western style clothing, including a short (although apparently not very short) skirt, and with bleached hair and lipstick, while being interviewed on Israeli television. She was interviewed because she had just completed an impressive fund raising campaign for her Druze community while living in New York. The 'notables' of the community met her earlier that day and were reportedly very grateful for the funds. The same 'notables', however, refused to condemn the murderer, and although one of her sisters who witnessed Ihlas' murder had a nervous breakdown, the rest of the family were reportedly proud of the brother who did 'his duty'. 'We have to protect our religion, our culture. She stepped over the line.'

Women, in their 'proper' behaviour, their 'proper' clothing, embody the line which signifies the collectivity's boundaries. Other women in many other societies are also tortured or murdered by their relatives because of adultery, flight from home, and other cultural breaches of conduct which are perceived as bringing dishonour and shame on their male relatives and community (see, for example, Chhachhi, 1991; Rozario, 1991). A weaker version of retaliation against women who betrayed the collective honour was the mass shaving of the heads of women, in various European countries after World War II, who were accused of befriending the occupying Nazi armies during the war (Warring, 1996).

Even when things do not reach these extreme and exceptional circumstances, cultural traditions and the (re)invention of traditions (Hobsbawm and Ranger, 1983) are often used as ways of legitimizing the control and oppression of women. In situations in which individual men as well as whole collectivities feel threatened by 'others' this phenomenon may intensify. Verity Staffulah Khan (1979) carried out a comparative study on women's purdah in Bradford in the UK and in the villages in Bangladesh from which the Bradford immigrants had originated, and found the practice of purdah to be much more extreme and rigid in Bradford than in Bangladesh. This is but one facet of a more general rigidity and 'freezing' of cultures which takes place in diasporic communities.

Cultural Difference and the 'Other'

International and intranational encounters with the 'other' are when management and control of cultural difference are called upon.

In his book on postmodern morality, *Life in Fragments*, Zygmunt Bauman (1995) claims that unlike the conventional outlook, which sees morality as a result of an internalization of specific cultural moral codes, morality needs to be seen as pre-social. It emerges once the individual becomes conscious that an 'other' exists and a choice arises concerning the way in which that 'other' should be treated. Bauman hastens to clarify that this does not mean that everyone is moral, but means that the need for human morality precedes rather than follows specific religious and other cultural systems.

Bauman's definition of morality puts management and control of boundary construction at the heart of the various cultural moral systems. All societies have a pool of cultural traditions, collective memories and 'common sense' in which the image of the 'others' and the 'rules' about how they should be handled are to be found. Of course, as in any other cultural production, cultural constructions of 'otherness' are dynamic, full of contradictions and differentially available to different social categories and groupings. Although usually the national and ethnic 'imagined communities' (Anderson, 1983) are supposed to transcend gender, class, regional and other differences, very often they can become signifiers, at least partially, of 'otherness', constructed as having come from a different 'stock'.

Women usually have an ambivalent position within the collectivity. On the one hand, as mentioned above, they often symbolize the collectivity unity, honour and the *raison d'être* of specific national and ethnic projects, like going to war. On the other hand, however, they are often excluded from the collective 'we' of the body politic, and retain an object rather than a subject position (see further discussion of this issue in Chapter 4). In this sense the construction of womanhood has a property of 'otherness'. Strict cultural codes of what it is to be a 'proper woman' are often developed to keep women in this inferior power position. The collective 'wisdoms' which are used to justify this state of affairs often sound very similar to other 'common sense' notions which are used to exclude, inferiorize and subjugate 'others' – such as 'women are stupid', 'women are dangerous' or 'women are impure and could pollute us'.

There are many different kinds of 'others'. In different situations and ethnic projects the collectivity boundaries might include some 'others' and exclude others. In contemporary Europe an 'other' could be, for example, a migrant, a black person, a member of an 'old' or a 'new' minority, somebody from another religion, someone who speaks with another accent, someone who comes from another region: in some situations and to some people, any, all or none of the above could become the 'other'. In other words, any culturally perceived sign could become a boundary signifier to divide the world into 'us' and 'them' (Anthias and Yuval-Davis, 1992).

It is not only the carriers of 'otherness' which are multiple. The patterns of relationships which can be developed with them are multiple as well. Aleksandra Ålund (1995) distinguishes between two models of 'the stranger' which have been portrayed in literature and in which 'the strangers' have a somewhat different relationship with the collectivities within which they live. 'The stranger' has been defined as 'a synthesis of nearness and remoteness' (Simmel, 1950: 407) and as such a challenge, if not actually a threat, to the sensibilities of orthodox orientation points. 'The stranger' portrayed by Alfred Schutz (1976) is in need of an escape, a refuge from his home base. He (the stranger in this literature is usually constructed as a 'he') is typically self-effacing and would seek to assimilate in his new environment so as to stop being a stranger. However, this assimilatory project is doomed to failure, as an insurmountable 'naturalised breach of cultural and psychological difference' (Ålund, 1995: 312) exists between him and the locals. The non-visibility of that difference is of no help ultimately because of the fear that, hiding his essential difference, he can take over what is not rightfully his: he is, and for ever will remain so, a stranger. The conspiracy theory against the Jews is an example of such a construction of 'otherness'.

The second model of 'the stranger' has been developed by George Simmel (1950). The stranger he is talking about is in a better power position than the Schutzist stranger. He seeks not to disappear within the native collectivity but to carry out a dialogue with it. Although he does not share the myth of common origin with the group, he can bring new qualities into it which might entitle him to group solidarity. However, tensions between this stranger and the collectivity tend to arise as well, because 'the stranger can become "itself", symbolizing the strangeness rather than an individual' (1950: 403).

The role of 'the stranger' as a social and cultural innovator will be explored later when the notion of hybridity will be discussed. Here it is important to emphasize that in order to be 'a stranger' as defined above, one does not have to be a newcomer to the society, a migrant or an immigrant. 'Old' as well as 'new' minorities constitute this 'synthesis of nearness and remoteness', including aboriginal people who have always been there. Moreover, the nearness of the stranger can be emotional, not necessarily only geographical. There are probably few relationships which could become as intimate as the relationship between the master and the slave, and at the same time so ultimately defined by otherness.

Moreover, in the discussion so far 'the stranger' has been portrayed to be not only in a minority position, but also in one of at least relative disempowerment. However, any non-westocentric discussion of relations between 'the community' and 'the stranger' has also to include relations with dominant strangers such as the conqueror, the colonialist, the settler, who might be in the minority but is by no means disempowered. Processes of construction and management of boundaries take place in these situations as well, as parts of processes of accommodation and/or resistance of the local population (Chatterjee, 1986; Stasiulis and Yuval-Davis, 1995), and women of the colonial 'others' play particular roles in these processes (Jayawardena, 1995). At the same time, for dominant minorities, the majority of the population can acquire characteristics of 'strangeness' and 'otherness'. Disempowered minorities, as well, have to develop strategies of survival and boundary management. These can sometimes take the form of oppositionary constructions of exclusion and demonization (see, for example, Shahak, 1994 on the attitude of the Jews to the Gentiles; and Gilroy, 1996 on the attitude of blacks to whites and Jews). Identity narrations of origin and destiny are crucial in this regard, as are rules and regulations about who 'belongs' and who doesn't.

Religious and other cultural codes concerning marriage and divorce are crucial in constructing those boundaries.

Racism occurs when the construction of 'otherness' is used in order to
exclude and/or exploit the immutable 'other' (Anthias and Yuval-Davis, 1983;
1992). Michel Wieviorka insists that what he calls 'the space of racism' (1994:
182) includes both elements, the first of which he connects with issues of
identities and difference and the second of which he relates to issues of
modernity and inequality. He distinguishes between four (ideal) types of
racism which are prevalent in today's world. The first is a universalist one
which inferiorizes others as unmodern or premodern. Another, which he
labels as 'the poor white response', derives from anxieties about losing out
and being excluded from the material benefits of the modern industrial world
and blaming the others for it. The third type has anti-modernist inflexions: it
appeals to traditions of community, religion and nation and demonizes those
thought to be excessively 'modern'. The fourth type emanates from specific
inter-group hostilities which have specific histories and complex, cross-cutting
relations with the conditions of modernity. The same objects of racism can be
the target of different or even opposing types of racism. The Jews, for
instance, have been accused of being both excessively modern ('the spirit of
capitalism', to use Marx's label) and premodern (clannish, religious, nationalist). Differential social positionings, however, as well as the identity of the
'other' and the specific traditions and collective memories which are associated with specific 'others', affect the contents of specific racisms which take
place as well as their intensity.

Although racism cannot be reduced to constructions of 'race', every racist
construction has at least some dimension of a mythical embodiment of the
'other'. This can relate to any part of the body. In an antisemitic poster in the
USA in the 1920s titled 'How Can We Identify Him?', for example, among
the parts of the body which are mentioned, in addition to the notorious
image of 'the Jewish nose', are the 'Jewish' elbows and knees!

However, skin colour has come to be the main racist signifier, establishing
mythical races which are 'red', 'yellow', 'white' and 'black'. Although in
Australia, for instance, it was the 'yellow peril' of South East Asians against
which most of 'white Australia' immigration legislation was established
(deLepervanche, 1989; Pettman, 1995), the association in western cultural
traditions of 'white' with 'good' and 'black' with 'evil' has given special
poignancy to the construction of blackness as a signifier as well as a legiti-
mator of racist ideologies and practices. As Tajfel points out:

> 'Black' and 'White', which represent so crudely the differences in the shade of
> skin between groups of human beings – are used to symbolize distinctions between
> vice and virtue, hell and heaven, devils and angels, contamination and purity.
> (1965: 130)

The racist association of 'blackness' with evil is an expression of a specific historical cultural tradition which operates on deeper, sometimes unconscious,
levels in western civilization, of demonological collective representation (de la

Campagne, 1983), and as such constitutes part of the Europeans' cultural resources and heritage¹. The very flimsy relationship between 'blackness' and the actual colour of the skin of the 'blacks' can be seen, for example, in the Metropolitan Police 'Identi Code Key' (given to me by a Metropolitan Community Relations Officer in 1987), in which category 3 was 'Negroid types (can be light or White-skinned)' (Anthias and Yuval-Davis, 1992: 146). As F. James Davis points out in his book *Who Is Black?* (1993), in the USA (and in Britain) the 'one-drop rule' operates which means that even 'one drop' of 'black blood' (which certainly is *not* visible) is sufficient in this society to construct a person as black. As Judy Scales-Trent (1995) points out, when dealing with blackness one has to differentiate between race and colour. Moreover, as Sander Gilman (1991) has pointed out, blackness has been constructed as a characteristic of 'non-black' minorities such as Jews and Moors (and I would add gypsies) in order to add the racialized connotation of blackness onto them. Blackness, however, like other racist cultural signifiers, can mark the category of people who are to be denigrated and discriminated against. Nevertheless, the specific contents of the racial stereotyping beyond its negativity, and the ethnic boundaries it draws, are not necessarily fixed or consistent. Different specific racist images would be attached to different 'black' ethnic minorities and their specific contents could even be contrasting (like the 'violent' Afro-Caribbean and the 'wimpy' Asian men).

Blackness has been associated with evil, monsters, and base sexuality. 'Half devil and half child' are the 'sullen peoples' who are 'The White Man's Burden' during Victorian times, according to the classic poem of Rudyard Kipling. As Winthrop D. Jordan has pointed out:

> English perceptions integrate sexuality with blackness, the devil and the judgement of God who had originally created man not only 'Angelike' but 'white'. (1974: 23)

These demonological traditions preceded Elizabethan Europe. Although the word 'black' did not acquire its negative connotations until the late Middle Ages, the preconceptions of Europeans on blacks were shaped by ideas transmitted through the medieval Church before there was any face-to-face contact with blacks. An extreme example of this is described by Sander Gilman (1985) concerning the Poles, who had very definite constructions of blacks without any direct contact with them. Daniel Siboni (1974) and, following him, Phil Cohen have linked this demonology to the unconscious sexuality of racism. In the words of Phil Cohen:

> Siboni . . . shows that the construction of The Other in racist discourses follows a route which is specific to its unconscious mode of functioning. Its surface structures of conscious reasoning are traced back to a phantasy system in which representations of sexuality and generation are organized in a peculiarly perverse way. Positions of racial superiority are associated with an ideal desexualized image of the body – an 'immaculate conception' of origins, an eternally regenerated destiny; whilst racial inferiority is associated with a degenerate or monstrous body, in which the power of sexuality, repressed at the other pole, returns as a purely negative principle. (1988: 8)

This ideology of split mind/body = superiority/inferiority and its racist/sexist double standards has been, claim Siboni and Cohen, part of the unconscious history of reason in western civilization and made to function as an instrument of class and ethnic domination over 'others'. This explains some of the deep-rooted resistance to 'reasoned' anti-racist strategies.

Racism and Sexuality

Similar sexualized demonologies which combine fear and envy towards racialized objects have existed not only in relation to blacks but also in most other racialized images of the 'other', as Siboni (1983) and Gilman (1991) have shown concerning the Jews, and Edward Said (1978) and others (see, for instance, Lewis, 1996; Lutz, 1991) have shown concerning the orientalist cultural tradition which has racialized the 'exotic' people of the Middle and Far East. The embodiment dimension of the racialized 'other' puts sexuality at the heart of the racialized imagery which projects dreams of forbidden pleasures and fears of impotency onto the 'other'.

These dreams, of course, are always highly gendered, although not always heterosexual (Kosofsky Sedgwick, 1992). In different social and political contexts the combination of sexuality and differential power relations manifests itself in a variety of ways – physical, political and/or economic. The interplay of the power relations between women and men as well as those between masters and slaves, the colonizers and the colonized, the locals and 'the strangers' has tended to create some common scenarios that have been played out in more than one context. A common literary theme, for instance (see, for example, Doris Lessing's novel *The Grass is Singing*, 1950 on Southern Africa; Amos Oz's *My Michael*, 1958 on Israel; and Harper Lee's *To Kill a Mocking Bird*, 1960 on the USA), is that of the disempowered and isolated woman of the hegemonic collectivity fantasizing and sometimes actually daring to develop sexual relationships with the available man of the racialized collectivity who is there as a servant or as a labourer. The men of the hegemonic collectivity in that narrative, while viewing the 'other' as inferior and uncivilized, would also fear and envy him, attributing to him omnipotent sexuality and lust. A common rationalization for lynching black men has been their actual but more often mythical sexual intercourse with white women which could only be constructed as a rape within this discourse. The myth of the 'other' as a rapist is a common tale in many racialized contexts. As Theresa Wobbe (1995: 92) argues, the gendered challenge that the stranger presents constitutes a physical-affective dimension which is central to the understanding of racist violence. It is structured around the common stereotype of the male stranger harassing, threatening or actually raping 'our women', whose honour has to be defended.

The prevalence of the myth of 'the stranger' as a rapist, however, should not prevent us from the realization that rape is a common violent practice aimed at women (and sometimes men) from other racialized collectivities

(see discussion in Chapter 5). As Theresa Wobbe also points out, the constructed collectivity boundary 'between "us" and "them" also indicates the
limits and intersections of social obligations and social norms' (1995: 94). She
sees this as a central dimension in the understanding of racist violence and
violence against women in everyday life, as the absence of social responsibilities towards the others often implies the freedom to violate and attack. The
targets for such attacks could be not only 'their' women, but also 'traitors'
such as wives of mixed marriages.

Relationships between racialized others, however, are not always embedded
just in violence. Cynthia Enloe (1989: Chapter 2) has described the elaborated
industries of sex tourism in which male orientalist dreams of inexhaustible
pools of sexual pleasures and 'exotic' sexual objects become the major source
of economic survival for impoverished post-colonial individuals and communities – in locations, incidentally, which have tended to be sites reserved for
the 'rest and recreation' of the American military, such as Thailand, South
Korea and the Philippines (1989: 36). Sometimes these relationships go
beyond the mere sexual. 'Mail-order brides' firms have been flourishing
because of the construction of oriental women as the 'perfect wives' – beau-
tiful, docile, hard working and dependent – for isolated and timid western
men. Such marriages can be seen to be the only opportunity for those women
(and often their families) to escape from lives of incredible hardship in their
societies of origin. Recently, the location of the 'mail-order brides' market has
been shifting to Eastern Europe, for a combination of economic and racist
considerations.

The 'Shirley Valentine' phenomenon where women are the tourists is somewhat similar to that of men, although here formal prostitution, in the form of
male gigoloism, is less common than just consenting casual or not so casual
sex. The exchange here is more on the basis of mutual pleasure than on
money for pleasure. The western women tourists are in search of sexual
adventures and experimentation while away from home, and the local men get
free sex not available to them from the local women who are under strict
social control. Sometimes these sexual relationships develop into love relationships and marriages in which one of the spouses immigrates. However, at
times other motivations would be more important. There have been studies
which indicate that the motivation of the men could often be similar to the
'mail-order bride' syndrome – the opportunity to gain a visa or a 'green card'
and immigrate (Cohen, 1971). Another study (Bowman, 1989) carried out
among shopkeepers in East Jerusalem has pointed to another motivation of
the local men – as an outlet for their generalized senses of frustration and disempowerment.

Bowman (1989) analysed the sexual relationships between the shopkeepers
and the tourists as between men who are feminized and women who have
taken upon themselves the classical male roles, as they are the ones who are
the mobile, the rich, the powerful. However, this framework of analysis is too
simplistic. Firstly, although the women tourists are powerful, are relatively
rich and mobile, the initiators of the sexual liaison are usually the men, whose

'machoism' – in a non-threatening because limited context – is one of their main sources of attraction to the women (as was revealed in a TV programme on this question: 'Esther', BBC2, 21 August 1995). Secondly, Bowman equates feminization with emasculinization and disempowerment. This is a model in which the feminine is the negative passive mirror image of the masculine, which of course (and 'even' Freud recognized this) femininity never is, even in the most constricting social systems.

Other authors (such as Meaney, 1993; Nandy, 1983) have attributed a more generalized feminized image to colonial societies:

> A history of colonisation is a history of feminisation. Colonial powers identify their subject people as passive, in need of guidance, incapable of self-government, romantic, passionate, unruly, barbarous – all of those things for which the Irish and women have been traditionally praised and scorned. (Meaney, 1993: 233)

Again, in this imagery, feminization and disempowerment are being equated. No wonder Fanon (1986) (and even more so many of his followers) have equated liberation with machoism – and it is in this conjecture that paradoxically the 'liberated' women can become disempowered.

Assimilationism and Separatism

Racialization of difference, even if prevalent, is by no means the only way in which cultural differences are managed in society; nor are the intensities – or the form – of all racisms the same. Wieviorka (1994) distinguishes between four levels of racism, from weak and inarticulate forms of racism, such as prejudice, to total racism. These should be seen as a continuum rather than as distinguished separate levels, and of course in concrete social realities different intensities and forms of racialization coexist and fluctuate constantly. This coexistence usually includes, however, not only the different levels and forms of racisms but also other forms of management of difference which might be more or less racialized, such as assimilationism, separatism, multiculturalism and hybridization.

If racism is all about excluding and/or exploiting the other, assimilation might seem to be its opposite. Rather than continuing to erect unsurpassable boundaries of segregation, assimilationism renders them invisible and passable. The American dream of 'the melting-pot' or the French dream of *liberté, égalité, fraternité* do not mention any specific membership in a community of origin as a precondition for membership in the collectivity and the benefit of all the rights which come with it. On the contrary. Professor Knopfelmacher (1984; Yuval-Davis, 1991c: 15–16), one of the main advocates of assimilationism in Australia, explicitly comes out against an essentialist connection between culture and origin: 'With anglomorphy firmly established in Australia and stable as a rock, the "British" character of the country is independent of the "race" of the immigrants.'

However, as has been pointed out (Balibar, 1990b), this supposed universal inclusiveness could be very misleading. Firstly, because while no formal criteria of exclusion might be in existence, the assumptions about the nature of the collectivity could be such that assimilation would simply not be possible. As Paul Gilroy (1987) has pointed out, if 'There Ain't No Black in the Union Jack', and in order to be British, or at least English, you need to be white, then no black people could really be assimilated into the English collectivity. Moreover, as Cathy Lloyd (1994) has pointed out, the construction of Enlightenment-derived universalism as developed by the new right includes claims for universal human nature which supposedly dictate that people like to interact only with their own (national-cultural) 'kind'. Even if assimilation is possible or welcome in principle, this universalism is misleading, as the newcomers would have many relative disadvantages stacked against them, in terms of formal and informal networks of support, knowledge of the language, the 'right kind' of education, and so on.

Secondly, the universal inclusiveness of assimilationism is misleading, because while individuals might gain entry on that basis to the hegemonic collectivity, their collective identity would not. Sartre (1948) has discussed 'liberal antisemitism' in which Jews might be accepted as people on condition that they stop existing as Jews. A similar logic lay behind the brutal act of the mass removal of Aboriginal children in Australia during the 1950s and their bringing up as white Australians. Public investigations are taking place in Israel at the moment concerning accusations that hundreds of Yemeni Jewish babies were abducted from their mothers who were told they were dead and they were given for adoption to Ashkenazi middle class families. Breaking up communities and families and separating children from their parents would often be central to practices of forced assimilationism. Such policies disempower the minorities and can reinforce their location in subjugated positionings.

Separatism is often a strategy of resistance to both racism and assimilationism. Separatist projects are ethnic projects, usually of disempowered minorities, which aim to better the relative positioning of the collectivity. Thus they promote the strengthening of the collectivity's boundaries, its collective identity and social cohesion and its social, economic and political self-sufficiency. The separatist projects are usually promoted by a particular grouping within the collectivity who are using a particular cultural ethos – religious, nationalist or racial – for their purpose. A separatist project which combines more than one such ethos, for instance, is the American – and now also British – black 'Nation of Islam', which combines the development of black economic self-sufficiency as producers and consumers, and their assertive self-identification as blacks, with the conversion of blacks into Islam, as a Third World alternative to the colonialist Christian tradition (Muslim slave traders notwithstanding). The 1995 'Million Men March' to Washington DC, initiated and headed by Louis Farrakhan, the leader of the 'Nation of Islam', which was joined by many of the established black leaders who had previously rejected separatism, such as Jesse Jackson, has pointed up how seductive and powerful such a movement can be.

One needs to differentiate between separatist and autonomous movements, which can have quite different ideologies although not always that different practices. While autonomous movements put the emphasis on grass-roots activism, autonomy and self-sufficiency, as an initial stage from which they can co-operate with others once they feel more empowered and confident, separatist movements construct their boundaries as absolute and accept others, if at all, only if they are ready to convert (that is, assimilate). One of the cornerstones of separatist policies is often to forbid sexual relationships between members of the collectivity and others.

The growth of autonomous and separatist movements among disempowered groupings has been closely linked to the rise of identity politics and the ethos of multi-culturalism.

Multi-Culturalism and Identity Politics

Trinh Minh-ha (1989: 89–90) has commented that there are two kinds of social and cultural differences: those which threaten and those which don't. Multi-culturalism is aimed at nourishing and perpetuating the kinds of differences which do not. As Andrew Jakubowicz concluded in relation to the Australian policies of multi-culturalism:

> Multi-culturalism gives the ethnic communities the task to retain and cultivate with government help their different cultures, but does not concern itself with struggles against discriminatory policies as they affect individuals or classes of people. (1984: 42)

Carl Schierup (1995) has claimed that multi-culturalism is an ideological base for transatlantic alignment whose project is the transformation of the welfare state. This alignment aspires to the position of the hegemonic credo in the contemporary era of postmodernity. He argues, however, that the paradoxes and dilemmas of existing multi-culturalisms present its ideological framework with problems similar to those 'real socialisms' present to 'socialism'.

Multi-culturalism has been developed in Britain as a major form of accommodation to the settlement of immigrants and refugees from the ex-colonial countries, and has broadly followed forms of legislation and political projects which were developed for this purpose in the USA as well as other ex-imperial settler societies such as Canada and Australia. In all these states there is a continuous debate about multi-culturalism, between those who want a continuous construction of the national collectivity as homogeneous and assimilatory, and those who have been calling for the institutionalization of ethnic pluralism and the preservation of the cultures of origin of the ethnic minorities as legitimate parts of the national project. A controversial related question is the extent to which the conservation of collective identities and cultures is important as a goal in itself or only becomes so as a result of collective will. Another is whether projects aimed at conservation of cultures can avoid the reification and essentialization of those cultures. As Floya Anthias has put it:

Debates on cultural diversity confuse culture and ethnicity . . . Is it the boundaries
that should be kept or the cultural artifacts that act as their barbed wire? However,
the question is not just about homogeneity, but also about western cultural hegemony. (1993: 9)

In Australia, for instance, the call of those who have objected to multi-culturalism has been for an 'Anglomorphic society' even if the members of the
Australian national collectivity are not of Anglo-Celtic origin, as the quote
above from Knopfelmacher (1984; see also Yuval-Davis, 1991c: 14) demon-
strates. In the USA, the ideological target has been the American 'melting-pot'.
However, those who have been objecting to multi-culturalism in the American
context have emphasized the primacy of its European cultural heritage: 'Would
anyone seriously argue that teachers should conceal the European origins of
American civilization?' (Schlesinger, 1992: 122). Collective cultural identity
rather than the ethnic origin and colour of the collectivity members seems to
be the crucial factor in these constructions.

   Nevertheless, it would be a mistake to suppose that those who support
multi-culturalism assume a civil and political society in which all cultural
identities would have the same legitimacy. In Australia, for instance, the government's document on multi-culturalism emphasizes 'the limits of
multi-culturalism' (Office of Multi-Cultural Affairs, 1989), and in all states in
which multi-culturalism is an official policy there are cultural customs (such
as polygamy, using drugs) which are considered illegal as well as illegitimate,
giving priority to cultural traditions of the hegemonic majority. Moreover, in
multi-culturalist policies, the naturalization of the western hegemonic culture
continues while the minority cultures become reified and differentiated from
normative human behaviour.

   John Rex describes multi-culturalism as an enhanced form of the welfare
state in which 'the recognition of cultural diversity actually enriches and
strengthens democracy' (1995: 31). This, he claims, is a result of three basic
factors: that the values of specific cultures might have important values in
their own right which might enrich the overall society; that the social organization of the minority communities provides them with emotional support;
and that the social organization also provides them with more effective means
of getting more resources and defending their collective rights. Questions
arise, however, concerning both the nature of these collective rights and what
specific provisions the state needs to make in order to fulfil them towards
individuals and collectivities in its heterogeneous population. Jayasuriya has
pointed out that two separate issues are involved here: 'One is the centrality
of needs in the collective provision of welfare and the other is the difficult
question of boundaries of need in claiming for one's right' (1990: 23).

   As will be discussed more extensively in Chapter 4, the most problematic
aspects of these questions become apparent when the provision relates not to
differential treatment in terms of access to employment or welfare but to
what has been defined as the different cultural needs of different ethnicities.
Jayasuriya (1990) distinguishes between needs, which are essential and which
therefore require satisfaction by the state, and wants, which fall outside the

public sector and are to be satisfied within the private domain in a voluntary way.

The differentiation between the public and the private domains plays a central role in delineating boundaries of citizenship in the literature (as will be discussed in Chapter 4), although not enough attention is being given to the fact that the public domain contains both the state and the civil society. Turner (1990), for instance, has anchored his typology of citizenship in the extent to which the state enters or abstains from entering the private domain. However, as the examples above show, in the dichotomous private/public construction the private and public spheres are culturally specific as well as gender specific (Yuval-Davis, 1991b). The whole debate on multi-culturalism stumbles on the fact that the boundaries of difference, as well as the boundaries of social rights, are determined by specific hegemonic discourses, perhaps using universalistic terminology, but definitely not universal. And as mentioned above, universalist discourses which do not take into account the differential positionings of those to whom they refer often cover up racist (and, I would add, sexist, classist, ageist, disablist, etc.) constructions.

One of the primary examples of a multi-culturalist perspective which reifies and homogenizes a specific culture is the book published in 1993 by UNESCO called *The Multi-Cultural Planet* (Laszlo, 1993). In this the world is divided into culturally homogeneous regions, such as 'the European culture' (but also 'the Russian and East European culture'), 'the North American culture', 'the Latin American', 'the Arab', 'the African' and so on, among which dialogues and openness should be developed.

Although multi-culturalism is generally hailed by its promoters as a major anti-racist strategy it has been criticized from the left for ignoring questions of power relations, for accepting as representative of minorities people in class and power positions very different from those of the majority members of that community, and for being divisive by emphasizing the differential cultures of members of the ethnic minorities rather than what unites them with other blacks (in the sense of the all-encompassing binary division of black/white) who share with them similar predicaments of racism, subordination and economic exploitation (Bourne and Sivanandan, 1980; Mullard, 1980). Other critiques from the left have been directed against both the 'multi-culturalist' and the 'anti-racist' positions (Rattansi, 1992; Sahgal and Yuval-Davis, 1992). These critiques have pointed out that in both approaches there is the inherent assumption that all members of a specific cultural collectivity are equally committed to that culture. They tend to construct the members of minority collectivities as basically homogeneous, speaking with a unified cultural or racial voice. These voices are constructed to be as distinct as possible (within the boundaries of multi-culturalism) from the majority culture in order to be able to be 'different'; thus, within multi-culturalism, the more traditional and distanced from the majority culture the voice of the 'community representatives' is, the more 'authentic' it would be perceived to be within such a construction. Within 'anti-racism' such a perspective also prevailed. The voice of the 'black' has often been constructed as that of the macho liberatory hero, rejecting all which might be associated with white Eurocentric culture.

Such constructions do not allow space for internal power conflicts and interest differences within the minority collectivity, for instance conflicts along the lines of class, gender and culture. Moreover, they tend to assume collectivity boundaries which are fixed, static, ahistorical and essentialist, with no space for growth and change. When such a perspective becomes translated into social policy, 'authenticity' can become an important political resource with which economic and other resources can be claimed from the state by those taken to be representative of 'the community' (Cain and Yuval-Davis, 1990). As Yeatman observes:

> It becomes clear that the liberal conception of the group requires the group to assume an authoritarian character: there has to be a headship of the group which represents its homogeneity of purpose by speaking with the one, authoritative voice. For this to occur, the politics of voice and representation latent within the heterogeneity of perspectives and interests must be suppressed. (1992: 4)

This liberal construction of group voice, therefore, can collude with fundamentalist leaderships who claim to represent the true 'essence' of their collectivity's culture and religion, and who have high on their agenda the control of women and their behaviour (Sahgal and Yuval-Davis, 1992).

Multi-culturalism can often have very detrimental effects on women in particular, as often 'different' cultural traditions are defined in terms of culturally specific gender relations, and the control of women's behaviour (in which women themselves, especially older women, also participate and collude) is often used to reproduce ethnic boundaries (Yuval-Davis and Anthias, 1989). An example of such a collusion, for instance, is the case in the UK in which the judge refused a request for asylum from an Iranian woman, who had to escape Iran after refusing to be veiled, because 'this is their culture' (case recounted by the solicitor Jacqui Bhabha). Another example is that of a young Muslim girl who fled her parents' home because of their restrictive control of her, and who was placed by the social services in another Muslim home, even more pious, against the wish of the girl and the advocacy of the Asian Women's Refuge (case recounted by the workers of Southall Black Sisters).

A contradictory multi-cultural practice is described by Jeannie Martin (1991), in which the practices of 'ethnic families' are weighed against a 'good society' model which becomes identical with some unspecified Anglo family norm 'on behalf of ethnic women', focusing on 'atavistic practices' such as clitoridectomy, child marriages, etc., as the 'limits of multi-cultural diversity'. Martin describes this approach as typical of the 'ethnicists' among the multiculturalist theorists in Australia, and points out that what motivates them is not a real concern for women – because the ethnicists assume women's subordination to be part of the natural order of things in which the family is at the forefront. Rather, this is a device for ranking the men according to the extent of their deviation from the Anglo model – constructed in this discourse as the ideal positive model.

An alternative dynamic model of cultural pluralism has been developed by Homi Bhabha (1990; 1994a; 1994b). Abolishing the division of space/time and structure/process, and emphasizing the constantly changing and contested nature of the constructed boundaries of the national 'imagined community' and of the narratives which constitute its collective cultural discourses, Bhabha notes the counter-narratives emerging from the nation's margins, from those national and cultural 'hybrids' who have lived, because of migration or exile, in more than one culture. Such 'hybrids' both evoke and erase the 'totalizing boundaries' of their adoptive nation. Such counter-narratives do not have to come, of course, from immigrant minorities. The growing voice of indigenous peoples, for example, is an instance of a counter-narrative which is heard from within. Furthermore, counter-narratives about the boundaries of 'the nation' have disintegrated the former Yugoslav and Soviet nations; and, while not as radical in other national communities, the construction of the nation and its boundaries is a matter of constant debate everywhere. It is important to note in this context what Homi Bhabha fails to consider: that 'counter-narratives', even if radical in their form, do not necessarily have to be progressive in their message. As Anna Lowenhaupt Tsing (1993: 9) claims, such counter-narratives have to be situated within wider negotiations of meaning and power at the same time as recognizing local stakes and specificities.

Another danger in Bhabha's approach is that it may interpolate essentialism through the back door: that is, that the old 'multi-culturalist' essentialist and homogenizing constructions of collectivities are attributed to the homogeneous collectivities from which the 'hybrids' have emerged, thus replacing the mythical image of society as a 'melting-pot' with the mythical image of society as a 'mixed salad'. Characteristic of such a position has been, for example, the description by Trinh Minh-ha of herself, in a Conference on Racisms and Feminisms in Vienna (October 1994), as standing 'on the margin, resisting both the majority culture and that of her own group', as if each of these two cultures were homogeneous fixed entities external to her own constructions.

Bhabha is aware, however, that one cannot really construct one's identity, even partly, on the basis of an 'authentic' pre-colonial experience. He points to the resulting danger, for the hybrids who attempt to do so, of easily slipping into essentialized nostalgia. In this way hybridity often takes the form of a mimicry of the hegemonized Eurocentre. Smadar Lavie (1992: 92) contrasts that hybrid model with the one developed by Gloria Anzaldua (1987). She claims that these two models present polar opposites concerning the textualization of the hybrid's lived experience that occurs in the inner border zones between nation and empire. Both models assert that the hybrid's ambivalence towards both nation and empire catalyses remappings of the blurred border zones between them. However, Bahbha's is a response-oriented model of hybridity. It lacks agency, by not empowering the hybrid. Anzaldua argues that when hybrids delve into their past, it need not be either essentialized nostalgia or the salvaging of an 'uncontaminated' pre-colonial past. On the contrary, reworking the past exposes its own hybridity, and to recognize and acknowledge this hybrid past in terms of the present empowers the community and gives it agency. Her emphasis on community contrasts sharply with Bhabha's assumption of the hybrid as a fragmented individual other as well as with Minh-ha's description of herself. The hybrids' refusal of individuation empowers them to agency as a community (with all the problematic this involves, of course: Yuval-Davis, 1991b; see also discussion in Chapter 4), to resist the hegemony of the Eurocentre, not only in reacting to it but also by opening a new creative space in the border zone.

It is this kind of communal hybridization which Jan Nederveen Pieterse (1994) sees as underlying the processes of globalization which are taking place today in the world, rather than the more common model of globalization which tends to portray it as growing homogenization.

Cultural Change and Modernity

Chatterjee (1986) observed that cultural decolonization has anticipated and paved the way for political decolonization – the major rupture which has marked the twentieth century. This process involved not so much going back to some mythical golden age in the national past but rather a growing sense of empowerment, a development of a national trajectory of freedom and independence. A central theme in this process of cultural decolonization has been the redefinition and reconstruction of sexuality and gender relations. Franz Fanon (1986) encapsulated some of it in his famous call for the black man to 'reclaim his manhood'. As Ashis Nandy (1983) has argued, the colonial man has been constructed as effeminate in the colonial discourse and the way to emancipation and empowerment is seen as the negation of this assertion. In many cultural systems potency and masculinity seem to be synonymous. Such a perspective not only has legitimized the extremely 'macho' style of many anti-colonialist and black power movements. It has also legitimized the secondary position of women in these national collectivities.

And yet, the 'emancipation of women' has come to signify much wider political and social attitudes towards social change and modernity in a variety of revolutionary and decolonization projects, whether in Turkey, India, Yemen or China (Kandiyoti, 1991b). As Chatterjee (1990) has pointed out, because the position of women has been so central to the colonial gaze in defining indigenous cultures, it is there that symbolic declarations of cultural change have taken place. It has been one of the important mechanisms in which ethnic and national projects signified – inwardly and outwardly – their move towards modernization. However, these changes did not lack ambivalence, as they have had to signify at the same time modernization and national independence. The process of mimicry was limited at best.

One of the focal points of related debates has been the extent to which modernization should be equated with westernization. For many national leaders of the colonial world, nationalism and socialism were measures of modernity which they had to adopt in order to successfully defeat the European colonial enemy. This is why Chatterjee (1986), for instance, has seen nationalism in the post-colonial world as a derivative discourse. However, this does not mean that the two should be equated. Anzaldua's (1987) collective model of empowered hybridization is a much better way of describing the process. Many indigenous cultural and religious traditions were appropriated, at least symbolically, as a resource to establish national emblems and symbolic 'border guards' of identity.

Because often the hegemony of the modern nation-state in the post-colonial world has been very limited and mostly confined to urban centres and the upper classes, the use of cultural and religious traditions as symbolic border guards has enabled, to a large extent, the continued coexistence of the 'modern' centre with the premodern sections of society. At a later period, it also enabled, in many cases, the rise of a new generation of leaders who could turn to those same customs and traditions and develop ethnic and national projects of a very different kind. In such projects, what symbolized progress and modernity in the older projects was now constructed as European cultural imperialism. As an alternative, a fundamentalist construction of 'the true' cultural essence of the collectivity has come to be imposed. These constructions, however, are often no more similar to the ways people used to live historically in these societies than the previous 'national liberation' ones, nor have they abandoned modernity and its tools, whether it is the modern media or high-tech weaponry.

Once again women occupy an important role in these projects. Rather than being seen as the symbols of change, women are constructed in the role of the 'carriers of tradition'. The symbolic act of unveiling which played centre stage in the emancipatory projects is now being surpassed by campaigns of forced veiling, as happened, for example, in post-revolutionary Iran. Even practices such as sati in India can become foci of fundamentalist movements which see in women's following of these traditions the safeguard of the national cultural essence, operating as a mirror image to the colonial gaze which focused on these practices to construct 'otherness' (Chhachhi, 1991; Mani, 1989).

Fundamentalism and Modernity

Fundamentalism is probably the most important social movement of our times (*Contention*, 1995). Fundamentalist movements all over the world, with all their heterogeneity, are basically political movements which have a religious or ethnic imperative and seek in various ways in widely differing circumstances to harness modern state and media powers to the service of their gospel. This gospel, which can be based on certain sacred texts or evangelical experiential moments linked to a charismatic leader, is presented as the only valid form of the religion, the ethnic culture, the truth (Sahgal and Yuval-Davis, 1992). Religious fundamentalist movements, therefore, need to be differentiated from liberation theologies which, while deeply religious and political, co-operate with, rather than subjugate, non-religious political struggles.

Fundamentalism can align itself with different political trends in different countries and manifest itself in many forms. It can appear as a form of orthodoxy, a maintenance of 'traditional values', or as a revivalist radical phenomenon, dismissing impure and corrupt forms of religion in a 'return to original sources'. Jewish fundamentalism in Israel, for example, has appeared in basically two forms, for which the state has very different meanings: a form of right-wing Zionism, in which the establishment of the Israeli state is in itself a positive religious act; and a non- if not anti-Zionist movement, which sees in the Israeli state a convenient source for gaining economic and political power to promote its own versions of Judaism. In Islam, fundamentalism has appeared as a return to the Koranic text (fundamentalism of the madrasa), and as a return to the religious law, the shariah (fundamentalism of the ulema). In the USA, the Protestant fundamentalist movements include both fundamentalists in the original sense – those who want to go back to the biblical texts – and those 'born-again Christians' who rely much more on emotional religious experiences (see Sara Maitland, 1992).

It is important to differentiate between fundamentalist movements of dominant majorities within states, which look for universal domination in society (such as the evangelical new right in the USA, Khomeini's Iran or Serbian Yugoslavia), and fundamentalist movements of minorities who aim to use state and media powers and resources to promote and impose their gospel primarily within their specific constituencies, which are usually defined in ethnic terms (such as the Jewish fundamentalists of the Lubavitche Hassids, and Hindu and Sikh fundamentalists in Britain). Identifying various heterogeneous forms of fundamentalist movements, however, does not invalidate the use of the term 'fundamentalism' as identifying specific social phenomena. All major social movements – such as national, socialist, and feminist movements – have been similarly heterogeneous.

The recent rise of fundamentalism is linked to the crisis of modernity – of social orders based on the belief in the principles of enlightenment, rationalism and progress. Both capitalism and communism have proved unable to deliver people's material, emotional and spiritual needs. A general sense of despair and disorientation has opened people to transcendental religions as a source of solace. They provide a compass and an anchor which give people a sense of stability and security, as well as a coherent identity. They shift the centre of the structuration of meaning from the individual to the religious leaders and institutions.

The control of women and the patriarchal family are usually central to fundamentalist constructions of social orders. They are often seen as the panacea for all social ills:

A widespread evangelical conviction is that stability in the home, is the key to the resolution of other social problems. Once wanderers came 'home' and the poor acquired the sense of responsibility found in strong Christian familiality, poverty would cease. (Marsden, 1980: 37)

And women's desertion of their proper social role might mean a social disaster:

Woman has such a degree of biological disability and such huge family responsibilities, as to preclude her leaving purdah in a well ordered society. (Pundah Mandrudi, quoted in Hyman, 1985: 24)

One of the paradoxes associated with fundamentalism is the fact that women collude, seek comfort and even gain at times a sense of empowerment within the spaces allocated to them by fundamentalist movements (see Yasmin Ali, 1992; Elaine Foster, 1992; Sara Maitland, 1992; and Nira Yuval-Davis, 1992a). It is a well known fact that in spite of the subservient place women generally occupy in religious institutions, they constitute the majority of their active members. This can be seen as linked not only to religion as a source of solace to the oppressed but to the emotional division of labour between the genders in which women, as part of their role as guardians of the emotional and moral well-being of their family members, would also be active in the religious domains (Beth-Halakhmi, 1996). Also, being active in a religious movement allows women a legitimate place in a public sphere which otherwise might be blocked to them, and which in certain circumstances they might be able to subvert for their purposes, as in, for example, the relationship between young girls and their parents. It can be also, at the same time, less threatening but still a challenge and a space for personal accomplishments to which unskilled working class women and frustrated middle class women might be attracted. For women of racial and ethnic minorities, it can also provide the means by which to defend themselves as well as to defy the racist hegemonic culture. However, the overall effect of fundamentalist movements has been very detrimental to women, limiting and defining their roles and activities and actively oppressing them when they step outside their preordained limits.

The reification and essentialization of identities which are linked to fundamentalist politics have also been presented as a defensive reaction to the processes of globalization. Both Stuart Hall (1996) and Verena Stolcke (1995) talk about cultural fundamentalism (although, considering its strong emphasis on immutable collectivity boundaries, it might be preferable to call it ethnic fundamentalism). Given the rise of global capitalism and the growing sense of disempowerment in a political world system in which political autonomy and sovereignty seem to mean less and less, more and more people feel the need for what Stuart Hall calls a symbolic retreat to the past in order to face the future. The myth of common origin and a fixed immutable, ahistorical and homogeneous construction of the collectivity's culture is used in a similar way to that of religious fundamentalism. Indeed, religion often plays a central role as cultural signifier in these cultural fundamentalist constructions.

As Verena Stolcke points out, the apparent contradiction in the modern liberal ethos, between an invocation of a shared humanity which involves an idea of generality so that no human being seems to be excluded, and a cultural particularism translated into national terms, is overcome ideologically. A cultural 'other', the immigrant or a member of other communities who do not share the same myth of common origin, is constructed as an alien and as such as a potential 'enemy' who threatens 'our' national cum cultural integrity and uniqueness. In yet a further ideological twist, national identity and belonging interpreted as cultural particularity become, thus, an insurmountable barrier to what, as humans, in principle comes naturally, namely communication. Total separation, preferably spatial, is considered to be vital for the common human welfare. As Aleksandra Ålund (1995) points out, the human being is 'the bordering creature who has no borders'. There is a subtle dialectical relationship between humankind's need to culturally demarcate its unique being and the ability to socially transgress borders between human beings.

Globalization and Culture

This transgression of borders, however, is never done in a symmetrical and comprehensive way. Wallerstein (1974; 1980; 1989), who first developed the model of the 'world system', described it basically in terms of the development of a world economy in which unequal relationships exist between the centre and the periphery. Other models of globalization (for example, Peter Beyer, 1994; John W. Meyer, 1980; Roland Robertson, 1992; and Bryan Turner, 1994) have added to this model aspects of a global polity, a global culture and a global society. Of particular significance in the development of the globalization process have been the development of the information technologies and the resulting time/space compression (Cohen, 1995). At the same time it is important to realize that the process of globalization does not necessarily lead to a process of homogenization as it has been understood in the modernization discourse, which views global differences basically as different locations/stages along the same pathway leading towards the western model. As Jan Nederveen Pieterse (1994) has pointed out, it leads rather to hybridization. Given that there are multiple globalization processes at work (economic, political, social and cultural), globalization should be seen as structural hybridization, the emergence of new mixed forms of co-operation and cultural hybridization, the development of translocal *mélange* cultures. Talal Assad (1993) has explored the anthropological notion of 'history' and the extent to which one can construct any notion of 'autonomous history' within the contexts of European expansionism and globalization. Like Pieterse, Assad finds absurd the notion of globalization and cultural borrowing as leading to total homogeneity. Instead he offers the notion of translation. Translation is never simply a reproduction of identity, and the mode and conditions under which the translation takes place (from forcible imposition to voluntary borrowing) affect the versions of power which are produced and the new possibilities which open.

> Yet, although the outcome of these possibilities is never fully predictable, the language in which the possibilities are formulated is increasingly shared by Western and non-Western societies, and so, too, the specific forms of power and subjection. (1993: 13)

This process of globalization, however, should not be necessarily analysed within the 'postmodern frame' (Rattansi, 1994). This might assume, erroneously, that globalization did not exist before the postmodern era, and moreover, that all societies involved in that process are 'postmodern' – that is, have already experienced an era of 'modernity'.

The notion of the 'global' is usually constructed as opposite to that of the 'local'. Local communities can have different relationships to the globalization process. They can, to a certain extent at least, still exist outside the globalization processes; they can coexist with the global environment/influence, and they can also be constituted as a reaction to the processes of globalization and become a site of resistance to it. However, it should not be assumed that the meaning and implications of these processes are necessarily the same to people who are located in different class, ethnic and gender positionings in these communities. Talal Assad (1993: 9–10), for instance, contrasts James Clifford's (1988) celebration of 'the widening scope of human agency that geographical and psychological mobility now afford' with the deep pessimism of Hannah Arendt (1975), herself a refugee from the Nazis, who spoke of 'the uprootedness and superfluousness which has been the curse of modern masses'.

Nevertheless, the technological developments in transportation and communication in recent years mean that 'communities' can be established by people who live far away from each other, especially those whose class and occupation positions give them access to these means of communication. Of particular significance in global/local relations is the existence of diasporic communities. Given the new communication technologies, it is easier than ever for immigrant communities to keep in touch with the country of origin as well as with other immigrant communities from the same country in other places. Videos, radio, television and the Internet, as well as relatively fast and cheap means of international travel, make the reproduction of language and popular culture, as well as the 'keeping up' with what is happening in the 'motherland' and in the diasporic communities in other countries, much easier than ever before. This can create its own painful paradoxes. Phil Cohen told (in the 1996 annual lecture of the New Ethnicities Unit, University of East London) of the Bangladeshi man they interviewed in the Isle of Dogs who spoke of how connected he feels to his village community in Bangladesh via e-mail, while at the same time he is afraid to open his front door for fear of racial attack.

Another dimension of 'non-territorial communities' is the phenomenon in communities where arranged marriages exist, like the South Asian and the

Orthodox Jewish communities, of the 'exchange of brides' between different diasporic communities as well as between them and 'the homeland'. This is a powerful device to continue the intimate links and the inclusionary construction of boundaries of 'the community'. They cross-cut the boundaries of the different geographical territories and the political borders of the different states in which the members of these diasporic communities are citizens.

The new communication technologies have added to the impact of global political changes (such as the decolonization of Africa and the victory of Zionism in Israel/Palestine). The result was a new role for the 'homeland', more central and concrete, for diasporic communities such as the Jews and the blacks, whose links with their country of origin had for many generations more of a symbolic meaning. Thus the processes of globalization and international migration have not necessarily weakened the powerful connection between the boundaries of the Andersonian (1983) 'imagined community' and specific territory. On the contrary, while diasporic communities get social and political legitimation in 'multi-culturalist' and pluralist societies, quite a few of the political projects which have emerged in various diasporic communities have been concerned with supporting political and military struggles in the homeland, whether in Ireland, Israel, India or Rwanda, which are aimed at 'liberating' the homeland from its 'others'. Such projects correspond with the rise of 'cultural fundamentalism' discussed above, as the prevalent form of contemporary racism in the West. Importantly, these cultural fundamentalist movements, which have been analysed as defensive reactions to the processes of globalization, assume an inherent attachment between culture and territory. Very often this connection is constructed around the notion of 'home' or – as articulated more accurately in German – *Heimat* (Rätzel, 1994). As Phil Cohen (1995) has pointed out, 'home' is a highly gendered structure – one other facet of the deep connection between gender relations and the construction of collectivities. The deeply gendered character of 'ethnic cleansing' (see discussion in Chapter 5) which, at worst, can emanate from such constructions, is one attempt to 'resolve' the contradictions between essentialized identity politics and a political and economic reality which pulls in other directions.

Conclusion

James Donald has argued that 'A nation does not express itself through its culture: it is culture that produces "the nation"' (1993: 167).

The position developed in this chapter (and the book as a whole) resists 'culturization' – that is, 'the colonization of the social by the cultural' – and recognizes the primary importance of the multiplex processes of power relations and micro and macro social, economic and political activities and structures. However, within this context, the utilization of various cultural resources, especially symbolic border guards (Armstrong, 1982), play crucial roles in the continuous (re)construction of collectivities and collective identities and the management/control of their boundaries. Culture here is perceived not as a reified fixed 'thing' but rather as a dynamic process, continuously changing, full of internal contradictions which different social and political agents, differentially positioned, use in different ways. However, the ability of 'cultural stuff' to withstand differential usage and meanings makes it easier for hegemonic cultural projects to become naturalized. The fundamental social, political and moral need to relate to social others often exacerbates the need to construct different cultures as completely different and separate. Historically, however, no contemporary culture has developed in complete isolation from other cultures (Lowenhaupt Tsing, 1993) and the direction of influences has been East–West and South–North as well as the other ways around. Similarly, counter-narratives and the plurality of projects promoted by those occupying different positions are not unique to the 'postmodernist era'.

The chapter examined constructions of culture and identity narrations and how they have been used in boundary management in both exclusionary and inclusionary ways. It also looked at the ways processes of cultural change, decolonization and globalization have been linked to different modes of hybrid and fundamentalist politics.

The centrality of gender relations and sexuality for the cultural construction of identity and difference has been drawn out in relation to all the issues discussed in the chapter. Hegemonic cultures present a specific view about the meaning of the world and the nature of social order. The relationships between women and men are crucial for such a perspective, and therefore in most societies also the control of women by men. Women are often constructed as the cultural symbols of the collectivity, of its boundaries, as carriers of the collectivity's 'honour' and as its intergenerational reproducers of culture. Specific codes and regulations are usually developed, defining who/what is a 'proper man' and a 'proper woman', which are central to the identities of collectivity members. Feelings of disempowerment which result from processes of colonization and subjugation have often been interpreted by the colonized men as processes of emasculation and/or feminization. The (re)construction of men's – and often even more importantly women's – roles in the processes of resistance and liberation has been central in most such struggles. However, as cultures are not homogeneous, and specific hegemonic constructions of cultures closely relate to the interests of the dominant leadership within the collectivity, these hegemonic constructions often go against the interests of women, who would therefore find themselves in an ambivalent position towards these hegemonic projects.

It is this ambivalence which is discussed in the next chapter in relation to women's citizenship and social difference.

4

CITIZENSHIP AND DIFFERENCE

'Citizenship' has become a very popular subject of debate in the last few years, appropriated by both left and right, nationally and internationally, as well as by feminists. Here 'citizenship' is used not just in the narrow formalistic sense of having the right to carry a specific passport, but as an overall concept which sums up the relationship between the individual and the state. As Melanie Phillips (1990) has put it, 'There appears to be a great yearning for it, even though no one actually knows what it is.'

And indeed, citizenship is an elusive concept (like so many others). It has been constructed in different ways in different societies and has undergone historical shifts within the same state and society. It has been subject to contesting ideologies from the left and the right, and used as an inclusive and exclusive organizing principle, as a political mobilization tool and as a means of the depoliticization of the population. Also, in spite of its universalist terminology it has been applied differently to different segments of the population in each country.

In this chapter I discuss citizenship as a multi-tier construct, which applies to people's membership in a variety of collectivities – local, ethnic, national and transnational. The basic claim of the chapter is that a comparative study of citizenship should consider the issue of women's citizenship not only by contrast to that of men, but also in relation to women's affiliation to dominant or subordinate groups, their ethnicity, origin and urban or rural residence. It should also take into consideration global and transnational positionings of these citizenships.

In doing that, the chapter addresses four major issues. It firstly explores the relationship between citizenship as an individual and as a collective phenomenon and how these relate to notions of nationalism and 'the community'. Following that, the chapter looks at notions of social rights and social difference and the ways these relate to debates on multi-culturalism and gender relations.

Bryan Turner (1990) has constructed an influential comparative typology of citizenship based on two dimensions – the public/private and the active/passive axes. Interestingly enough, although Turner's typology is gender blind (Yuval-Davis, 1991b; Walby, 1994), these two dimensions have often been used to describe gender differences in general and differences in relation to women's citizenship in particular (Grant and Newland, 1991; Pateman, 1988). This chapter, therefore, proceeds to explore these two dimensions and how they should be theorized when seeking to construct a comparative non-westocentric framework of analysis of gendered citizenship. The third major question addressed in this chapter concerns the relationship of the private/public dichotomy to the divisions between the family, civil society and the state.

In the final part of the chapter, notions of active citizenship are explored as well as the ways in which they have been constructed by right and left within the political and social domains and how these relate to citizenship rights and duties.

A word of warning, however, is necessary before the exploration of the various issues considered in the chapter can begin. When dealing with the notion of citizenship it is also important to remember that, as Floya Anthias and myself have commented before (Yuval-Davis and Anthias, 1989: 6), on its own the notion of citizenship cannot encapsulate adequately all the dimensions of control and negotiations which take place in different areas of social life, nor can it adequately address the ways the state itself forms its political project. Studying citizenship, however, can throw light on some of the major issues which are involved in the complex relationships between individuals, collectivities and the state, and the ways gender relations (as well as other social divisions) affect and are affected by them.

Citizenship, Nationalism and the Community

In the liberal tradition citizenship has been constructed in completely individualistic terms. Citizenship is defined as a

> set of normative expectations specifying the relationship between the nation-state and its individual members which procedurally establish the rights and obligations of members and a set of practices by which these expectations are realized. (Waters, quoted by Peled, 1992: 433)

This definition differs significantly from the definition of citizenship of T.H. Marshall (1950; 1975; 1981) who has been the most influential theorist of citizenship in Britain. According to Marshall, citizenship is

> a status bestowed on those who are full members of a community. All who possess the status are equal with respect to the rights and duties with which the status is endowed. (1950: 14)

These rights and responsibilities relate to civil, political and social rights. Marshall developed an evolutionary model of citizenship in which the circle of those who received rights expanded historically as did the type of rights which they have enjoyed. Marshall pinpoints the formative period of civil rights as being during the eighteenth century, political rights during the nineteenth century and social rights during the twentieth century with the development of the welfare state.

The most important difference between these two definitions is that the liberal definition constructs the citizen as an individual member of a state, while Marshall's definition constructs the citizen as a member of a community.

This is important because Marshall's definition raises the possibility of multi-tier citizenship in both sub- and supra-state collectivities as well as the question of the relationships of these collectivities to the state.

Hall and Held (1989) have pointed out the usefulness of Marshall's definition as relating citizenship to 'the community' rather than to 'the state' which avoids identifying citizenship in its wide social definition simply with the nation-state. Citizenship originally emerged as an ideology in the Greek polis, where it was confined to cities. These days as well, there is a need to be able to relate citizenship to local politics, especially around ventures such as the Greater London Council (GLC) and other radical local authorities in Britain during the 1980s, which developed new mechanisms of accountability between the local state and different segments of the local population. Similarly, in many countries, the state has managed to penetrate only partially into civil society. There traditional ethnic communities have partial autonomy and their rules and regulations construct most dimensions of everyday life (Suad Joseph, 1993). At the same time, with the development of the European Union and with the processes of economic and communication globalization which progressively limit the autonomy of nation-states, as well as mass voluntary and forced migrations, citizenship must also be analysed in international if not actually global terms. 'Global citizenship' has also been mentioned in relation to increased international interdependency concerning ecological issues, as well as in relation to the New World Order and the growing political, military and legal role of the United Nations.

The notion of 'the community' used in Marshall's definition is so vague as to extend from a village into the 'global village' and is thus able to reflect this multi-dimensionality of citizenship. At the same time, however, the notion of the 'community' in the definition of citizenship evokes a strong 'sense of belonging' and of national identity that citizenship can provide. The Andersonian (1983) notion of the nation as the 'imagined community' and the Marshallian community of citizenship are being unified in a non-problematic way. This raises the question of the relationship between 'the community' and the state and how this affects people's citizenship. The debates in the literature between the 'liberals' and 'communitarians' (see, for example, Avineri and Shalit, 1992; Daly, 1993; Nimni, 1996; Phillips, 1993) and the 'republicans' (Oldfield, 1990; Peled, 1992; Roche, 1987; Sandel, 1982) relate to these issues.

As Roche (1987) describes it, in the liberal tradition the individual citizens are presumed to have equal status, equal rights and duties, and so on, so that principles of inequality deriving from gender, ethnicity, class or other contexts are *not* supposed to be of relevance to the status of citizenship as such. The citizens are therefore constructed not as 'members of the community' but as *strangers* to each other, although they are sharing a complex set of assumptions and expectations about each other which, when not fulfilled, can be enforceable by the state.

This liberal abstraction of self has been criticized, however, by the 'communitarians' who claim that notions of rights and duties, as well as those of equality and privacy, have no meaning outside the context of particular communities (Ackelsberg, forthcoming). We shall further discuss this relativist argument later in the chapter (the discussion in Chapter 3 on multi-culturalism is also relevant here). However, on different grounds, the proponents of republicanism such as Sandel (1982) also find the individualistic construction of citizenship highly unsatisfactory. They argue that such a construction denies the possibility of citizenship constituting a membership in a 'moral community' in which the notion of the 'common good' is antecedent to the individual citizenship choice. Liberal construction of citizenship, according to Sandel, assumes the priority of 'right over good'. Republicanism, on the other hand, constructs citizenship not only as a status but also as a means of active involvement and participation in the 'determination, practice and promotion of the common good'. The will and capacity to participate constitute one's civic virtue and are not only an expression but also a condition of citizenship.

However, as Peled comments, 'This raises the question how the republican [moral] community is constituted and what qualities are required for active participation in it' (1992: 433). According to him, two distinct notions of community can be discerned in the current revival of republicanism: a weak community, in which membership is essentially voluntary, and a strong, historical community that is *discovered*, not formed by its members. In a strong community its 'ongoing existence is an important value in and of itself' and becomes one of the most, if not the most, important imperatives of the 'moral community'.

Membership in a 'strong community' is, therefore, not completely voluntary or a matter of choice, but is bound together by 'enduring attachment', which often is, but not necessarily so, a result of a myth of common origin and is clearly bonded by a myth of common destiny. In other words, this 'strong community' is the national 'imagined community'. As a strong community, there is no difference between republican constructions of the 'moral community' and the *Gemeinschaft*-like constructions of the 'national community'. The communitarians go as far as arguing that, 'It does not make sense to speak of individuals constituting a community: rather, communities constitute individuals' (Ackelsberg, forthcoming: 5).

The question arises, then, what should happen to those members of the civil society who cannot or would not become full members of that 'community'. In virtually all contemporary states there are migrants and refugees, 'old' and 'new' minorities, and in settler societies (where colonialist projects constituted new independent national collectivities: Stasiulis and Yuval-Davis, 1995) also indigenous people who are not part of the hegemonic national community. In addition there are many other members of the civil society who exist fully or partly in what Evans (1993) calls 'the marginal matrix of society' and who, although they might share the myth of common origin of 'the community', do not share important hegemonic value systems with the majority of the population in sexual, religious and other matters and are therefore, at least partly, not part of the 'moral community'.

For Peled (1992) this reality is not sufficient to reject the republican position, which sees in the continued historical existence of 'strong national communities' a moral dictate in its own right even if it means the continued exclusion of all those 'outsiders'. His solution (following Oldfield, 1990) is a two-tier construction of citizenship: a full membership in the 'strong community' for those who can be included; and for people who cannot, 'a residual, truncated status, similar to the liberal notion of citizenship as a bundle of rights. Bearers of this citizenship do not share in attending to the common good but are secure in their possession of what we consider essential human and civil rights.'

In other words, Peled is suggesting the institutionalization of an exclusionary two-tier system of citizenship as a way of solving the discrepancy between the boundaries of the civil society and the boundaries of the hegemonic national collectivity. This solution, of course, is far from satisfactory politically, as it openly condones discrimination and racialization of citizens on national grounds (Peled cites Israel and its treatment of the Palestinians, who have been citizens of the state since 1948, as an ideal case of a state that has successfully managed such a system). It is also unsatisfactory theoretically, because it dichotomizes the population into two homogeneous collectivities – those who are in and those who are out of the national collectivity – without paying attention to other dimensions of social divisions and social positionings, such as gender, intranational ethnicity, class, sexuality, ability, stage in the life cycle, and so on, which I would argue are crucial to constructions of citizenship, as well as individuality.

Yet, with all these reservations, the above position at least recognizes the potentially inherent contradictory nature of citizenship as individual and communal, inclusionary and exclusionary. In Marshall's works (1950; 1975; 1981), these issues were not problematized at all and there has been an automatic assumption of an overlap between the boundaries of civil society and the boundaries of the national community. Not incidentally, Theodor Shanin (1986) once remarked that in English, unlike in other languages (such as Russian or Hebrew), there is a missing term which expresses the notion of ethnic nationality, to differentiate from nationality which is equivalent to formal citizenship in the state. In different states and societies the relationship between the two hugely differs and can be structured formally, or informally, in a way which prioritizes one hegemonic ethnic/national collectivity or several; in a way in which such a membership would or would not be primarily important for one's identity; in a way which would provide members with easier or more difficult access to a whole range of social, economic and political facilities; in a way which would or would not actually ground in law that members in different collectivities would be entitled to a differential range of civil, political and social citizenship rights. A common status in Europe, for instance, is that of the 'denizen' who is entitled to most social and civil rights but is deprived of the political national voting rights. Paradoxically, although Marshall's theory of citizenship does not relate to any of these issues, his conceptual definition of citizenship as a membership of the community rather than of the state can provide us with the framework to study specific cases of the differential multi-tier citizenship that people have in their ethnic community, their local community, the state and, more and more often these days, also in supra-national organizations.

A word of caution is necessary here, however. As I have elaborated elsewhere (Cain and Yuval-Davis, 1990; Yuval-Davis, 1991b) it is important not to view 'the community' as a given natural unit to which one can either belong or not. As Chantal Mouffe rightly comments, 'Politics is about the constitution of the political community, not something that takes place within it' (1993: 81). Collectivities and 'communities' are ideological and material constructions, whose boundaries, structures and norms are a result of constant processes of struggle and negotiation, or more general social developments (Anthias and Yuval-Davis, 1992). This is especially important if we consider, as Stuart Hall and David Held (1989) point out, that in real politics the main, if not the only, arena in which questions of citizenship have remained alive until recently, at least in the West, has been in relation to questions of race and immigration – in other words, questions which have challenged both the identity and the boundaries of 'the community' in relation to both nations and states.

The problems, however, do not relate only to external boundaries. As a given 'natural' social unit, any notion of internal difference within the 'community', therefore, can be subsumed to this organic construction. Such a difference can be attributed to a functional need so that the difference contributes to the smooth and efficient working of 'the community'. Otherwise, differences acquire the character of an anomaly, a pathological deviation which threatens the community. Therefore, although the notion of 'the community' can incorporate gender divisions, and to a certain extent even class divisions of labour, it would be intolerant of cultural, political and sexual diversities.

Accordingly, the republican moral imperative which interprets the 'good of the community' as a support for its continuous existence as a separate collectivity, and the communitarian collective argument which interprets the social construction of individuals as a support of traditional 'communal values', can become extremely conservative ideologies which would see any internal or external change in the community as a threat. This is where the link between nationalism and racism would be most intense. Political mobilizations against this, however, would have to take into account that people's identity is constructed in relation to collectivities. They would also have to take into account the fact that the different collectivities people are members of are usually positioned differently in relation to the state.

We shall turn next, therefore, to examine some of the issues which are raised when Marshall's notion of citizenship is applied to notions of difference.

Social Rights and Social Difference

The liberal definition of citizenship constructs all citizens as basically the same and considers the differences of class, ethnicity, gender and so on as irrelevant to their status as citizens. This view, incidentally, was also shared by Marx (1975) as developed in his article on the 'Jewish question'. On the other hand, the whole notion of social rights, as it has developed in the welfare state and been described by Marshall and others, assumes a notion of difference, as determined by *social needs*. In the words of Edwards: 'Those with similar needs ought to get similar resources and those with different needs, different resources, or – more succinctly – treatment as equals rather than equal treatment' (1988: 135).

As originally envisaged by Beveridge (1942) and others, social welfare rights were linked directly to class difference. Welfare rights were aimed at improving the quality of life of the working classes as well as the smooth working of capitalism. Marshall (1981) calls it 'the hyphenated society', in which there are inevitable tensions between a capitalist economy, a welfare state and the requirements of the modern state. As Harris (1987) described it, welfare was conceived as the institutionalized recognition of social solidarity within the political community of the citizens.

As Evans points out, this social solidarity is being threatened by a variety of groupings, such as ethnic, racial, religious and sexual, which exist within the marginal matrix of society:

> These are sub-collectivities which experience informal and formal discrimination consonant with their credited lower social worth, and in the case of sexual minorities in particular, their relative immorality within the British moral community. (1993: 6)

Debates around the citizenship of ethnic and racial minorities (Paul Gordon, 1989; Hall and Held, 1989) have touched on all levels of citizenship – civil, political and social. However, as mentioned above, the primary concerns of many relevant struggles and debates have been around an even more basic right – that is, the right to enter, or, once having entered, the right to remain in a specific country. Constructing boundaries according to various inclusionary and exclusionary criteria, which relate to ethnic and racial divisions as well as to class and gender divisions, is one of the main arenas of struggle concerning citizenship that remain completely outside the agenda of Marshallian theories of citizenship. The 'freedom of movement within the European Community', the Israeli Law of Return and the patriality clause in British immigration legislation – are all instances of ideological, often racist, constructions of boundaries which allow unrestricted immigration to some and block it completely to others.

Even when questions of entry and settlement have been resolved, the concerns of people of ethnic minorities might be different from those of other members of the society. For example, their right to formal citizenship might depend upon the rules and regulations of their country of origin as well as those of the country where they live, as well as the relationship between the two. Thus, people from some Caribbean islands who had been settled in Britain for years were told that they could not have a British passport because their country of origin did not recognize dual citizenship and because they had not declared on time their intent to renounce the citizenship of their country of origin after it received independence. Concern over relatives and fear of not being allowed to visit their country of origin prevent others (such as Iranians and Turks) from giving up their original citizenship. Thus, although they might spend the rest of their lives in another country, they would have, at best, limited political rights in it (contradicting the evolutionary model of Marshall, according to which social rights always follow civil and political rights). An issue which has been a specific focus of migrant women's campaigns has been the rule that women workers who have children in other countries would often be ineligible to receive child benefits like other mothers. Also, given specific combinations of nationality laws, children can be born stateless in countries like Israel and Britain. Such countries confer citizenship on those whose parents are citizens rather than on those born in the country.

Immigrants can also be deprived of social rights enjoyed by other members of the society. Often, the right of entry to a country is conditional on a commitment by the immigrant that neither s/he nor any other member of their family will claim any welfare benefits from the state – which might affect especially the position of immigrant women who become the major carers of their relatives. In most cases, a high class position, such as proof of a sizeable fortune in the bank, can be used to override national/racial quotas for the right to settle in a country. As Bakan and Stasiulis have argued in relation to women who are foreign domestic workers in Canada, constructions of citizenship have to be reconceptualized in ways

> that simultaneously reflect both global and national relations of power . . . the acceptance of the regulatory authority of hegemonic states in determining access to citizenship rights is not only reflected in the racialized and gendered definition of who is and who is not suitable to obtain such rights. It is also apparent in the assumption of the non-hegemonic status of third world states . . . The unequal distribution of citizenship rights within the advanced/liberal democracies, principally along the lines of class, race and gender inequalities, becomes blurred and recedes in importance when considered in counterposition where far greater proportions of citizens suffer from chronic poverty and privation. (1994: 26–8)

Citizenship needs to be examined, not just in terms of the state, but often in relation to multiple formal and informal citizenships in more than one country. Most importantly, these citizenships need to be viewed from a perspective which would include the different positioning of the different states as well as the different positionings of individuals and groupings within states. (On the importance of the international dimensions in imperial pasts for the construction of differential citizenships see Catherine Hall, 1994.)

A whole different set of citizenship issues would relate to indigenous minorities in settler societies (Dickanson, 1992; Stasiulis and Yuval-Davis,

1995). It is not just that in many societies indigenous populations have been very late entrants, if entrants at all, to the formal citizenship body of the state. It is that were their claim on the country – in the form of land rights, for instance – taken seriously to a full measure, this would totally conflict with the claim of the settler national collectivity for legitimacy. Attempts to solve the problem by transforming the indigenous population into another 'ethnic minority' have usually met with strong and understandable resistance (deLepervanche, 1980). Formal treaties, which would institutionalize and anchor in law the relations between what Australian Aboriginals have been calling 'the imposing society' and the indigenous people, often create a complex situation in which there exist two national sovereign entities over the same territory – one which owns the state and one which attempts to establish a sovereign stateless society within it. Somewhat similar, if less racialized, struggles are present in the many regionalist secessionist movements which claim the right of national self-determination *vis-à-vis* their states which themselves have been constructed as nations.

This situation can be seen as symptomatic of the present state of affairs in which individual and collective rights are no longer determined exclusively by the state, while identities are still perceived as particularized and territorially bound. As Yasemin Soysal (1994) argues, this state of affairs has come about in the post-World War II era as a result of several factors, such as the internationalization of labour markets and massive decolonizations. The latter brought about new forms of migratory flows. Even more importantly, however, they have established new states which asserted their rights in universalistic parameters and participated in international agencies, such as the UN and UNESCO, in the development of international human rights discourse as well as legislation. This international human rights discourse was largely strengthened by the development of new social movements in the North as well as in the South which protested against both discrimination towards and disadvantage of various marginal sectors and collectivities in society, such as women, blacks, Fourth World people, disabled people and so on. At the same time, the executors of these international codes of rights and the members of international bodies are still the states and no international agency has the right to 'interfere in the internal affairs' of other states.

The most problematic aspects of citizenship rights for racial and ethnic minorities relate to their social rights and to the notion of multi-culturalism (see, for example, Bhiku Parekh, 1990; Laksiri Jayasuriya, 1990; Yuval-Davis, 1992b). For some (like Harris, 1987; Lister, 1990) the problem remains within the realm of individual, though different, citizens. As Harris claims:

> The goal is to provide everyone with the wherewithal to enjoy and participate in the benefits of pluralism . . . there are common elements underlying cultural variations which can effectively define minimum standards. (1987: 49)

The homogeneous community of Marshall is being transformed into a pluralist one by the reinterpretation of his emphasis on equality of status into mutual respect (Lister, 1990: 48). However, such a model does not take into account potential conflicts of interest among the different groupings of citizens, nor does it consider the collective, rather than the individual, character of the special provisions given to members of ethnic minorities (Jayasuriya, 1990: 23).

The question of a collective provision of needs relates to policies of positive action aimed at group rather than individual rights. Multi-culturalist policies construct the population, or rather, effectively, the poor and working classes within the population, in terms of ethnic and racial collectivities. Those collectivities are attributed with collective needs, based on their different cultures as well as on their structural disadvantages. Resistance to these policies has been expressed by claims that constructing employment and welfare policies in terms of group rights can conflict with individual rights and are therefore discriminatory. However, at least in countries which officially adopted multiculturalist policies, such as Canada, Britain and the USA, it has been widely accepted, at least until recently, that in order to overcome the practical effects of racism rather than just its ideology, collective provisions and positive action, based on group membership, are the only effective measures to be taken (see Burney, 1988; Cain and Yuval-Davis, 1990; Young, 1989). Similar policies have been constructed in other pluralist states, such as India and South Africa.

The question becomes more problematic when the provision relates not to differential treatment in terms of access to employment or welfare, but to what has been defined as the different cultural needs of different ethnicities. These can vary from the provision of interpreters to the provision of funds to religious organizations. In the most extreme cases, as in the debates around Aboriginals on the one hand and around Muslim minorities and the Rushdie Affair on the other, there have been calls to enable the minorities to operate according to their own customary and religious legal systems. While the counter-arguments have ranged from the fact that this would imply a *de facto* apartheid system to the case for social unity and political hegemony, those who support these claims have seen them as a natural extrapolation of the minorities' social and political rights. This raises the question of how one defines the boundaries of citizens' rights.

Will Kymlicka (1995) suggests to differentiate between 'two kinds of group rights': one which involves the claim of a group against its own members and one which involves the group's claim against the larger society (or the state). Kymlicka opposes the use of state powers in the support of claims of the first kind, because he suspects that very often individuals within the group would be oppressed in the name of culture and tradition. On the other hand, in the second case, the issue often involves protection of a disadvantaged group by others: in such a case, state intervention should be welcome. While the general line of argument of Kymlicka can be supported, he reifies and naturalizes the groups' boundaries and does not differentiate between people with specific power positionings within the groups (which are not homogeneous and can have differing and conflicting interests) and 'the group'.

Jayasuriya (1990), using a somewhat different terminology when grappling with the same question, suggests a distinction between what he calls needs, which are essential and which therefore require satisfaction by the state, and wants, which fall outside the public sector and are to be satisfied within the private domain in a voluntary way.

The differentiation between 'wants' and 'needs' as objective differences between essential and non-essential cultural demands of specific sub-collectivities within the civil society is, of course, highly suspect. Cultures and cultural needs are not fixed ahistorical essentialist characteristics of collectivities. As was explored in some detail in Chapter 3, cultures are highly heterogeneous resources which are used selectively, and often in contradictory ways, in different ethnic projects which are promoted by members of specific collectivities. These projects are affected both by the specific positionings of those who promote the ethnic projects within the collectivity, and by the specific positioning of the collectivity as such *vis-à-vis* the state. Women often suffer from the acceptance by the state of the definition of what constitutes 'the cultural needs of the community' in matters of education, marriage and divorce and other provisions such as women's refuges (Sahgal and Yuval-Davis, 1992). In South Africa, women members of the ANC fought hard and long to have the principle of 'non-sexist South Africa' accepted (just 24 hours before the finalization of the constitution) as having a superior constitutional authority to the principle of 'respect for custom and tradition'. A special conference was organized which included women from different post-colonial states who gave evidence on how women's citizenship rights were taken from them after independence in the name of indigenous culture (Amy Biehl, 1994).

Jayasuriya establishes the boundary of provision by the state between the public and private domains, as if this boundary was natural and static. However, this boundary is highly problematic and is both gender and culture specific (Kandiyoti, 1991a; Yuval-Davis, 1991b). The next section of the chapter explores notions of the public/private dichotomy and the ways they have been used to construct gender relations and divisions of labour as well as to construct different types of citizenship.

The Private and the Public

There is a high degree of inconsistency in the ways that different authors discuss the public/private boundary and its relationship to other concepts such as political and civil society, the family, the economy, the voluntary sector and so on.

In the way feminists like Carole Pateman (1988; 1989), Rebecca Grant (1991) and Ursula Vogel (1989), for instance, talk about the public and the private spheres, it is clear that in their writings the public sphere is identical to the political sphere, while the private sphere relates primarily to the family domain where women are primarily located.

Carole Pateman examined the writings of social contract theorists as 'the most famous influential political story of modern times' which were written as 'an explanation for the binding authority of the state and civil law and for the legitimacy of modern civil government' (1988: 1). Her claim is that only half of the story has been told by these theorists, because they have talked about the *social* contract, while she sees it as based on and legitimized by the *sexual* contract – that is, the power that men exercise over women.

'Fraternity' (one element of the slogan of the French Revolution, which also called for liberty and equality) for Pateman is not just about social solidarity or even male bonding among the citizens. It is about the transformation of the hegemonic power relations in the society from a patriarchy, in which the father (or the king as a father figure) ruled over both other men and the women, to a fraternity, in which the men get the right to rule over their women in the private domestic sphere, but agree on a contract of a social order of equality among themselves within the public, political sphere. Women, therefore, were not excluded from the public sphere incidentally but as part of the bargain between the new regime and its member citizens. The whole social philosophy which was at the base of the rise of the notion of state citizenship, therefore, far from being universalistic, was constructed in terms of the 'rights of man' (actually as the 'rights of the white man', for the enslavement of black people, according to Pateman, 1989, is also part of the story that is rarely told).

Ursula Vogel (1989) has shown that women were not simply latecomers to citizenship rights, as in Marshall's evolutionary model. Their exclusion was part and parcel of the construction of the entitlement of men to democratic participation which 'conferred citizen status not upon individuals as such, but upon men in their capacity as members and representatives of a family (i.e. a group of non-citizens)' (1989: 2). And indeed, in Britain during Victorian times, women lost their citizenship when they got married; they continued to lose it if they got married to 'foreigners' until 1948; and it wasn't until 1981 that they got the independent right to transfer their citizenship to the children (Bhabha and Shutter, 1994; WING, 1985) – at the same time, however, that babies born in Britain to non-citizen or settled mothers lost their rights for British citizenship at all.

In contrast to this construction of the private as the domain of the family, in Jayasuriya's (1990) writings, mentioned above, the private domain is that which is not financed and/or controlled by the state and includes, for example, religious institutions. Bryan Turner (1990) uses the public/private dichotomy as one of the axes for his typology of citizenship, and includes in the private domain self-enhancement and other leisure, as well as spiritual activities. Sylvia Walby (1994: 383) criticizes him for adopting 'the male viewpoint' in this by conflating two meanings of 'private' – one which relates to the autonomy of the individual, and one which relates to freedom from the interventions of the state. She argues that while the family can or cannot be free from the intervention of the state, it is not an autonomous and free space for women, nor has it a unitary set of interests, as husbands and wives (and,

I would add, children and other relatives in cases of extended families) have different social positionings, powers and interests within the family.

If we accept the meaning of 'private' as that in which the individual is autonomous, then this can be exercised to a lesser or greater extent in all social spheres, where people – and not just women – can act both as part of social structures and collectivities with all the constraints these provide, and as autonomous individual agents, whether in the family, in the civil domain or in the political domain. Similarly, depending on people's preferences and hobbies, leisure and self-enhancement activities can be spent with the family or other personal friends, with the trade union, church or ethnic sports associations, or as a councillor in local government. At the same time, especially in the modern welfare state, there is no social sphere which is protected from state intervention. Even in cases where there is no direct intervention, it is the state which has usually established, actively or passively, its own boundaries of non-intervention. In other words, the construction of the boundary between the public and the private is a political act in itself. Political power relations with their own dynamics exist in each social sphere. The most important contribution of feminism to social theory has been the recognition that power relations operate within primary social relations as well as within the more impersonal secondary social relations of the civil and political domains.

The recognition that power lines operate horizontally as well as vertically has given rise to the Foucauldian perspective that there is no need to theorize the state as a separate unitary sphere. However, as discussed in Chapter 1, while the state is not unitary in its practices, its intentions or its effects, there is a need to retain the state as a separate sphere, 'a body of institutions which are centrally organized around the intentionality of control with a given apparatus of enforcement at its command or basis'. Different forms of the state will involve different relationships between 'the control/coercion twin which is the residing characteristic of the state' (Anthias and Yuval-Davis, 1989: 6). While state powers can be more or less autonomous both internationally and intranationally, and ideological production, like education and the media, can lie both inside and outside the state, the exercise of individual and collective rights continues to be tied to the state (Soysal, 1994) and control over the state continues to be the primary political target.

Bryan Turner (1990), as mentioned above, has included the public/private dichotomy as one of the main axes for a comparative model of citizenship. Specifically, however, Turner defined this dichotomy as 'public and private definitions of moral activity in terms of the creation of a public space of political activity' (1990: 209). This definition, in actuality, relates closely to what we discussed earlier about the individual/collective construction of citizenship and the relative place of the 'moral community' and the 'common good' vis-à-vis the rights of the individual.

Given all these inconsistencies and confusions in the determination of the private domain, I would like to suggest that rather than retaining the public/private distinction, we should differentiate between three distinct spheres: the state, the civil society, and the domain of the family and kinship relations. Because Turner, as Walby has pointed out, conflated the individual and the family, he missed the additional important comparative dimension of different kinds of citizenship which is focused on the relative importance of each of these spheres in the construction of citizenship.

Feminist critiques of the influential comparative analysis of welfare states by Esping-Andersen (1990), like Ann Orloff (1993) and Julia O'Connor (1993), have pointed out that there is a need to add the family domain to that of the state and the market when examining the ways countries organize the provision of welfare. This is an important correction. However, the family domain has also to be added when we discuss different locations for political organization and power. This is especially important if we expand the comparative span of citizenship beyond the very limited western examples Turner has used.

It is misleading to see in the rise of the 'modern nation-state' a completely different form of social organization from the 'premodern' ones. In many states, especially post-colonial states, for example, extended family and kinship relationships have continued to be used as foci of loyalty and organization, even when constructed as ideological political parties. Political, social and probably even civil rights might depend on the familial positioning of the particular citizen (Saudi Arabia or Jordan are probably good examples of such states, but in more dilute forms this phenomenon is spread much more widely, especially among ruling parties' elites). In these states, traditional social and especially familial relations continue to operate and often either women do not have any formal citizenship rights at all, or those rights are very minimal. Paradoxically, however, where familial relations are important in the politics of a country, women who are widows or daughters of political leaders have the highest chance of becoming political leaders, as has been the case in the Indian subcontinent, for instance.

At the other extreme of the family/civil society/state agencies domination continuum we have the states of the former Soviet bloc, in which there was an attempt to incorporate into the state all facets of the civil – and to some extent also familial – domains. All political, economic and cultural activities were aimed to be controlled by the state; all forms of organization or expression which did not follow the state (and the Communist Party) line tended to be repressed and controlled; and membership in the party brought with it higher civil, political and social rights. Also in the realm of the family there were far-reaching changes in terms of family laws, the virtually complete recruitment of women into the labour force (although mostly in positions lower than those of men: Voronina, 1994: 733), formal legal and political equality (although women were absent from the central Politburo throughout its history), and the collectivization of certain aspects of domestic labour, such as child care facilities and public canteens (although women continued to do the bulk of domestic labour in addition to their work load). Natalya Kosmarskaya (1995), commenting on this, actually claims that in Russia it is women who are visible in the public domain – as they are the ones who do the shopping and so on while men are locked in the 'private space' of their work places.

In western welfare states, such as, for example, the Scandinavian countries, the state has supplied public facilities to help with women's domestic responsibilities and child care, so as to enable women to go out into the labour market. Women work more than men in the public sector and, unlike in the former Soviet bloc, have had high rates of political representation. However, as Helga Hernes (1987) and Anne Showstack Sassoon (1987) argue, in countries like Norway the corporations in civil society are those which carry the most significant economic and social powers, and they have tended to be controlled by men.

Welfare states are considered to be those where the influence of civil society is the greatest in terms of the location of political as well as economic power. Marshall (1981) described the capitalist society as the hyphenated society in which there are inevitable tensions between a capitalist economy and the welfare state. Esping-Andersen (1990) described the variations between different welfare state regimes as dependent on the extent to which market forces or the state have the upper hand in the struggle for domination.

It is important to remember, however, that the civil domain is not just the market. It is not only economic relations, but political and social as well, which operate there and which inform and are informed by the state. Political parties, social movements and trade unions are not part of the state even if they are often organized and focus their activities on the state. Education and media can be owned or not by the state and can have ideological projects which are to a larger or lesser extent autonomous from the state.

Of particular importance to our concern here are formal and informal organizations, associations and institutions in civil society which are organized by/for members of particular ethnic/racial/national collectivities. Any comparative model of states would also have to differentiate between states in which such collectivities play a larger or a smaller role in the construction of state policies and in social and political relations in the country. The formal ethnicization of the different regions in Yugoslavia in the revised constitution approved by Tito during the last years of his life was a major development in that country's history and a partial explanation of later developments and its disintegration. The degree to which various social and educational services should be given to the public via various ethnic organizations in 'multi-cultural societies' is a point of political debate in many.

In general terms the above examples demonstrate the relative importance of the different domains – the familial, the civil and that of state agencies, which vary in different states and societies – in the determination of the social, political and civil rights of its citizens, although not exclusively so (for example, in post-revolutionary China, state agencies and familial structures have been in a contest for hegemony throughout its history). Obviously each of these spheres is never homogeneous: different parts of the state can act in contradictory ways to others, and their effects on different ethnic, class, gender and other groupings in the society could be different. For example, the immigration authorities in a country like Britain or the USA might ask immigrants to sign a waiver of their social rights so that other people in the familial domain, rather than the state, would be responsible for supporting them if they are not successful in the civil economic sphere. Another example is that, usually, marriages which are carried out by ministers of certain religions automatically obtain the formal sanctification of the state, while those which are officiated by others are invalid and need to be performed in addition by the authorized authorities. In the Soviet Union there were certain areas (for example, places in higher education institutes) in which people of different national origin were given priority in their 'homelands'. On the other hand, Russian 'settlers' were often those who had control over political power in the different territories. In the aftermath of the fall of the Soviet bloc and the rise of the independent republics, a situation is arising which has already existed for many years in some of the oil countries, in which formal state citizenship is becoming a privileged status which can be conferred only on a minority of the population – those of the 'right origin'.

Any comparative theory of citizenship, therefore, has to include an examination of the individual autonomy allowed to citizens (of different gender, ethnicity, region, class, stage in the life cycle and so on) *vis-à-vis* their families, civil society organizations and state agencies.

Active/Passive Citizenship

The other axis of Bryan Turner's comparative typology of citizenship is that of active/passive, which he defines as 'whether the citizen is conceptualized as merely a subject of an absolute authority or as an active political agent' (1990: 209). The conventional differentiation, then, between 'citizen' and 'subject' is removed in Turner's definition, and instead there is a continuum of passivity and activity.

The history of citizenship is different in different countries. In some countries, like France and the USA, it has been a result of popular revolutionary struggles, while in others, like Britain and Germany, it has been more of a 'top to bottom' process. Similarly, in some post-colonial countries, like India or Kenya, national independence was achieved after a long period of popular struggle, while in others, like some Caribbean islands, that transition was much more peaceful and political rule was passed more or less smoothly from the colonial elite to the local one.

Today, virtually the entire world population lives in countries in which some form of citizenship exists, at least in the Marshallian sense of being a member of a community. As to the Aristotelian definition (Allen and Macey, 1990), in which citizenship means participating in some form in ruling as well as in being ruled, the picture is, of course, very different, and only a minority of people, in probably a minority of world states, can be said to have such active citizenship status. The question of activity and passivity, of course, is not just a question of the formal constitutions of specific states. Even in the most democratically active societies there are strata of the population which are much more passive and, even if they have some social rights, either have no political rights of participation or, if they have the formal rights, are too disempowered and/or too alienated to participate even in the formal act of voting. Among them can be not only children, migrants, ethnic minorities and indigenous people in settler societies, but also what has come to be known as the 'underclass', which in the USA is to a large extent black, but which in Britain and other countries can also be largely white, and in which lone mothers are looming large (Lister, 1990; Lydia Morris, 1994). Gender, sexuality, age and ability as well as ethnicity and class are important factors in determining the relationship of people to their communities and states.

The notion of the 'active citizen' has been a focus of debates and policies in recent years within both the 'left' and the 'right', especially in Britain. The recent growth of interest in citizenship among the left has coincided with the growing crisis of the welfare state, just when there are signs that many of the social rights which have come to be taken for granted in the welfare state have come under threat, in the areas of health care, education, retirement, child benefits and so on. This crisis has taken place at the same time as significant elements of the working classes have started to vote for the conservatives in several western countries, and also at the same time as the fall of the Soviet bloc and the demise of its model of state socialism.

Rather than concentrating on social rights, however, the left (and the centre) has used citizenship as a call for political mobilization and participation. In Britain it also became part of a campaign for a written constitution (Charter 88) in which citizenship entitlement would be enshrined so that a radical rightist government, as was the Thatcherite government, would not be able to transform the relationship between people and state without being accountable.

The language of citizenship has also been a major discourse of the right. In Britain 'the active citizen' has been put forward as an alternative to the welfare state, in which 'the citizen' – constructed as an economically successful middle class male head of a family – would fulfil his citizenship duties by giving his spare money and time 'to the community' (Evans, 1993; Lister, 1990).

In this discourse, therefore, citizenship stops being a political discourse and becomes a voluntary involvement within civil society, in which the social rights of the poor, constructed as the passive citizens, would be transferred, at least partly, from entitlements into charities. Lister (1990: 14) quotes the Conservative minister Douglas Hurd as defining active citizenship as a necessary complement to the enterprise culture. 'Public service may once have been the duty of an elite, but today it is the responsibility of all who have time or money to spare.' And she claims that in the name of social cohesion, obligations are being shifted from the public sphere of tax-financed benefits and services to the private sphere of charity and voluntary services. And charity, usually, assumes the dependency and passivity of those given the charity. Rights become gifts and active citizenship assumes a top-down notion of citizenship. Typically quangos, which are appointed rather than elected, have come to be the means by which various public services, like health and welfare, are being managed.

This depoliticization of the notion of citizenship has been enhanced with the publication of the government's Citizens' Charter in 1992 which constructs citizens as consumers whose prime rights are to have the freedom to make well-informed choices of high quality commodities and services in the public and private sectors and to be treated with due regard for their 'privacy, dignity, religious and cultural beliefs' (Evans, 1993: 10). As Bauman (1988: 807) claims, 'In our time individuals are engaged (morally by society, functionally by the social system) first and foremost as consumers rather than producers.' The balance of citizenship rights has shifted, then, away from social rights of welfare towards civil rights of an economic kind (that is, market access related) such as the right to buy council houses, shares and so on. There is a debate, however (Oliver, 1995), about whether or not such a construction of citizenship can still be included in the definition of citizenship, as its aim is to promote the individual persona and autonomy rather than the relationship between the individual and the community (although it would clearly fall within the liberal mode of citizenship which was described above). What is clear, however, is that this construction of citizenship is highly class biased and cancels out the construction of citizenship in the welfare state which aimed at, as Edwards (1988) put it, 'treatment as equals rather than equal treatment'. Under the new right mode of citizenship, as Peter Golding remarks (foreword to Lister, 1990: xii), 'To be poor is to endure conditional citizenship.'

The Thatcherite notion of citizenship as consumerism is not based, of course, on completely free market models, in spite of its universalist rhetoric. As Ruth Lister comments,

> We are now conceived as customers rather than as citizens. Yet this does not empower us as sovereign consumers so much as it limits our value and our rights to our purchasing power. (1990: 1)

There are legal and moral constraints which prevent a variety of marginal or minority groups from pursuing their religious and cultural beliefs or economic needs in equal measures (Evans, 1993: 6). The state's management of these 'moral aliens', who are to be found in the marginal matrix of citizenship, is exercised in social, political and economic arenas and results in both formal and informal discrimination. This is the twilight zone between the liberal and republican constructions of citizenship, where religious, ethnic and sexual minorities are located – outside the national 'moral community' but inside the civic nation.

To those who can afford it, this is not a completely closed-off system. Evans (1993) describes how sexual minority groups developed, as a result, socio-economic 'community' infrastructures of varying degrees of complexity around their identities. They organized to obtain further housing, insurance, medical, parenting, marital rights and so on, and spent a significant proportion of their income on, for example, gay commodities and distinctive lifestyles in segregated or specifically gay social and sexual territories. According to him,

> Specific forms of sexual citizenship are largely confined to the moral and the economic and are largely part-time leisure and lifestyle spaces which encircle the moral community between the boundaries of immorality and illegality. (1993: 8)

Multi-culturalism which is aimed at ethnic minorities can be described in similar terms. As discussed elsewhere (Sahgal and Yuval-Davis, 1992), multi-culturalist policies are aimed at simultaneously including and excluding the minorities, locating them in marginal spaces and secondary markets while reifying their boundaries. These marginal spaces, however, both ethnic and sexual (as well as those of other marginalized groups such as the disabled), have become the terrain for contested ideologies of the right and the left around identity politics as the basis for citizenship rights: segregation and separatism on the one hand and collective as well as individual rights of minorities on the other hand (Eisenstein, 1993; Phillips, 1993; Young, 1989).

The existence of these spaces in civil society for constructions of citizenship is very important. The transformation of what is described in one discourse as the specific social and economic needs of people, into another discourse in which they become signifiers of collectivity boundaries, is what can transform 'active citizenship' from the social arena into the political one.

Iris Young (1989) has suggested that representative democracy should treat people not as individuals but as members of groups, some of them more oppressed than others. She argues that a discourse of universal citizenship which would ignore these differences would just enhance the domination of groups which are already dominant, and would silence the marginal and oppressed groups. She suggests, therefore, that special mechanisms have to be established to represent these groups as groups. Although Iris Young's insistence that difference and differential power relations should be recognized in the practice of citizenship is very important, her approach is problematic in several ways. As elaborated elsewhere (Anthias and Yuval-Davis, 1992; Cain and Yuval-Davis, 1990; Phillips, 1993) such an approach can easily fall into the pitfalls of identity politics, in which the groups are constructed as homogeneous and with fixed boundaries. The interests of people who are positioned in specific positions within the groups is going to be constructed as necessarily representing the interests of the whole group, and the advancement of the powers of the specific group *vis-à-vis* others would become the primary aim of political activities which concern and relate to the citizenship body as a whole.

Thus, Anne Phillips argues that

> when so many of the problems that face us are general in nature and require a vision that looks beyond what is local – the prospects for a better democracy lie not in dissolving distinctions between public and private but in more actively revitalizing the public sphere. (1993: 13)

In that Anne Phillips claims that she is following the arguments of Hannah

Arendt. However, unlike Arendt (1975), she recognizes that notions of difference cannot just be ignored. She suggests, therefore (following Mary Dietz,
1987), that the participation in the public arena of politics should be based on
what she calls 'transformation', getting beyond one's immediate sphere, rather
than transcendence. The former she sees as rightly stressing the limits of
localized and specific identities, while the latter involves pursuing this to the
point of jettisoning all group differences and concerns. John Lechte (1994),
when discussing Arendt's approach to the political, argues that Kristeva's
theory of the relationship between the semiotic and the symbolic can be used
to posit the private domain, which is the domain of difference, and the public
political domain, not as a dyad of opposites, but as the first being the mate-
riality of the second, which gives it its particular meaning. In other words,
every discussion of individual differences already involves the public domain.
Young's construction of 'oppressed groups' is no more 'natural' than any
other political discourses, and the transformation/transcendence process is
inherent in the act of naming.

Suggestions of other feminists and activists who attempted to deal with the
question of citizenship rights and social difference focus differentially on the
social and on the political. Correa and Petchesky (1994), for instance, advo-
cate that political rights should be enhanced by social rights. They argue that
rather than abandoning rights discourse, we should reconstruct it so that it
both specifies differences, such as gender, class, cultural and other differences, and recognizes social needs. Sexual and reproductive (or any other)
rights, understood as private 'liberties' or 'choices', are meaningless, especially for the poorest and most disenfranchised, without enabling conditions
through which they can be realized. While, like Young, such an approach recognizes the crucial importance of collective disadvantages and discrimination,
these do not become reified in the construction of the political subjects and
remain distinguishable from them. In the post-GLC era in London, with the
massive backlash against the identity politics which was practised there as a
basis for resources allocation, some black and other radical activists came to
the conclusion that the alternative to group politics should be the politics of
disadvantage which would mean confronting these disabling conditions. The
argument has been that if black people suffer disproportionately from unemployment, for instance, political discourse which focuses on unemployment
will also benefit black people disproportionately, without it being formally
directed specifically at them. However, this approach would not exclude, or
create a construction of 'otherness' for, the other unemployed (Wilson, 1987).

Zillah Eisenstein's approach to questions of difference is that

> The concern here is not with differences *per se*, but rather with how we can start
> with differences to construct a particularist understanding of human rights which
> is both universal and specific. (1993: 6)

Her solution in her 1993 book is to construct a woman of colour as an alternative, inclusive standard norm to that of the white male. It might be more
difficult, but I much prefer her former position (Eisenstein, 1989) in which she

argues that while we cannot do without some notion of what human beings have in common, we can and must do without a unitary standard against which they are all judged. Her latter position can assume that the needs of a woman of colour are greater than, rather than different from, those of a white man. It is also a position which cannot necessarily be used internationally.

Instead of a given unitary standard, there has to be a process of constructing it for each specific political project. Black feminists like Patricia Hill-Collins (1990) and Italian feminists like Raphaela Lambertini and Elizabetta Dominini (see Yuval-Davis, 1994b) have focused on the transversal politics of coalition building, in which the specific positionings of political actors are recognized and considered. As will be elaborated upon in Chapter 6, this approach is based on the epistemological recognition that each positioning produces specific situated knowledge which cannot be but an unfinished knowledge, and therefore dialogue among those differentially positioned should take place in order to reach a common perspective. Transversal dialogue should be based on the principles of rooting and shifting – that is, being centred in one's own experiences while being empathetic to the differential positionings of the partners in the dialogue, thus enabling the participants to arrive at a different perspective from that of hegemonic tunnel vision. The boundaries of the dialogue would be determined by the message rather than its messengers. The result of the dialogue might still be differential projects for people and groupings positioned differently, but their solidarity would be based on a common knowledge sustained by a compatible value system. The dialogue, therefore, is never boundary free.

Of course, in 'real politics', unlike in grass-roots social movements, there is often no time for extensive continuous dialogue. When the Women's Unit in the GLC in the early 1980s tried to work in this manner, it ended up being completely ignored by the ongoing hierarchical structures of decision-making which were working at a much faster pace. Transversal politics should not be seen as necessarily opposing the principle of delegation, as long as the political delegates are advocates, rather than representatives, of specific social categories and groupings and as long as their message is a result of transversal dialogues.

Citizenship's Rights and Duties

The various definitions of citizenship emphasize that citizenship is a two-way process and involves obligations as well as rights. This, of course, raises not only the thorny issue of whether specific rights should be conditioned by carrying out specific duties but also the more general question of the boundaries of citizenship. What, if any, should be the criteria for selecting people who want to immigrate into a specific country and become its citizens? Recently, Helen Meekosha and Leanne Dowse (1996) presented a challenging paper in which they argued that, according to this model of citizenship, disabled people who cannot carry out any obvious citizenship duties are excluded automatically from entitlement to citizenship rights.

A correlated question is what are or should be the specific citizenship duties. This has been a contested and shifting terrain, and sometimes citizenship rights and duties can get mixed up. For example, voting is considered a primary citizenship right. However, there are quite a few states – not the most democratic ones but those in need of legitimation of their powers – in which voting has become the duty of the citizens (or some of them, as in Egypt where this is the duty only of the men: women have had to ask for this right specifically and in writing, proving that they are literate), and if they do not comply with that duty they can be heavily fined.

Keeping the law, for instance, cannot be seen strictly as a citizenship duty because even those who are not citizens or residents are required to keep the law wherever they are – although the laws can differ from one grouping of people to another, and the state's and community's ability to enforce the law may differ as well. On the other hand, in many cases, especially concerning unwritten and customary laws, keeping them becomes not just members' duty but also a marker of boundaries, and those who do not comply can be ousted from the community as well as punished for non-compliance.

Defending one's own community and country has been seen as an ultimate citizen's duty – to die (as well as to kill) for the sake of the homeland or the nation (Yuval-Davis, 1985; 1991b). This duty has given rise to Kathleen Jones' (1990) claim that the body is a significant dimension in the definition of citizenship. Traditionally, she claims, citizenship has been linked with the ability to take part in armed struggle for national defence; this ability has been equated with maleness, while femaleness has been equated with weakness and the need for male protection.

Some feminist organizations (such as the National Organization of Women in the USA, ANMLAE in Nicaragua, and others) have fought for the inclusion of women on a footing equal to that of men in the military, arguing that once women share with men the ultimate citizens' duty – to die for one's country – they would also be able to gain citizenship rights equal to those of men. In the recent Gulf War women fought together with the men in the American army, in almost indistinguishable ways as well as uniforms: these uniforms have been designed for ABC (atomic, biological and chemical) warfare and seem to be quite indifferent to the 'type' of human 'body' inside them. This experience raises several sobering thoughts in relation to this kind of argument.

Firstly, the experiences of some of the women who had to leave small babies behind (mostly in the care of their own mothers, as often the husbands of these women serve in the army as well) show that feminist equal opportunity slogans can be used to create further pressures for women, rather than promote their rights. Secondly, their experiences show that the differential relations of power between men and women continue also within the military domain, including sexual harassment, and therefore it cannot automatically be considered as empowering women. Thirdly, and probably most importantly, this argument ignores the general social and political context of the military and its use. Empowering women to play global policemen on a footing equal to that of men is not what feminists (at least not socialist anti-racist feminists) should be engaged in.

Probably even more importantly for our concern here is the fact that virtually none of the soldiers who fought in the Gulf War in the western allies side did so as part of national service¹. Both women and men were professional soldiers who see the military as their professional career. I've elaborated more on this elsewhere (Yuval-Davis, 1991b; see also discussion in Chapter 5), but the clear implication is that in modern warfare, fighting is often not a citizen's duty any more.

Originally, citizenship was conditioned by owning property and therefore the universal duty was to pay taxes. With the expansion of citizenship over the different classes, this duty is now conditioned by the amount of earnings a person has, and therefore again cannot be seen as a universal duty.

For propertyless people, earnings are based on employment. Carole Pateman (1989) points to the fact that Marshall mentions 'the right to employment' as one of the citizenship rights, just at a time when architects of the welfare state were constructing men as breadwinner-worker and women as dependant-wife. A major fight of the feminist movement has been for equal pay and equal opportunities in employment. In spite of certain achievements in this field, the gender gap and the segregated labour market have largely remained and women continue to be primarily constructed as wives and mothers. Similar, often less successful, results have been achieved in fights against discrimination in the labour market for racial and ethnic groupings.

Moreover, it became clear that equal opportunities policies can be effective only in relation to those who have actually entered the labour market. As mentioned above in the discussion on 'active citizenship', citizenship duties can become a marker of the privileged. This, of course, tallies historically with the emergence of citizenship in the Greek polis, in which citizenship rights and duties were the privilege of the few, at the expense of women, slaves and denizens who were excluded from citizenship.

Recent discussions on 'workfare' as a substitute for 'welfare' have used the discourse of citizenship duties as a condition for citizenship rights, and 'community service' is constructed as the way the 'have-nots' can fulfil their duties. Probably the motives of many of the people who call for this shift are positive (although, of course, those of many are not) and are based on a sincere desire to break the perpetual cycle of dependency, deprivation and alienation. However, 'workfare' – in addition to its inherently coercive and selective nature, and the side-effects that its execution can bring to other sections in the labour market – shifts the primary ground of the debate on citizenship from the political to the social arena, from personal and collective empowerment into unskilled forced labour.

Conclusion

The chapter has discussed some of the issues which are relevant to the development of a theory of citizenship which will be not only non-sexist, non-racist and non-westocentric but also flexible enough to deal with the far-reaching changes in the global (dis)order.

One such issue has been the multi-tier construction of citizenship. If citizenship is defined as a 'full membership in a community', then usually people are members in more than one community, sub-, supra- and cross-states. Very often people's rights and obligations to a specific state are mediated and largely dependent on their membership in a specific ethnic, racial, religious or regional collectivity, although very rarely are they completely contained by them. At the same time, the development of ideologies and institutions of 'human rights' means that ideologically, at least, the state does not always have full control of the construction of citizenship's rights; also usually it is left for the state to carry them out. It is important to remember in that respect that people are not positioned equally within their collectivities and states, collectivities are not positioned equally within the state and internationally, and states are not positioned equally to other states. In order to study, for instance, the citizenship of a Palestinian woman who is a citizen of Israel, it is important to study her membership in the Israeli Palestinian community, that of the Israeli Palestinian community in relation to Israel – but also in relation to other Palestinian and Arab communities – and the positioning of both the state of Israel and 'the Arabs' internationally.

However, citizenship is not just a question of being or not being a member in a community(ies). Different social attributes would construct the specific positioning of people within and across the communities in certain social categories. The fact that the citizenship we want to study is that of an Israeli Palestinian is crucial, and radically affects her citizenship in all its tiers. However, other factors, such as her gender, class position, religion, her coming from the city or from a village, her ability, her stage in the life cycle and so on – would also all determine her citizenship. Many of these different attributes are not spread evenly or randomly in the different collectivities, but membership in any specific collectivity can only rarely, if at all, be reduced into any of these attributes.

Citizenship, therefore, cannot be analysed as a completely individual or collective phenomenon. Although usually the boundaries of collectivities, societies and states are being continuously reconstructed, membership in them and identities can often be forced rather than voluntary (Chhachhi, 1991). An important question which relates to states, collectivities and individuals would be their degree of autonomy – the extent to which their roles and activities are not determined by other social agents.

If privacy is to be equated with autonomy, then the family domain cannot usually be defined as private as well. Most members of most families, usually the children, the sick, the elderly and women, can determine very little of their lives even within the family domain, let alone outside it. These lives are determined both by those who are more powerful within the family, and by outside ideologies and practices which are located wholly or partly within the civil society domain and/or the state.

The family domain, however, is not just enacted upon. In different societies and states, family affiliations and structures, especially within the elite, can determine more or less the structure and power relations in the state and civil society. When they do, then even those who are relatively powerless within the family, like women, can gain power positioning over the state as a whole and become queens or prime ministers.

In governing a society, many of the issues concerned go beyond or might even be irrelevant to the particular concerns of the collectivities and social categories from which the political agents have come. However, this does not mean that people's different attributes and social positionings are left behind and are not relevant once they participate in the political domain and that they do not or should not inform and affect their ideologies and practices. As in science, there are no 'ivory towers' within politics.

Transversal politics, which are based on knowledge acquired by dialogue carried out by people who are differentially positioned, using the techniques of rooting and shifting, should be, then, the political guidelines for all political activism, whether at the grass-roots level or in state and supra-state power centres.

Citizenship rights are anchored in both the social and the political domains. Without 'enabling' social conditions, political rights are vacuous. At the same time, citizenship rights without obligations also construct people as passive and dependent. Citizens' most important duty is, therefore, to exercise their political rights and to participate in the determination of their collectivities', states' and societies' trajectories.

5

GENDERED MILITARIES, GENDERED WARS

Wars, claims Giddens (1989: 340, 346–7), do not exist as such in stateless societies: there is not enough surplus value produced in such societies to sustain systematic and long armed conflicts and militaries. And yet, constructions of manhood and womanhood which are assumed to have arisen in stateless hunter-gatherer societies have been the basis for the naturalization of the gender divisions of labour in militaries and wars. John Casey claimed:

> Males were selected for the role of warriors because the economical and physiological sex-linked differences that favoured the selection of men as hunters of animals favoured the selection of men as hunters of people. (quoted in Kazi, 1993: 15)

Moreover, Chris Knight (1991) has argued that men have bonded together and developed their roles as hunters and fighters to empower themselves with the brotherhood of blood as a defence against women's magical powers in their menstrual blood!

Notwithstanding the above, the argument of this chapter is that militaries and warfare have never been just a 'male zone'. Women have always fulfilled certain, often vital, roles within them – but usually not on an equal, undifferentiated basis to that of the men. The sexual division of labour within the military has often been even more formalized and rigid than that in the civil sector. This is important, because there have often been arguments, both by feminists and by those who opposed them, that the entry of women into the military is the precondition for women's achievement of full citizenship rights. As sacrificing one's life for one's country is the ultimate citizenship duty, citizenship rights are conditional on being prepared to fulfil this duty. Nevertheless, as in the case of the entry of women into the civil labour market, the entry of women into the military labour market – and as we shall see later, even in cases where they have obtained formal equality – has changed the context of the sexual divisions of labour and power, but has not erased them.

This chapter looks at the participation of women in both informal liberation struggles and in modern militaries and considers the ways this has had wider implications for the position of women in society. As in all other facets of gender and nation, women and men in the military are not homogeneous entities. Different groupings of men and women are positioned differentially and participate differently in militaries and war. It is important to emphasize this aspect in relation to warfare even more than most other aspects, because of the naturalization of the construction of men as warriors (and of women as worriers?) across all social divisions.

This does not mean, however, that there have not been constructions and images of women as warriors throughout history – from the Amazons to the American women soldiers in the Gulf War. These images usually have either enhanced the constructed unnaturalness of women as fighters, or been made in such a way as to collude with more generalized notions of femininity and masculinity in the society from which the women fighters have come.

In contemporary societies, the civil and military domains are closely inter-wound. And this is not just in relation to notions and representations of femininity and masculinity. It is a known phenomenon, for instance, that generals and heads of militaries are often among the people more cautious to start a war (Giddens, 1989). Modern militaries are huge bureaucratic organi-zations whose smooth workings could often only be disrupted by the intensity and unpredictability of war (although small 'safe' wars like the Gulf War could be used very beneficially, from the point of view of the leaders of the military machine, to test new weaponry as well as other dimensions of mili-tary operation such as communication and human organization). Of particular contemporary importance are those wars which Miriam Cooke (1993: 181) calls 'post-modern wars' – such as those which have taken place in Lebanon, Somalia and former Yugoslavia and in which the warring parties exist usually within rather than between states. These wars, and the contend-ing warring parties in them, are usually continuously being renegotiated and redefined. They can be seen as a direct or indirect outcome of post-colonial-ism and of the end of the Cold War. The chapter explores some of the gendered dimensions both of the militaries and of wars. The latter, especially, until recently (Jones, 1994) have been the subject of very little systematic study.

While men have been constructed as naturally linked to warfare, women have been constructed as naturally linked to peace. The image of women resisting war has been in existence in the western public imagination at least since *Lysistrata* was first shown in Athens in the fifth century BC. This Greek comedy by Aristophanes describes the coming together of Athenian, Spartan and Corinthian women to declare a sex strike against their husbands until they stop fighting each other. A major debate within the feminist movement has been the extent to which feminist activism should be automatically linked to peace activism. The chapter ends with the examination of this debate and its implications for women's citizenship.

Military Service and Citizenship

Fighting, whether physical, verbal or by other means, seems to be an (almost?) universal social behaviour. Freud claimed that aggression and sex are the two universal human instincts which are being controlled and regulated in one way or another in all human societies. Ritualized fights, to preserve or change certain social hierarchies or to secure access to territorial or water resources, have been part of routinized social repertoires throughout human history together with other means of negotiating settlement for various conflicts. While women did not always participate directly in the fighting (although it was not uncommon for them to do so), they always had specific roles in the combat, whether it was to take care of the dead and wounded or to become the embodied possession of the victorious. Sometimes the two roles went together: Cynthia Enloe (1983: 4) quotes Samuel Hutton who describes the great demand in the seventeenth century for women who took care of the soldiers. A good carer, like Kate Keith, the pretty Scotswoman, was not allowed to remain outside wedlock more than two days after her soldier husband died. Similarly in the Iraq–Iran War, the Ayatollah Khomeini instructed war widows to marry war invalids and to become their carers.

Clear sexual division of labour in war, however, usually disappears when there is no clear differentiation between the 'battle front' and the 'home front' or 'rear' (Yuval-Davis, 1985). The Spanish reported, for instance, that in the fight against the Incas they saw women fighting alongside the men using slings. However, as Penny Dransart comments (1987: 62–77), slings were commonly used by both men and women in that society for doing herd work, and thus the way women fought during that war for survival cannot be assumed to represent a routine military role for the Inca women. Similarly, during the siege on Jerusalem by the Romans, Jewish women participated in the fighting activities such as pouring boiling oil on the Roman soldiers – again an adaptation, but not a routine part, of their usual social roles.

Once a separation between 'front' and 'rear' exists, and when the social collectivity accumulates enough surplus value to be able to sustain war and the absence of the warriors from the 'home front', even for the short periods of conducting seasonal raids on neighbouring tribes and villages, there is an emergence of more routinized sexual division of labour between men and women in the military.

Mythical or historical figures of women who led the men to battle, like Boadicea or Jeanne d'Arc, have existed for many centuries in the western collective imagination. However, like the Amazons, their main function has usually been not to point out that women are capable of warfare heroism like men, but rather to construct them as unnatural if romantic women (unless they are seen as witches, of course). In the twentieth century, however, since women started to be incorporated formally into militaries, whether of national liberation armies or of nation-states and empires, romantic images of women heroines have become more common. In Israel, for example, Khana Senesh, the Hungarian-Jewish Zionist settler poetess who was parachuted by the British behind enemy lines during World War II, and who was caught, tortured and eventually executed, has been canonized as a heroic counter-image to that of the millions of European Jews who have often been epitomized by Zionists as going to their extermination by the Nazis 'like sheep to the slaughter'. In Russia, Irina Sibrova was a bomber pilot during

World War II who survived 1006 missions against the Germans, and in Palestine Leila Khaled has been hailed as the heroine behind the hijacking of American planes to Amman in Jordan in the early 1970s.

Any contemplation of gender relations in the military, however, should not lose sight of the fact that it is never all men and all women in the society who fill particular roles within the military or outside it. Ethnic membership, class, age and ability play crucial roles in determining who is included and who is excluded from these roles. Of course, as mentioned above, these differentiations become blurred when the war takes place on the 'home front'. Reports from the Russian army's attack on Chechnya in 1994–5, for example, point to the fact that although the operation was directed against the Chechens demanding national independence, local Russians did not escape the systematic destruction directed towards the whole of the local population.

One of the pioneering studies of Cynthia Enloe has been *Ethnic Soldiers* (1980). In this book she shows how specific ethnic and racial minorities are used in specific ways by the militaries. And different minorities can be used in very different ways. Alison Bernstein, for example, has described how native Americans had one of the highest rates of combat fighting in World War II (next to American Japanese), more than any other ethnic or racial grouping in the USA. This is in complete contrast to American blacks who were virtually excluded from the front during that war (WREI, 1992: 86). In Israel, soldiers from the Druze ethnic community often belong to the low status but highly dangerous units of the border guards; the Bedouins are used as trackers; while at the same time Palestinians from other ethnic/religious groupings who are citizens of Israel are virtually completely excluded from the military.

Militaries of different empires were often composed of ethnically specific units. Usually these units were loyal to their specific commander with whom the emperor had a contract. These commanders could even have been part of the militaries defeated by the emperor. In the army of Alexander the Great, for example, Persian generals acquired a great deal of influence which went against the grain of some of the Greek generals. The larger the military, the more heterogeneous its units would be, with a myriad of the different nationalities and groupings incorporated into it.

However, the imperial military did not just rely on voluntary participation, for ideological or monetary reasons. Often ethnic or regional collectivities had to produce certain quotas of 'cannon fodder' for the military, and where not enough volunteers came forward, coercive tactics were used, whether it was by the Turks, the Russians, the French or the British (Peled, 1994: 61–78).

This historical reality is important because it goes against the grain of the ideological construction of participation in the military as giving automatic access to citizenship rights. The coupling of citizenship rights with participation in the military has existed since the French Revolution, carrying on the tradition of the Greek polis. However, before and after the French Revolution, serving in the military has never been universal, even among the citizens of the state, who virtually never encompass the whole population living in the state's territory. Citizenship rights have only very partially, if at all, corresponded with active service. On the contrary, even among citizen soldiers, a repetitive theme in the aftermath of wars is the complaint of those who come back from the front that they find that those who remained behind have managed to accumulate economic and political resources denied to them.

Military power constitutes the basis of the coercive power from which states claim and contest, inwardly and outwardly, the legitimacy of their claims to rule particular territories and people. For this reason, rulers and governments, especially in countries where the legitimacy of the state is in question, cannot afford to completely alienate the military, or they risk losing their positions either by revolutions (as happened in Russia in World War I) or, more directly, by military coups (as has happened often in post-colonial Africa and Latin America since the 1950s). Establishing a 'people's army' or introducing national draft has been one major way to legitimate particular regimes and governments for a wide variety of individuals and groupings.

This said, there is still not necessarily a direct link between participation in the military and citizenship rights. What determines one's rights and position in society is not whether one participates in the military, but in what capacity, and what alternative sources of civil power one has. Sometimes the ability of groupings to avoid being recruited into the military is a sign of the rising power of their social and political resistance – for example when the British decided to avoid confrontation with the Irish and did not forcefully recruit them into their military in World War I. On the other hand, the growing number and positions of African Americans in the USA's military is a sign not just of the strengthening of their general civil position, but also of the still very limited number of options for upwardly mobile careers open to most of them in the American civil society. Interestingly, Women In Black in Belgrade report (Zajovic, 1994) that the first women recruited into the Serbian army were women from the refugee camps.

The formal incorporation of women into the military can only partially be related to their social empowerment and depends on the nature of the political project which brought about this social change. Significantly, in western militaries, especially the USA, the question of the rate and quality of participation of women has arisen just when military service as a signifier of citizenship – that is, the national draft – has been terminated.

Modern Warfare and the Incorporation of Women into the Military

Modern militaries have tended to fulfil two, potentially contradictory, roles. On the one hand, especially in times of national crisis and war, they became a focus for national bonding and patriotism, which cuts across differences of class, region, origin, and sometimes age and gender. On the other hand, they developed as a modern efficient corporation, structured and geared towards the perfection of the ability to produce death and destruction in the most efficient and innovative ways. The incorporation of women into the military can

take very different forms when one rather than another goal is the first hegemonic political priority.

As was discussed in Chapter 3, women often become the symbolic bearers
of modernity. Deveiling women in Atatürk Turkey's revolution of 1917, which
was aimed at constructing Turkey as a modern nation-state, was as important
as veiling them has been to Muslim fundamentalists in the contemporary
Middle East. The incorporation of women into the military has fulfilled similar roles, for example, in Libya, Nicaragua or Eritrea. Incorporating women
into the military under such conditions contains a double message: firstly,
that women, at least symbolically, are equal members of the national collectivity; but secondly, and probably more importantly, that *all* members of the
national collectivity are incorporated, at least symbolically, into the military.

This inclusive construction of women in the military is very different, for
instance, from their incorporation into contemporary NATO militaries, especially the USA. There, women started to be encouraged to enter the military
in high numbers just when the national draft was stopped and the military
became completely professional. Women, in that instance, are not so much
symbols of social openness but the least undesirable human pool of the
reserve army of labour. One of the most important reasons for the decision to
mass recruit women into the US military has been in order to keep it voluntary rather than one based on the draft, so as to prevent a recurrence of the
popular revolt against the Vietnam War. In other words, women's recruitment
to the military, rather than enhancing their citizenship, was aimed at transforming the military service from a citizenship duty into a 'job', and to make
it less dependent on the co-operation of all citizens – women and men.

Cynthia Enloe (personal correspondence mentioned in Yuval-Davis,
1991a) claims that, following the decision to make the military based on 'vol-
untaries', one of the most important considerations in opening the American
military ranks to women was to avoid 'flooding' it with blacks.

> Women were being weighed as a counter-balance to a foreseen non-white mili-
> tary . . . women's recruitment was expanded in 1973 at a time when many White
> and Black policy makers were predicting that, if left a primarily male force, the all-
> voluntary army would soon become a primarily Black male force because it was
> Black young men who had the fewest economic alternatives to military enlistment
> in post-Vietnam America.

This type of sexist/racist thinking is a common phenomenon. bell hooks
(1981) has pointed out that in such a construction the assumption is that all
blacks are men, and all women are white. At the moment, 48 per cent of
American women soldiers are black.

The most important factor, however, which has enabled the entry of women
in mass numbers into more and more military tasks has been the changing
nature of modern warfare. As discussed above, women have always fulfilled
vital and specific roles in militaries, but have been excluded from the public
military domain. Modern warfare has brought with it, first of all, the need to
formalize and control the military's channels of sustenance and support. It

was Napoleon who is rumoured to have declared that 'the military marches on its stomach.' With the modernization of the military, feeding, clothing, nursing, clerical and communication services, ammunition production and sexual services have all needed, at least to an extent, to establish formal relationships with the military.

Moreover, with the continued development of military technology, engaging in face-to-face combat has become a smaller and smaller part of military action. Differences in physical strength between men and women have become, therefore, of significantly less importance as a block to women's participation in the military on an equal footing.

Not all militaries followed the same route of incorporating women. As I discuss elsewhere (Yuval-Davis, 1985: 32), one of the factors which makes comparison between militaries and the number of women they include difficult is that the classification of what is a civil and what a military task varies from one military to another. For example, in West Germany in 1980, only the 50 female military medical officers were considered to be formally part of the military, while all the female clerical workers servicing the army were considered to be civilians (Chapkis, 1981: 89). In Israel, on the other hand, all clerical workers were considered to be part of the military, while doctors and nurses could be civilians. In other words, apparent changes in the number of women in the military could be just a side-effect of a bureaucratic or ideological redefinition of the boundaries of the armed forces. Another example is statistics based on veteran registration, as has been the case in post-independence Algeria. As Helie-Lucas (1987) has commented, the complex documentary requirements attached to registration requests have made it very difficult for the bulk of peasant or working class illiterate people to register. This has been especially the case for women, not only because a larger percentage of them have been illiterate and because of their partial social seclusion, but also because the prime motivation for registration has been for paid employment benefits which would not have been relevant to many of these women.

The more sophisticated the weaponry, transport and communication systems in the military, the more elaborate the bureaucracy, the more specialized and professional the members of the military forces need to become, and the more similar the organization of the military becomes to that of large civil corporations. An inclusive definition of 'people's army' under such conditions can become constructed as inappropriate and wasteful. The connections between patriotism and militarism become obsolete. Such a debate, for instance, is being carried out at the moment in Israel, where there are growing voices to end the so-called universal draft, especially of women, in favour of constructing a 'leaner', more professional military.

The military in Israel, which is composed of a relatively small professional army and a large regular one, has always played a central role in the nation's formation and reproduction. After two or three years of regular service, men continue to be called for reserve service for one or two months a year until the age of 50. Women have also been drafted by law, usually for a somewhat shorter period to that of men, and their reserve service is usually minimal and stops altogether once they get married or become pregnant. As elaborated elsewhere (Yuval-Davis, 1985), the Israeli military has never been universal and all-encompassing, even for the Israeli Jewish men. Allowing ultra-ortho-dox Jewish men to avoid serving in the military by continuing religious studies has been one of the ways in which a major contradiction in the construction of the Israeli Jewish nation – as secular but dependent on orthodox religious definition for its boundaries – has been negotiated and contained (although, over the years, this practice itself has produced its own contradictions). In relation to women, the formal inclusiveness of the draft encompassed, in reality, no more than 60 per cent of the Jewish women of recruitment age and none of the non-Jewish citizens of the state. Significantly, women were excluded, not only on national, religious and reproductive grounds (which affect women from different ethnic and class backgrounds in different degrees) but also on 'quality' grounds. They were required to obtain higher educational levels than the men in order to be called for national service. The military was never prepared to invest in women's education what it was pre-pared to invest in that of men.

Recently, however, even these differences between the incorporation of men and women in the Israeli military have not been deemed sufficient. Some voices have started to emerge, within and outside the military, calling for the abolition of the mandatory recruitment of women, citing this as one of the main causes of hidden unemployment and inefficiency in the military, given computer and other technological developments which radically reduce the demand for clerical workers in the military. A discussion on whether the Israeli military should be transformed from 'the people's army' into a differ-entialist military which recruits 'whoever it needs' has become part of the agenda of the Parliamentary Committee for Foreign and Security Affairs. One of the most important arguments against such a change has been that

> in a society which absorbed 700 thousand new immigrants during the last five years, the military is significant as part of the process of absorption and identifi-cation with the Israeli society. (MP Or, Chairman of the Parliamentary Committee for Foreign and Security Affairs, as reported in the daily *Davar*, 13 February 1995)

The fact that new female immigrants above the age of regular service, unlike new male immigrants, have not been called to serve in the military, is notwith-standing.

The construction of the 'people' in 'the people's army' reflects the major gendered character of the social relations within the military, even in the rare cases where formally equal access supposedly exists.

Women as Soldiers

In spite of the fact that women have always constituted an integral part of military life, the formal incorporation of women into the military as soldiers has encountered a lot of prejudice and male fear, although the overwhelming majority of women soldiers are positioned in roles which largely reflect the gendered civil labour market – that is, they are usually secretaries, nurses and teachers. Only very few (although the computer revolution, if not the feminist one, is slowly changing this) fulfil roles which are specifically military and/or which directly relate to the military's main 'business' – that is, fighting and killing (Enloe, 1983; 1989; 1993; Yuval-Davis, 1985; 1991a).

It is not incidental that in the celebrated novel *Portnoy's Complaint* by Philip Roth, the American Jewish hero, who is continuously randy, becomes impotent when he tries to have sex with an Israeli woman soldier. If the experience of the military is supposed 'to make men from the boys', womanhood cannot be easily incorporated within such imagery. Jacky Cock, who studied military women on both sides of the South African war against apartheid (1992), describes how, in the South African army, woman hating and homophobia have been active parts of the male soldier's training: 'Recruits who do not perform – who are not up to standard – are often labelled "faggots" or "homos" or "murphies"; they are told to "go back to your mothers and play with the girls"' (WREI, 1992: 65). Sandra Gilbert (1983: 436) describes how, in World War I, the military women nurses evoked images of omnipotence and sinistry ('Does male death turn women nurses on?'), as well as being portrayed as ministering angels.

These dichotomous images of women soldiers have been central to the ways in which women have usually been incorporated into the military. They are threatening unless controlled and distinguished from male soldiers by emphasizing their femininity. In Israel, for instance, the only state in which women have been regularly recruited to the military in a national draft, the women's corps has been called by its initials 'Khen' which in Hebrew means 'charm'. One of the formal duties of the members of Khen, as described by an Israeli military spokesperson, has been 'in the areas of crystallizing the morale of the units and taking care of the soldiers of the units' (Yuval-Davis, 1985: 661). It is arguable that the high rate of rape and sexual harassment of women in the American military (recent reports in the press put the rate of rape as high as a third of women soldiers), in which separate women's corps and tasks have been abolished to a large extent, is intended to distance the male soldiers from and secure their fears of the omnipotent woman soldier.

In national liberation armies, where the hierarchical and organizational framework of the forces is much less formal, a strong common ideological stance might help to transcend some of these tensions, especially where women's emancipation is seen to symbolize the emancipation of the people as a whole. Still, strict rules of non-fraternization, or the execution of soldiers who are found guilty of rape, might be found to be necessary components to enhance the ideological elements of 'political correctness', as has been the case, for instance, in the Eritrean national liberation army (Zerai, 1994; see also Urdang, 1989).

Although I have no doubt that very few women soldiers see themselves in the 'castrating' roles in which male imaginations might position them, it is clear that one of the main motivations for women to join the military is an opportunity to empower themselves, both physically and emotionally. As Gilbert points out,

> A number of texts by men and women alike suggest that the revolutionary trans-formations wrought by the [First World] war's 'topsy turvy' role reversals did bring about a release of female libidinal energies, as well as a liberation of female anger, which men usually found anxiety-inducing and women often found exhilarating. (1983: 436)

Interviews with women soldiers, especially those who have joined various national liberation armies, reveal how many of them have escaped to the guerrilla camps from intolerable personal situations caused by both colonial and loyalist forces and/or their own families (Bennett et al., 1995; Zerai, 1994). In the military they have been able to establish for themselves new identities, skills and respectable social positions, as well as to struggle for causes they believed in.

The film *Private Benjamin* with Goldie Hawn has tried to portray joining the American military in such a light (Chapkis, 1981). The film tells the story of a 'poor little rich girl' who feels lonely and rejected and who finds her salvation by joining the American military and surviving the tough military training. (The difference between Private Benjamin and women in the Eritrean or Tigrean armies, however, is that her position in the military is described in completely personal terms, rather than in the context of what the American military does – but more on that later.) The military in *Private Benjamin*, as in the propaganda campaigns of most western militaries, is seen purely in terms of a good career move – an opportunity to get training, to see the world and to earn more than in another career.

A study by Elizabetta Addis (1994) has shown that, indeed, women usually benefit economically, individually and collectively from becoming soldiers. She claims that the military as a rule is an equal opportunities employer in terms of wages, and that the relative benefit of the women soldiers depends on the differential level of payment for men and women in the civil labour market. As male soldiers do not have such a wage benefit from becoming a soldier, the marginal benefits for women becoming soldiers are higher, therefore, than those for men. Moreover, to the extent that women get opportunities to train and to be upwardly mobile once they leave the military and go into the civil labour market, women soldiers achieve collective benefits for women in the labour market as a whole.

One of the additional reasons, Addis claims, that women benefit more than men from serving in the military is the fact that they run less risk of being killed or maimed than men, as they are forbidden from joining combat roles. This is a controversial point, not only because the definition of combat becomes narrower and more meaningless with time and the technological advancements of warfare, but also because that technology means that the chance of being hit at the battle front is not necessarily larger than it is at the rear. In the Gulf War most of the American casualties were the result of a hit by an Iraqi missile on a bunker in Saudi Arabia rather than during the strikes in Iraq itself.

Feminists fighting for equal rights of women in the military argue that it is their exclusion from combat roles which prevents them from benefiting fully from promotion opportunities in the military (and consequently outside it) on a footing equal to that of men. Recently in the USA a whole legal battle took place regarding the right of women to participate in combat roles, especially concerning the right of women pilots to bomb the enemy, rather than just being allowed to fuel bombing aeroplanes in the air which has not been defined as a combat role and which women pilots performed during the Gulf War. After a long and arduous process of political lobbying and the establishment of a presidential commission to investigate this issue, the Clinton administration conceded the right of women to participate in all combat positions except those of ground infantry and submarines. The extent to which these policies are going to be implemented on the ground, especially after the victory of the Republicans in the Congress, is still an open question.

The degree to which this development needs to be seen as a major new achievement for women's rights in the USA becomes a little doubtful when one evaluates it given the background of the general backlash in women's positions in the USA (Faludi, 1992). Moreover, a whole new light could be thrown on the issue when one remembers that in World War II Russian women pilots successfully performed thousands of bombing missions, and many survived to tell the tale. Unsurprisingly, perhaps, their nickname was 'the night witches' (Yevgenny Kaldei's exhibition, Riverside Studios, London, May 1995). What is probably even more significant in this tale, however, is the fact that after World War II women became virtually excluded from any significant positions in the Soviet Union.

Such a reversal in the nature of women's participation in the military, after a national crisis such as war or national liberation, is not uncommon. However, liberation armies have differed in the ways they initially incorporated women into the struggle. Valentine Moghadam (forthcoming) differentiates between two kinds of revolutionary movements: one which uses women as a symbol of liberation and modernization, in which case women would be encouraged to participate actively in the military; and one which uses women as a symbol of the national culture and tradition which is to be reclaimed, in which case women are virtually excluded from formal participation, and the nature of their supportive roles is highly controlled.

Constructing the position of women in the military around the dichotomies of combat/non-combat and front/rear are, therefore, more a result of ideological constructions of womanhood and manhood in society than a reflection of considered decisions based on objective difficulties of incorporating women into combat roles. One would think that no specific male muscles are required in order to be able to press the button to send off the missile or the bomb. However, as Caroline Cohn (1993: 227–46) discovered when she conducted field work in a community of North American nuclear defence intellectuals and security affairs analysts, the discourse of American national security policy is permeated by gender discourse in which so-called male values are considered supreme and in which those who fail to stick to 'objective' non-emotional non-moral considerations are labelled contemptuously as 'wimps' or as 'pussies'.

One of the unresolved debates about women's participation in the military has been whether or not it would be better for women to be part of women-only units or to be incorporated into the general (that is male) military units. On the one hand, moving from separate women's corps into integrated units has meant that many of the formal barriers for women to perform certain military tasks (and get the appropriate rewards and promotion attached to them) have been removed and their equal potential as soldiers has been recognized. One of the signs of this development, for instance, has been devising specific fitness tests in order to determine suitability for certain military combat tasks rather than conditioning these *a priori* upon the sex of the soldier. However, as those with experience in this area have commented (WREI, 1992: 43), this in itself might not secure an equal chance for men and women, because the determination of which tests should be chosen as the decisive ones is often political. For example standards in stretching, in which women do better than men, would be lowered, while standards of physical strength, in which men do better, would be kept high. One can argue that both of these abilities might be necessary for successfully fulfilling a specific military task contemplated, such as getting out of hatches in ships.

Those who oppose the abolition of separate women's units point out that these units often provide safe and comfortable social environments for the women. Often women, especially as they tend to be the minorities in mixed units, have to prove themselves more than men to show that they are equal. For instance, in the Palmakh (the military units of the Hagana, the pre-state military units of labour Zionism), after a long and eventually successful struggle to gain the right to be included in mixed fighting units, women soldiers met again and decided to ask for separate women's units in view of their experience in the mixed units (Yuval-Davis, 1985).

Beyond this question, of course, is the issue of sexual harassment, which is much more prevalent in mixed units. One of the safeguards for women soldiers in the Israeli army has been the fact that at least it is women officers rather than their male officer bosses who have been responsible for disciplining them, thus making them a bit less dependent on the whims of their bosses if frustrated in their sexual advances. An alternative to such a partial or formal separation has been an imposition of strict rules on fraternization. In the Eritrean liberation army, for instance (Zerai, 1994), men and women were strictly forbidden to fraternize, and the punishment for rape has been execution.

Another factor mentioned in the literature (Gilbert, 1983: 440–1) in relation to separate women's corps has been that these corps are more conducive for the development of a comfortable lesbian sub-culture. Lesbianism and male homosexuality have been a major topic of debate in western militaries recently, and the regular practice of discharging anybody who is 'discovered' to be gay in the US and British militaries is being challenged in court on the basis of equal rights.

The issue of homosexuality is but the latest one of public debates in the West concerning the incorporation of people's – but especially women's – other facets of 'normal life' into the military, such as marriage and mother-hood. In Britain the military has had to pay millions of pounds in compensation to women who were automatically discharged from the military once they became pregnant. For many years most militaries have relied on the 'military wives' to bear and rear the children of the soldiers as well as to carry out other supporting roles for the soldiers. In some cases, such as in the guerrilla wars in Eritrea and Palestine, the liberation armies have taken it upon themselves to rear collectively the children and orphans of the fighters. However, in most armies 'normalizing' motherhood for women soldiers is but one facet of the professionalization of the military and the transformation of soldiering from the ultimate civic duty (of the male citizens) into just another professional career.

Military Service and Women's Rights

Elizabetta Addis (1994) claims that the participation of women in the military also has a beneficial economic effect on the general position of women in society, because the military in many countries is one of the largest employers of the male sex and an equivalent public expenditure programme to employ women would dramatically decrease women's unemployment figures. Moreover, the large number of men employed in the military labour market creates a relative scarcity of them in the civil labour market which raises civil wages.

It can also be assumed that if high military position is an assured upwardly mobile route in society in general, then women who have been promoted in the military have a higher chance of getting higher economic and, probably even more importantly, political positions in society. Indeed, in some post-revolutionary societies, such as Eritrea and South Africa, being part of the guerrilla fighters has earned women significant social and political authority. However, unlike male political leaders, virtually none of the small but growing body of women national political leaders in different states have achieved their position via serving in the military. (Quite a few of them, however, such as Golda Meir, Margaret Thatcher and Indira Gandhi, earned the reputation of being 'the only men in the cabinet', and tended to pursue pro-militaristic policies.)

The construction of women soldiers as models for women's autonomy and empowerment reached a high point during the Gulf War. American broadcasters learned to say 'our boys and girls in the Gulf' rather than just 'our boys', and Saudi women were emboldened by this presence in their country and attempted to break the prohibition on women driving. One of the things that participation of women soldiers in the Gulf War illuminated was the fact that the relationship of the military with, and their effects on the daily lives of, the civil population in different communities is highly variable. While in some communities in the USA there were virtually no people sent to the Gulf, in others they constituted significant percentages of the population. It was during the Gulf War, for instance, that black activists came out against the anti-war movement, in order 'to defend their brothers and sisters' who went to fight there. There are also many specific local communities in which a relatively high proportion of men and women belong to the military. Such communities necessarily would have a very different relationship with the political/military centre of the state than communities which have no or very few members in the military.

This social phenomenon, which positions different segments of the population in different relations to the military, is the result of the end of the national draft and the professionalization of the military forces. It is more widespread among women than men because, except in Israel, women everywhere are asked to volunteer for the military, even in countries where the men are recruited by national draft.

It is highly plausible to assume that communities where a large number of the civil population have relatives in the military or belong to militias often emerge in areas surrounding large military bases. It has been commented upon (Wheelwright, 1991) that most of the American women soldiers who were sent to the Gulf and had children had husbands who were also in the military. It was, therefore, often the grandmother rather than the father who took responsibility to care for the child of the missing parents. It is also a known fact that many sexual partnerships and even marriages take place wherever an army is stationed for long periods of time. Many stories were told, for instance, about the social effect of local British girls bearing children by black American soldiers during World War II, and similar things happened in Germany, Vietnam and so on.

Of course, marriages and voluntary sexual partnerships are only one facet of the effect the sexuality of soldiers in places of long term military presence can produce. Cynthia Enloe (1983; 1989) has written about the long term effect on local communities of the establishment of mass prostitution houses in the Philippines. Of course, the determination of the exact nature and form of the relationship between the military base and its neighbouring civil population would depend, among other things, on their relative political and economic power relations. Recently there has been a major campaign in Japan against their American bases after eighteen American soldiers were brought to trial for raping a twelve-year-old girl (*The Guardian*, 30 September 1995). Somewhat similar sentiments have been expressed in Cyprus towards the British bases after the trial of soldiers who raped and murdered a tourist on the island.

It has often been found that militarization of the population raises the general level of domestic and other violence in society. In spite of the growing similarity between the military and the modern sophisticated industrial complex, the military is explicitly organized around principles of aggression and obedience. Personal identities and modes of interpersonal and intergendered behaviour cannot but spill over into the civil society once the military gains prominence in society.

In the discussions of the potential benefits for women becoming soldiers it is often forgotten that unlike the civil labour market, the ultimate function of the military is to fight in wars. Wars produce massive destruction of human lives, social fabrics and physical environments. And although different military conflicts and wars can hugely differ from each other, their effects tend always to be highly gendered.

Wars as Gendered Constructions

In discussions about women soldiers' lives and their aspirations for equal rights in their profession, it is easy to forget what the nature of that profession is. Jeanne Holm, a retired woman major-general, found it necessary to remind the participants at a conference on women in the military organized in Washington, DC that

> Anyone, male or female, who considers joining the armed forces, must be made aware, before taking the oath, that contrary to some of the recruiting razzle-dazzle, being in the military is not about uniforms and parades and it's not about benefits or adventure. The military is about going to war and war is about killing and maybe dying for your country. (WREI, 1992: 59)

And, indeed, it was reported in the press how shocked some of the women soldiers who were sent to the Gulf in 1992 were to find out that they were actually sent overseas to fight. So many of them joined the national guards as a way of getting fit, earning extra income and having a bit of adventure in their lives.

The Gulf War was for the American soldiers, however, an experience very different not just from that of the Iraqis – both soldiers and civilians, who were the other party in that war – but also from that of American soldiers in other wars. It has been said (Boose, 1993) that one of the main reasons the USA was so keen to go to the Gulf War was in order to win the Vietnam War there – notwithstanding the fact that Sadam Hussein continued to rule Iraq after the war, and the inept and impotent interventions of the USA and other NATO and UN armies in former Yugoslavia, Somalia and so on. An interesting study (Boose, 1993) compared the experiences of bomber pilots in World War II with those in the Gulf War and discovered that while the dominant emotion of the World War II pilots was terror, that of the Gulf War pilots was the excitement of playing games in an arcade.

It is not only the sophisticated technology but the national security discourse as studied by Cohn (1993), mentioned above, which has created this difference. It has created the illusion that the directed missiles can hit only their predestined targets, that the exact location of these targets, as in arcade games, is fully known, and that it is all about hitting objects rather than people. Indeed, the official discourse never mentioned people getting hit, but spoke about 'collateral damage'.

The official discourse of the Gulf War has also been much more gender neutral than that of previous wars. As was noted at the time, the women soldiers dressed in battle fatigues were hardly distinguishable from men under all the protective layers. (Similar images appeared again with the delivery of British forces to Bosnia.) Also, unlike the usual discourse of war, this war was not constructed as a war fought by men for the sake of the 'womenandchildren' (Enloe, 1990) but was carried out by 'our boys and girls'. Indeed, in Israel, this was the first war in which 'the boys' were not able to fight, but were locked in sealed rooms together with the women and children. This created a deep national trauma that was swiftly repressed. At the same time that reports on domestic and other violence in Israel grew significantly, the masculinist image of the Israeli fighters as invincible superheroes was seriously damaged and probably created the space that enabled Rabin's government to engage in the 'peace process' with the PLO, however limited and subversive.

Most wars, however, are experienced very differently from the Gulf War. Even given the available sophisticated technology, it was enough for the Bosnian Serbs to catch a few UN officers and use them as a human shield in order to render the technological discourse completely inept and for the air bombing to stop. While the enemy can become (and some say necessarily becomes) dehumanized, it is different when 'the human shield' is made with one's own 'boys'.

This feeling of loyalty to 'one's boys' serves a central role in the experience of the fighting men. Whatever the context and scale of the war, it is the 'warriors' camaraderie', often also referred to as 'male bonding', which is almost universally emphasized by whoever discusses what makes soldiers able to withstand the tremendous efforts and suffering involved in warfare. While ideological patriotic convictions on the one hand, and material and status rewards on the other, can be more or less important in different experiences of fighting, it is always the feeling that one can rely on one's fellow soldiers and on mutual loyalty in situations of life and death which is mentioned as the continuously nurturing sentiment in the daily lives of the warriors. In Israel, this reluctance to betray fellow soldiers has been given by many Israelis as the main reason why they continue to serve in the reserve army, despite objecting to Israel's continuous occupation of the Palestinian territories, or its invasion of Lebanon.

In the same way American generals objected to the recruitment of women into (until then male-only) combat roles in the military, giving as their reason the fear that 'male bonding' would be disrupted. Indeed, given the nature of most soldiers' socialization of either sex, such a sense of bonding is easier to achieve in men-only or women-only groupings. However, long common training and emphasis on professionalization tend to neutralize these feelings significantly, as has been the case in the civil labour market, although the latter rarely involves such intense engagement. It is an open question to what extent rules forbidding fraternization can enhance or complicate such processes.

The experience of fighting a war, however, can be very different in different wars, as can be its distance from military lives when not in war. It can involve short, orderly periods of 'going on a mission'; it can involve endless months of living in trenches or bunkers; and it can involve desperate chaotic and hellish situations of fighting for survival, mutilating and being mutilated, killing and being killed. It can also involve working in roles supportive to the actual fighting, on or off the battleground. A study (Janowitz, 1991: 41) found that only 15 per cent of soldiers ever fired a weapon, even once, during World War II. Given the nature of modern warfare technology, this ratio would probably be even smaller now. In guerrilla and other small scale warfare the situation, of course, is quite different, and the warriors themselves might be required to fulfil themselves many more of the maintenance roles of preparing food and providing education, for instance, when not actually fighting.

Wars can also affect the lives of the people on the 'home front' in many different ways. At one extreme, the war can have little or no effect if it is taking place away from the home front, the military involved is professional, and there are very few casualties. Much of the experience of the colonial countries has been of that nature. While some women have had husband soldiers, especially officers, who have visited them from time to time, most of the gendered support network has been composed of local people and a few colonial women, in or outside the military.

At the other extreme, war becomes a total experience which completely transforms and often destroys the lives of the people in the country. Most or even all of the determinants of one's daily life and personal identity before the war came can disappear in a few hours: place of work, properties, homes, personal effects and, worst of all, friends, relatives and members of one's family. Even if one is not injured, abused or tortured by the enemy, the brutal stripping of all that has been nearest and dearest has devastating long-term if not permanent effects on people's lives. Life becomes solely about survival.

Becoming a refugee is a gendered experience. Up to 80 per cent of the total refugee population (to differentiate from the percentage of refugees who actually make it to the West – the majority of whom are males) is composed of women and children. As Adam Jones (1994) has pointed out, this is a result of the fact that being killed, as well as killing, is gendered in war. It is not that women and children do not get killed but that, when selective killing does take place – such as during ethnic cleansing in former Yugoslavia – it is the men who are selected, are taken away, and then 'disappear', sometimes to re-emerge from a detention camp, but often to be discovered in a mass grave (as has been the case in Srebrnica).

Even when men are not selectively arrested and/or murdered (I almost wrote 'executed', falling into the formal discourse of 'legitimate wars'), they are often absent, even when the war is local, as they are attached to fighting units and/or hiding in order not to be caught (1994: 120–9). Women and old men are left in villages to look after the house and children, to work the land, and to keep the social fabric of the community going.

The women left become vulnerable to rape by the enemy soldiers. A lot has been written in the last few years about rape in war, especially since the systematic rape of women by Bosnian Serbs has been exposed by the media (for example, Amnesty International, 1995; Pettman, 1996; Zajovic, 1994). Similar reports were heard about Rwanda (Bonnet, 1995) and the war in Bangaladesh in 1981 (Gita Sahgal's film *The War Crimes Files*, shown on 3 May 1995 on Channel 4). Significantly, as feminist human rights activists like Rhonda Kopelon have pointed out in debates at the NGO Forum of the UN Conference on Human Rights in 1994 in Vienna, rape has been defined by the Geneva Convention as 'a crime against honour' rather than as a mode of torture. Here the 'honour' is that of the men and the community, rather than necessarily that of the women themselves.

It has to be recognized, nevertheless, as the Women In Black in former Yugoslavia have pointed out (Zajovic, 1994), that although rape in war is an extreme example of its gendered effects, often the most devastating experience of the war for the women involved has not been the rape but the loss of the entire basis of their former lives. However, in cases of pregnancies resulting from these rapes the effects could become much more devastating, because paradoxically, once the pregnancies are public knowledge, the women may lose the respect and support of their surviving families and communities as a result of traditional notions of honour and shame. This is the reason that the overwhelming majority of the reported cases of systematic rape have been of widowed or single women rather than married ones who have often preferred to keep their experiences to themselves.

The experience of becoming a displaced person can vary a lot. Being left with some material resources, or having a family elsewhere in the country or overseas who are prepared to receive and sponsor the refugee and her surviving family, can make the transition to a rehabilitated new life much easier than becoming stranded in a refugee camp without any extra resources other than the charity of international aid organizations, and having most of one's emotional and physical resources spent on the daily struggle for survival (Forbes Martin, 1992). A common phenomenon among most refugees, whatever their personal circumstances, however, is a state of 'permanent temporariness' in which life and identity before the war and the displacement gain a status of validity and permanence which any new life, constructed for however many years, can never replace. Being a permanent 'outsider' in the new place of living sustains such a feeling. Often this is a sentiment which can be transferred to the second generation. Thus, for example, children born in Palestinian refugee camps in the Lebanon might identify their place of origin as the village from which their parents were exiled. Although that village might not have existed for 30 or 40 years, the dream of 'return' is still a passionate sentiment around which one's identity has been constructed.

When discussing war and its aftermath, it is important to remember what a gendered and class-based experience this usually is. A study comparing the experiences of sisters and brothers in World War I, for example, has very much highlighted this factor (Woollacott, 1993; see also Accad, 1990 on the gendered character of the war in the Lebanon).

But it is not just experiences of war which are different between men and women. As Cynthia Enloe (1989; 1993) and others have pointed out, militarized images of femininity at war – whether they call women to stay at home and be good wives and mothers, or to volunteer to the military industry and become 'Rosie the Riveter' – are highly necessary for the militarized images of masculinity, which themselves can vary. Wars are seen to be fought for the sake of the 'womenandchildren', and the fighting men are comforted and reassured by the knowledge that 'their women' are keeping the hearth fires going and are waiting for them to come home.

One of the interesting questions which needs exploring is the relationship between these images of femininity, which have been so necessary for war discourse, and the link between women and peace which has been central to feminist and other war resisting movements.

Women's Politics and Anti-War Movements

The British Greenham Common women's groups (Roseneil, 1995), the Argentinian Mothers of the Disappearing Children (Fisher, 1989), and the Israeli, Italian and former Yugoslavian Women In Black groups (Lentin, 1995; Zajovic, 1994) are but some of the better known women's groups which have been active in the last fifteen years. These groups have constructed anti-militarism not as a women-only issue but as an issue in which women, owing to their specific positioning in society, have a specific message to transmit, around which they should organize separately from men. While some women in these and other movements have colluded with the essentialist notion of 'women as the peaceful sex', most of the women in these movements have rejected such notions which are so prevalent in militaristic constructions of femininity (Enloe, 1983; 1989; Leonardo, 1985; Pettman, 1996).

The essentialist construction of men as aggressive and violent fits the nationalist-militaristic myth in which men fight for the sake of the 'womenandchildren' (Enloe, 1990), the 'protected–protector' myth (Stiehm, 1989). While some feminists, like Judith Stiehm, have argued that the best way to demolish this myth is for women to participate in the military on a footing equal to that of men, others, like many German feminists, continue to object to the inclusion of women in the military (Seifert, 1995). Many feminists, from Virginia Woolf onwards, have argued that women should publicly reject the claim that the men are fighting for their sake and withdraw their support and legitimation. Thus in Israel, for example, during the war in Lebanon in 1982 a group organized under the name of Mothers Against Silence claimed that they were not prepared any more to support the state sending their sons to the war and sacrificing their lives for the sake of an occupation which they did not agree was vital for the survival of Israel.

Motherhood has played a very important role in feminist anti-military thinking. One of the most developed and theoretically sophisticated voices in this camp has been that of Sara Ruddick (1983; 1989), who has claimed that some characteristics inherent in the ideology and practice of mothering can become the foundation of an anti-militaristic movement. She called it

'maternal nonviolence: a truth in the making' (1989: Chapter 7). According
to her, the centrality of life preservation in the task of mothering colludes
with peace-making practices and would be against life destruction.

Although Sara Ruddick denies her arguments are essentialist, they nevertheless have an essentialist tinge to them, similar to the decoration with
nappies of the fences of the American missile base in Greenham Common in
the early days of the peace movement at that site. What is particularly problematic in Ruddick's inherent connection of mothering with anti-militarism is
her attachment of life preservation to the kinship system. Ruddick, like Carol
Gilligan (1982) from whom she draws inspiration, presents a certain paradox
in her construction of women's morality. On the one hand, Ruddick presents
women's psyche, especially mothers', as universal, not constructed historically
by ethnicity, class, age, culture and so on. Although Ruddick recognizes that
not all women behave as she would like them to behave, she continues to use
the generic 'women' 'out of respect' (for the many women who do pursue
nonviolence) as much as out of what she calls 'stylistic laziness' (1989: 163–4).
In this what Ruddick calls 'idiom of achievement' (1989: 164), women are
assumed to view the world and to judge it in a particularistic way which differs from the more abstract universalistic way in which, she claims, men's
view of the world is constructed. However, if women's view of the world is so
particularistic, then obviously their family, community, ethnic and national
collectivity should matter to them much more than to men. The archetype of
such a construction of motherhood is that of Bertolt Brecht's Mother
Courage, whose sole interest and struggle during wartime is the survival of
her own children. Such a construction of 'preservative mother's love', to use
Ruddick's term, heroic as it could be, can hardly become a basis for an anti-
militaristic women's peace movement which opposes war because of a general
worry about human lives, not their own children's only, but also those of the
'enemy'.

And in reality, of course, there are many women and mothers whose
'preservative love' transcends their love for their children. A recent example
is mothers of soldiers in Chechnya who travelled from Moscow to Chechnya
to plead with the Russian soldiers, their sons, to stop their atrocities in
Chechnya – only to be taunted and pushed away by those same soldiers (1995
leaflet by the National Peace Council).

The specific positioning of women in peace movements can be explained as
a result of some very different rationales rather than biological and social
constructions of women as mothers. Firstly, unlike men, women are virtually
nowhere drafted and forced to fight in wars which they don't approve of.
They always join the military as volunteers. Even in Israel, where they are
drafted, they are not drafted to the reserve army which constitutes the bulk
of the military, nor are they allowed to serve in the front line. MP Geula
Cohen has pointed out (Yuval-Davis, 1985) that in Israel all women, if they
are not soldiers, are mothers or sisters or wives of soldiers and as such are
entrenched in the military system. However, civilian women are nevertheless
a bit freer to protest against militarism and war without being subjected to

the same pressures and sanctions that those who are actually members of the military would be.

Secondly, some women would prefer to organize autonomously within the anti-war and anti-militaristic movement, as part of their more general feminist convictions that as such they would be able to be more assertive and not shadowed and intimidated by men in a mixed organization. However, they would tend to co-operate and work closely with men's and mixed groups and organizations with similar political goals.

Thirdly, some women's anti-militaristic and anti-war groups would see their anti-militaristic fight as a spearhead in their fight against the patriarchal social system as a whole which they see as dominated by male machoism and violence. 'Take the toys from the boys' – one of the slogans of the Greenham Common women – could typify such an approach.

Such a standpoint might lead to an automatic link between feminism and anti-militarism and pacifism (Feminism and Nonviolence Study Group, 1983). A debate around this question has often tended to arise in international conferences whenever First and Third World feminists come together. Feminists from the Third World justifiably argue against simplistic universalized notions of 'the terrorist' and an automatic condemnation of all acts of violence (Robyn Morgan, 1989) without taking into account who carries out the violent campaigns and why. They would also argue that they could not afford the luxury of being anti-militaristic, because the national liberation of oppressed people can only be carried out with the help of an armed struggle. Interestingly, Sara Ruddick (1993) has been sympathetic to this claim, because 'the right to fight . . . is significant for any powerless or stigmatized group' (1983: 472). Such a concession might be interpreted, however, as encouraging women to resist patriarchy by using violence, which seems to be very far from her general politics.

There is no space here to enter into this debate in detail. However, as discussed in Chapter 3, this Fanonite ideology of the oppressed, who are called 'to reclaim their manhood' by violence, has been to the detriment of many black and Third World women who have suffered from the misogyny which has been central to the machoist ideologies sustained by most interpretations of this sentiment. As long as the struggle of the powerless is to gain power rather than to transform power relations within the society, so-called 'national liberation' has often just brought further oppression to women and other disadvantaged groupings within the new social order. While armed struggle might sometimes be the only way open to fight against oppression and occupation, the ways this struggle is organized, its targets and social organization, are crucial. These are some of the issues which are going to be discussed in the next chapter.

Conclusion

This chapter has discussed the gendered characteristics of militaries and wars. While the specific tasks that women fulfil in different militaries in different

historical contexts vary, as does the extent to which they are formally incorporated into the military, it is only very rarely, if at all, that differential power
relations between men and women have been erased, even within the most
socially progressively organized national liberation armies or western professional militaries. Moreover, except for a few liberation armies, as in Eritrea
and Tigre, while women are 'allowed' to a lesser or greater extent to fulfil
'men's roles', some sexual division of labour continues to operate even when
technological innovations in modern warfare have deemed biologistic ratio-
nalizations of women's exclusions mostly obsolete. These technological
innovations not only have made physical strength less important in combat
roles, but also have defined out of existence many of the manual clerical roles
women have traditionally tended to fill in the military.

These considerations, however, are still only marginal in most contemporary wars, especially those which Cooke (1993) has called the postmodern
ones. It is men, in these wars, who are mostly selected to fight and to be
killed, and it is women who continue to sustain all other facets of social life,
often finding themselves in the aftermath of brutal attacks and rape as displaced refugees where they have to continue their fight for survival for
themselves and their children.

Feminists have been divided on the question of whether, as feminists, they
should struggle for the entry of women into the military on a footing equal to
that of men in order to gain equal access to the social power and social
resources it can offer, and thus to become citizens in the Marshallian sense of
'full members of the community'. Others have argued that, as feminists, they
have a special role to influence their community and state against militarism
and war. Some, like Sara Ruddick, have called for both – for women to volunteer for the military in order to stop it being militaristic:

> Many people support a draft on the grounds that conscripts are less eager for
> battle than self-selecting volunteers. Women conscripts might be especially reluc-
> tant to fight, their families particularly appalled to see them on the battlefield. A
> 'peaceful' army would fight only the most necessary and clearly just battles, fights
> them as humanely and briefly as possible, and in its fighting does nothing to
> increase chances of escalation to more destructive conventional weapons or to
> nuclear arms. (1983: 476)

This is, of course, a hopelessly idealized notion of womanhood, as it has
been found again and again (and not just by pointing at Margaret Thatcher)
that when women's positioning is not different in power terms to that of men,
their behaviour is not necessarily different to men's.

However, this does not mean that women's presence in the military could
not affect its social and political role. If wars are fought for the sake of 'womenandchildren' (Enloe, 1990), then the presence of women next to the men on
an equal footing might undermine at least part of this machoistic myth
(Stiehm, 1989). I do not see, as many feminists do, the necessary connection
between women 'fulfilling their patriotic duty' and their entitlement to full
citizenship rights. However, I do feel that citizenship, as full membership in
the community, does and should involve responsibilities and duties which

might involve a national draft in a specific historical context, and that being excluded from the military, like being excluded from night shifts and other so-called dangerous jobs in the civil labour market, has been paternalistic and often to the detriment of the social positioning of women.

However, no discussion of gender relations in the military can remain on this general level of discussing 'women' and 'men'. National, ethnic, race, class, regional, age and ability divisions are crucial in the positioning of specific individuals and groupings of women – as that of men – in militaries and wars, and, without exploring these specific social relations, our understanding of how women or men would affect and be affected in these major social and political arenas could only be partial and misleading.

6

WOMEN, ETHNICITY AND EMPOWERMENT: TOWARDS TRANSVERSAL POLITICS

The previous chapters in the book have looked at some of the major ways gender relations affect and are affected by national and ethnic processes. One such aspect (explored in Chapter 2) has been the biological reproduction of the nation. Although often legitimate fatherhood would be the gatekeeper for membership in a national or religious collectivity, women are the bearers of the collectivity. As such, within different national discourses on reproduction, they would be encouraged or discouraged, and sometimes forced, to have more or fewer children. As a result of the discourse that 'people is power' they would be called upon to have more children, so that the nation could flourish and defeat its enemies; while within the terms of the Malthusian discourse their children would be seen as a threat, taking more resources than the nation has available. The call for women, however, to have more or fewer children is hardly ever uniform to all women, from all class, ability and ethnic groupings. This differentiation is formulated in particularly extreme terms within the eugenicist discourse, which, 'for the sake of the quality of the nation', calls upon upper class, educated women from the 'right' ethnic origin to have more children, while as much as possible preventing poor, disabled and ethnic minority women from having children.

Women, however, are not just the biological reproducers of the nation, but also its cultural reproducers, often being given the task of guardians of 'culture' who are responsible for transmitting it to the children and constructing the 'home' in a specific cultural style. Chapter 3 explored the ways 'culture' is used as a resource in various ethnic and national projects and how, in such projects, women are constructed as symbols of national 'essence', unity and emancipation as well as border guards of ethnic, national and racial difference. These constructions of womanhood are often used as resources for national relations of both domination and resistance.

Not all women in any society are constructed in the same way. Differential positionings in ethnic, racial, class, age, ability, sexual and other social divisions interface with gender divisions, so that although women usually are constructed and treated by various agencies as different to men, 'women' as well as 'men' do not constitute homogeneous categories as either social agents or social objects. This theme is explored in Chapter 4 on citizenship and difference. Citizenship, defined as 'full membership in the community', is analysed as a multi-layered construct, in which one's membership in local, ethnic, national and supra-national communities constructs, although is not reducible to, gendered state citizenship. The chapter also examined some of the accepted divisions of citizenship types into private/public and passive/active.

Citizenship involves both rights and duties. Being prepared to die for one's country has been considered to be the ultimate citizen's duty, which until relatively recently has been formally the specific domain of the male citizens, central in the construction of masculinities. Chapter 5 analysed the gendered character of militaries and of wars, and – as in the previous chapters – explored the differential effects of those on women and men who are differentially positioned in the society.

In this concluding chapter I want to explore some of the political conclusions that can be drawn out of the analysis in the previous chapters. More specifically I want to examine the extent to which feminist solidarity is possible given women's social and especially national divisions. In order to do so I first examine the interrelationships between nationalist and feminist movements. I then turn to look at the general question of solidarity across difference and introduce the notion of transversal politics.

Feminism and Nationalism

In 1986 Kumari Jayawardena published her book *Feminism and Nationalism in the Third World*. It was an important book, not only because of its considerable contribution to our knowledge and understanding of the particular movements she was discussing, but also because it constructed these two social movements as interrelated in a way that very few, if any, feminist scholars had done before.

Since the rise of second-wave feminism in the West, during the 1970s and 1980s, there has been a recurrence of non-dialogue between women from the 'First' and 'Third' Worlds at international conferences. One side would call for women's liberation as the primary/only goal of the feminist movement. The other side would respond that as long as their people are not free there is no sense for them in speaking about women's liberation: how could they struggle to reach equality with their menfolk while their menfolk themselves were oppressed? It was a dialogue of the deaf. For western feminists, as members of a hegemonic collectivity, their membership in the collectivity and its implications for their positionings was often rendered invisible, while Third World women acutely experienced their being part of a subjugated collectivity and often did not see autonomous space for themselves to organize as feminists. To the extent that the western feminists did relate to their national collectivities it was usually from an oppositional point of view. Not only did they agree with Virginia Woolf's claim that 'as a woman I have no country' but they were also often involved in anti-government political movements such as the anti-Vietnam War, civil rights and other anti-colonial and leftist movements and later on in women's peace movements such as at Greenham Common. This created in both sides very different assumptions concerning relationships between individual women and their collectivities – and their governments at the time.

Moreover, often in this non-dialogue, Third World women would feel that western women were constructing them solely in terms of what seemed to them to be barbaric customs and subjugation, without taking into account the social and economic context in which they existed. Third World women would thus be defined in terms of their 'problems' or their 'achievements' in relation to an imagined free white liberal democracy. This had the effect of removing them (and the 'liberal democracy') from history, freezing them in time and space, and eternally constructing them as politically immature women who need to be versed and schooled in the ethos of western feminism (Amos and Parmar, 1984: 7).

For example, Mohanty (1991: 57–8) describes how, in the writings of feminists, Third World women are 'frozen' into archetypal victims in discussions of issues such as genital mutilation and various forms of male violence. Lata Mani (1989) has commented on a similar phenomenon concerning sati in India. Focusing on certain social and cultural practices in isolation ignores some of the trade-offs that the continued existence of certain practices might have had on the lives of women in these societies. For example, in a society in which women are not allowed to live on their own, and divorce/repudiation is easy for the men, the continued existence of polygamy might be a much better option for older women who under such a system would not lose their social status and livelihood, compared with monogamy in which they would end up repudiated and left to the mercy of their brothers' families.

Kumari Jayawardena's book signalled a possible break in this deadlock between 'the feminists' and 'the nationalists'. It pointed out to western feminists that loyalty to one's national liberation movement does not necessarily mean that women do not fight within it for the improvement and transformation of the position of women in their societies. At the same time it also pointed out the fact that feminism has not been a specifically western phenomenon.

During the 1980s and 1990s the international feminist scene has undergone far-reaching changes in both the West and the Third World, as well as in the relationship between them. Owing to a large extent to the rise of the black feminist movement in the West which challenged the ethnocentrism, often racism, of western feminists from within (see, for example, *Feminist Review,* 1984; hooks, 1981; Mohanty et al., 1991), a growing sensitivity to issues of difference and the multi-positionality of women has started to develop among white western feminists. This was largely aided by the development of post-structuralist and postmodernist deconstructionist critical theories which reached hegemonic positions within cultural, literary and social academia (Nicholson, 1990; Weed, 1989). However, this sensitivity for difference often took on the form of a feminist version of multi-culturalism with all its problematics.

Identity Politics and Multi-Culturalism

The feminist version of 'multi-culturalism' developed as a form of 'identity politics' which replaced earlier feminist constructions of womanhood which had been informed by the hegemonic experiences of white middle class western women. In spite of the politically important (although theoretically somewhat problematic: see discussion in Chapter 1) introduction of the differentiation between sex and gender – the former being described as a fixed biological category and the latter as a variable cultural one – the feminist technique of 'consciousness-raising' has assumed, as a basis for political action, a *de facto* fixed reality of women's oppression that has to be discovered and then changed, rather than a reality which is being created and re-created when practised and discussed (Yuval-Davis, 1984). Moreover, this reality of women's oppression is assumed to be shared by all women who are perceived to constitute a basically homogeneous social grouping with the same interests. Women's individual identities have become equated with women's collective identity, whereas differences, rather than being acknowledged, have been interpreted by those holding the hegemonic power within the movement as mainly reflections of different stages of raised consciousness. Although to a large extent the fallacy of this position has been acknowledged by many women's movements in recent years, the solution has often been to develop essentialist notions of difference, such as, for example, between black and white women, middle class and working class women or northern and southern women. Within each of these idealized groups, the assumptions about 'discovered' homogeneous reality usually continue to operate. 'Identity politics' tend not only to homogenize and naturalize social categories and groupings, but also to deny shifting boundaries of identities and internal power differences and conflicts of interest. It is important to emphasize, as Paul Gilroy has done (in his introduction to his 1994 book *The Black Atlantic*), that such an essentialist construction can also be a result of a 'strategic essentialism' of the Guyatari Spivak (1993) variety, where, while it is acknowledged that such categories involve 'arbitrary closures' (to use a term I've heard used by Stuart Hall) for political mobilization, these categories become reified via practices of social movements and state policies. Rejecting such reified construction of categories does not negate, however, the primary importance that considerations of individual and collective positionings, power relations between and within collectivities, and the cultural, political and economic resources which they carry, should have in the construction of any political alliances.

One of the differences which these 'arbitrary closures' have helped to obscure has been class differences. These do not relate simply to the fact (which has been often pointed out) that western feminists have usually been represented by highly educated white middle class women, representing a very specific view of 'women's interests', even of women from their own societies. Third World women are often represented by women who come from even more exclusive circles in their societies: in post-colonial societies they often come from the families of the ruling elites. One of the differences between First and Third World feminist women, therefore, that is very rarely pointed out, is that the Third World women come from homes where domestic servants, for instance, are a much more usual practice than in the homes of the western feminists. At the same time, of course, the practice by western middle class professionals of hiring au pairs, nannies and housekeepers, who often come from subjugated ethnic and migrant collectivities, is also growing. An endemic problem in national as well as international identity politics is that of representation. As I have argued elsewhere (Cain and Yuval-Davis, 1990; see also discussion in Chapter 4), the only way feminist and other community activists can get over this pitfall is to see themselves as advocates rather than as representatives of their constituencies. However, even as advocates, it is important that they should be conscious of the multiplexity of their specific positionings, both in relation to other women in their societies, as well as in relation to the other participants in the specific encounter.

International Women's Activism

As in the West, there has been in the 1980s a development of feminist awareness and an autonomous organization of women in a variety of revolutionary and liberationist social movements in the Third World (see, for example, Rowbotham, 1992; Wieringa, 1995). This has brought a new sense of legitimacy to the pursuit of the promotion and transformation of the position of women in many Third World societies. Of particular importance in this regard has been the UN Decade on Women, and the growth of a variety of women's non-governmental organizations (NGOs) which were particularly aimed at empowering local women in various countries (Afshar and Dennis, 1992; Ashworth, 1995; Vargas, 1995). These NGOs often emanated from grass-roots women's organizing around 'traditional' women's preoccupations, such as health, reproductive rights and child care, but there were also initiatives which were aimed directly at empowering women to be independent economically, such as women's co-operatives and even women's banks. Some women's NGOs started organizing around traditional concerns and then developed into powerful political grass-roots organizations, such as the women's communal kitchens in Peruvian cities. Others have brought pressure for the establishment of 'women-friendly' state institutions such as the women's police stations in the state of Andhra Pradesh in India and in Brazil, or have lobbied for changes in law which would still be seen as acceptable within the boundaries of the country's 'traditions' but which would guarantee women's rights (as was the case, for instance, in Sri Lanka: see Helie-Lucas, 1993; on the role of Sri Lanka's women's organizations in the war, see Abeyesekera, 1994). One of the things which has enabled the long term survival of many of these NGOs, as well as their relative level of autonomy from local pressures, has been the funds provided by aid organizations from overseas as well as the more personal support and solidarity of feminist organizations and networks in other countries (such as, for instance, the net-works of Women Living Under Muslim Laws and Women In Black). This has often provoked the accusation, especially by local patriarchal groups opposed to the activities of these organizations, that they are nothing but traitors and offshoots of western imperialism. Indeed, some of these organizations, as was discussed in Chapter 2 in relation to issues of women's reproductive rights, have proved to be nothing more than instruments of population con-trol which have caused a lot of harm to a lot of women. However, many other NGOs, as became clear at the UN Cairo conference in 1994, have been organized to resist exactly such policies. NGOs, like other political organiza-tions, have to be judged according to their specific projects and practices rather than *en bloc* as positive or negative phenomena.

However, it would be a westocentric stereotype to view women associated with NGOs in the South as puppets of western feminists. At recent UN con-ferences, like the 1993 Rio Conference on the Environment, the 1994 Vienna one on Human Rights, the 1994 Cairo one on Population and Development Policies, as well as the 1995 Beijing one on Women, it has often been groups of women from post-colonial countries, especially South Asia and Latin America, who have been the most organized and who have been operating with the clearest political agendas. At the same time, the level of co-operation between them and western women's groups with compatible agendas has also grown. Good examples of such co-operation have been the tribunals orga-nized in Vienna, Cairo and Beijing around the slogan of 'Women's rights are human rights', which were organized by the Center for Women's Global Leadership in Rutgers University in the USA in close co-operation with a variety of women's organizations in the North and the South including the Japanese campaign for the compensation of World War II 'comfort women'; the Peruvian Flora Tristan organization; the Algerian association for the promotion of equality between men and women; the Shirkat Gah centre in Lahore in Pakistan; and many more. As a result of the campaigns of these groups, 'women's issues' as such have become officially part of the UN human rights agenda, and rape in war, for example, is not seen any more just as a 'crime of honour' but has been included as a form of torture.

The above picture, however, might give the impression that the state of both women and feminist movements in the world today is rosy. This is far from being so.

The Backlash

The term 'backlash' was used by Susan Faludi (1992) to describe what she saw as a significant retreat in and threats to women's position in the USA. (Ann Oakley and Juliet Mitchell (1997) have edited a collection on the same theme in Britain.) But clearly this is a phenomenon which is happening much further afield than the USA and Britain or even the West as a whole. A lot of this scenario has to do with men's fear of feminism, of losing control over their women and of generally having less collective power in the society where women would gain access to positions and roles which were previously the exclusive domain of men. However, as was discussed in Chapter 3, this also has a lot to do with the crisis of modernity, the reinvention of particularistic essentialist identities and cultures associated with the rise of religious and ethnic fundamentalist movements, and the central place that control of women plays within these constructions as pivotal to their symbolic social order. One of the most significant political developments at the 1994 UN Cairo conference was the (un)holy alliance between the Catholic Pope and Islamist Iran, in their common fight against reproductive rights for women.

While women's progress to positions of power in countries where 'equal opportunities' legislation has been operating is blocked by what is known as 'the glass ceiling', the crisis and restructuring of welfare states has meant that many of women's social rights which have been gained in earlier struggles are being lost, whether child care facilities, social security benefits or health care. Of particular importance – both politically and symbolically, in this regard – have been women's reproductive rights and especially their right to legal abortions. But the issue is much wider than that. One of the paradoxes of the 'new liberalism' has been that while formally encouraging 'freedom' and 'democracy', in its pursuit of the 'free market' and a 'minimal state' (in the countries of the former Soviet Union as well as in post-colonial states), it has also promoted traditional familial ideologies which would enable the radical weakening of the welfare state. In practice this, of course, means the exclusion of women from full participation in these 'democracies' (Molineux, 1994). There is a rumour, for instance (which I've heard from Algerian women in London, members of SWASWA), that when American diplomats went a few years ago to Algeria, torn between the terrorist campaigns of Muslim fundamentalists and a military government, they explicitly let it be known that they would not care about the specific ideology/religion of the Algerians they supported, as long as they were assured that they would 'demolish the public sector'.

One of the most observed differences between the 1995 Beijing UN Conference on Women and the 1985 Nairobi one is the prevalence and organization of fundamentalist, religious and other 'traditionalist' groups at the conference. I was told, for instance, that there were at least seven Islamist workshops a day during that conference and that even organizations like the Salvation Army put a lot of energy into its presence and lobbying at the Beijing conference. It seems that the category 'woman' which used to signify emancipation and progress, first by modernizing national liberation movements and then specifically by feminists, is now being (re)claimed by fundamentalists and other anti-modernist agencies whose version of the 'equality versus difference' debate is very far from even the most essentialist versions of feminist positions.

No doubt part of these developments has to do with these organizations competing for the specific resources available for 'women's issues' these days. Activists from Southall Black Sisters (SBS) tell how when they first started to work on issues of domestic violence among Asians in London, 'community leaders' objected to their activities on the grounds that there is no such thing and, if there is, it should be hushed in order not to give ammunition to racists. However, within a few years their attitudes changed completely when it became clear not only how important and successful was the work of SBS in the area, in a way which threatened traditional networks of control in 'the community', but also that it was a source of money from the local authority. They started to compete for these monies and to organize alternative, much more co-optive counselling services for such women, claiming that SBS are not 'authentic' representatives of 'the community' (Sahgal and Yuval-Davis, 1992; Southall Black Sisters, 1990). Similarly in other places, 'community leaders' and 'fundamentalists' are feeling threatened by the relative political and economic autonomy of some of the women's NGOs described above.

The reason which is often given by those who object and try to repress autonomous women's organizations is that they represent a betrayal of the community's 'customs and traditions'. There is an ongoing debate among feminists, especially from the South, as well as between feminists and others, about the extent to which their discourse should be constructed by these customs and traditions.

Postmodernist Feminism?

On one side of the debate stand those who feel that unless feminists talk and legitimate their struggles using the popular religious traditions, they would never have any chance of progressing beyond a limited urban educated middle class grouping. A leading voice in this camp is, for instance, Riffat Hassan (1993), the Muslim feminist liberation theologist. She claims that no equality for Muslim women is possible until the constitutive myth that women were created inferior to men, from crooked ribs, is challenged. According to her, the myth about Eve being made of Adam's rib is not included in the Koran, and Adam is used in it as a generic concept for humanity, which is related both as male and as female, because it was originally undifferentiated. The prejudice against women in Islam comes from the Hadith which is not always considered authentic and can be fought against once the Koran is understood properly.

Another example is the South African lawyer who suggested a way of getting rid of polygamy without explicitly coming out against it. She was speaking at a women's conference organized by some activists in the ANC in 1993, a short time before the South African constitution was to be finalized, when they realized that equal weight was promised to the principles of 'non-sexist South Africa' and 'respect for customs and tradition' and were afraid that the first principle would be sacrificed to the second one. The lawyer suggested that the traditional custom of polygamy (about which many women participants in the conference, especially from the 'homelands', bitterly complained in terms of its exploitative and degrading effects on women) should not be forcibly or legally abolished. However, there should be an adoption of the law that in marriage, the wife becomes entitled to 50 per cent of the property of the couple. If the man marries again, he can share only his 50 per cent with the new wife, and so on.

Similar strategies of struggle in Iran, where Muslim feminists, for instance, have been arguing for women's more equal participation in public offices, such as becoming judges, have been called by Afsane Najmabadi (1995) 'postmodern feminism'. (A similar argument has also been developed by Haleh Afshar, 1994.) Najmabadi's argument, somewhat different to that of Riffat Hassan, is that between what she calls 'modern feminism' and 'Islamism' there are no overlapping points for even tactical co-operation. On the other hand, the 'piecemeal' approach of 'postmodern feminism' enables co-operation around specific issues without making generalized claims for women's equality or women's rights:

> I want to propose that the Islamicist onslaught cannot be resisted by defensibly hanging onto a competing set of foundational truths, but by a willingness to suspend such groundings, and to risk the impurity of pragmatism for the possibility of an often elusive conversation, a conversation centred, for instance, on the effects of the Enlightenment rather than on its claims to a superior Truth. (1995: 7)

An important motivation for this 'postmodernist' approach is the tendency, mentioned above, of labelling feminism as an offshoot of western cultural imperialism. However, many feminists from the South, such as those who belong to the international network of Women Living Under Muslim Laws (WLUML), do not agree with this approach. Although anti-imperialist and anti-racist themselves, fighting against the ethnocentrism and racism of western feminists, they feel that giving up feminism as a secular discourse results in accepting that there is an essential homogeneous 'Islamic' position on women in which women's difference is constructed in their primary social roles as wives and mothers (Helie-Lucas, 1993). This, they fear, can delegitimate a lot of the important work that feminists in their societies have accomplished during the last century and more. Moreover, many also feel that constructing women's struggles within the boundaries of their communities' religion and culture creates racialized exclusions towards women who are not part of those collectivities, but are part of their pluralist societies. Some Egyptian feminists, for example (from the organization The New Woman), have refused to formally associate themselves with WLUML, although they generally support their politics, because they feel that association with any organization in whose title the word 'Muslim' appears would have the effect of excluding Copt and other Egyptian women of non-Muslim origin from becoming full members of the organization. Gita Sahgal (1992) discusses the need for 'secular spaces' (which Homi Bhabha, 1994b has titled 'subaltern secularism') in which women from different communities can coexist and struggle together while having the space and the autonomy to choose which elements of their traditions (and what interpretation of those traditions) to keep and which to cast aside.

There is probably no one 'right' tactical answer to this debate, in the sense that in different societies, states and communities the possibility of women to enter such 'secular spaces' is highly variable. While in Egypt, for instance, a crucial struggle is taking place at present on the principle of the continued existence of secular spaces, small and threatened as they may be, in Iran this struggle, for the moment at least, has been lost. Specific historical conditions should dictate the form and substance of particular feminist struggles. Co-operation and solidarity among feminists positioned differentially in different societies and in the same society should be informed by these differences. This is what transversal politics is all about.

Transversal Politics

I first heard the term 'transversal politics' when I was invited by Italian feminists from Bologna to a meeting they organized between Palestinian and Israeli (both Jewish and Palestinian) women which took place in 1993 (Yuval-Davis, 1994b). I had been searching for such a term already beforehand. In a conference organized by Valentine Moghadam at the United Nations University in Helsinki in 1991 I gave a paper which was a critique of identity politics in which I used the term 'universality in diversity' (Yuval-Davis, 1994a: 422; see also Jayawardena, 1995: 10). Transversalism, which, apparently, has been promoted by a certain strand of the autonomous left in Bologna (the Transversalists) for many years, expresses the same idea in a much less clumsy way.

As mentioned in Chapter 4, transversal politics aims to be an alternative to the universalism/relativism dichotomy which is at the heart of the modernist/postmodernist feminist debate. It aims at providing answers to the crucial theoretical/political questions of how and with whom we should work if/when we accept that we are all different as deconstructionist theories argue.

Etienne Balibar (1990b) has pointed out the inherent racism and ethnocentrism of supposed 'universalism' which ignores the differential positionings of those to whom the universalist rules are supposed to apply. bell hooks has pointed out this truth in regards to the supposed universal feminist idea of sisterhood. She claimed:

> The vision of sisterhood evoked by women liberationists was based on the idea of common oppression – a false and corrupt platform disguising and mystifying the true nature of women's varied and complex social reality. (1991: 29)

As we have seen throughout this book, there are many examples of this varied and complex social reality of women. As a result, any simplistic assumptions about what is 'the feminist agenda' need to be problematized. Debates relating to these issues can be found in all areas of feminist politics, whether it is the debate on reproductive rights and prioritizing forbidden abortions versus forced sterilizations; the attitudes feminists should have towards 'the family' as an oppressive or protective social institution; or the extent to which women should come out against all forms of violence or should campaign for participation in the military (Anthias and Yuval-Davis,

1983; 1992; Hill-Collins, 1990; Kimble and Unterhalter, 1982; Spelman, 1988).

If we add to membership in particular ethnic, national and racial collectivities other dimensions of identity and difference among women, such as class, sexuality, and stage in the life course, it would be very easy to reach a postmodernist deconstructionist view and a realization that 'everyone is different'. This raises doubts about whether any collective political action in general, and feminist collective action in particular, is possible once such a deconstructionist analytical point of view is conceded as valid (see the critique by Michele Barrett and Mary McIntosh, 1985 of Anthias and Yuval-Davis, 1983; see also bell hooks, 1991). Are effective politics and adequate theoretical analysis inherently contradictory to each other? My basic answer to this question is the same as that of Gayatri Chakravorty Spivak when she claimed:

> Deconstruction does not say anything against the usefulness of mobilizing unities. All it says is that because it is useful it ought not to be monumentalized as the way things really are. (1991: 65)

Or, to put it in Stuart Hall's succinct way, 'all identity is constructed across difference' (1987: 44).

Adopting such a political perspective of boundary construction of 'units' or 'unities' can keep us aware of continuous historical changes and keep our perceptions of the boundaries between collectivities sufficiently flexible and open so that exclusionary politics are not permitted. At the same time it still enables us not to be paralysed politically. Concretely this means that all feminist (and other forms of democratic) politics should be viewed as a form of coalition politics in which the differences among women are recognized and given a voice, in and outside the political 'units' and the boundaries of this coalition should be set not in terms of 'who' we are but in terms of what we want to achieve. As Caryn McTighe Musil says:

> The challenge of the nineties is to hold on simultaneously to these two contradictory truths: as women, we are the same and we are different. The bridges, power, alliances and social change possible will be determined by how well we define ourselves through a matrix that encompasses our gendered particularities while not losing sight of our unity. (1990: vi)

The question is, of course, how to go about this task concretely. To help in clarifying the issues involved, several approaches which attempted to tackle that task will be examined. Two of these, although creative and thoughtful in many ways, have, I believe, some major flaws relating to some of the issues discussed earlier in the book; two others, although very different from each other, might point the way forward in effectively tackling the problem.

The first approach has been presented in the article by Gail Pheterson (1990) in the *Bridges of Power* collection. It describes an experiment in the Netherlands in which three mixed women's groups (more or less in half-and-half proportions) were constructed: one of black and white women, one of Jews and gentiles, and one of lesbian and heterosexual women. The groups operated very much within the usual pattern of feminist conscious-ness-raising tradition. Pheterson found that

> in every group, past experiences with oppression and domination distorted the participants' perceptions of the present and blocked their identification with people in common political situations who did not share their history. (1990: 3)

She talks about the need to recognize and interrupt how we internalize both oppression and domination in order to create successful alliances. Her posi-tion constructs ethnicity as including a power dimension – of oppression and domination and not just as made of 'cultural stuff'. She also shows that women can experience internalized oppression and domination simultane-ously as a result of different experiences: people and identities are not just unidimensional. On the other hand her approach implies that there is such a thing as an 'objective truth' that can be discovered rather than a constructed one. I would say that rather than using a discourse of 'distortion', one should use a discourse of ideological positioning. I will come back to this point later.

The discourse of 'distortion' creates its own distortions. Pheterson dis-cusses, for instance, the reluctance of some women (black women born in the colonies rather than in the Netherlands; Jewish women who have only one Jewish parent) to identify with their groups and sees it as a distortion and 'blocked identifications'. Such a perspective assumes essentialist homogene-ity within each category (such as 'blacks' and 'Jews') and refuses to accept that these women are genuinely located in different positionings from other members of their groups. Moreover, it assumes that the centrality and signif-icance of these categories would be the same for different women members and disregards differences of class, age and other social dimensions among the participants as inherently irrelevant for the group.

Such an approach is typical of the 'identity politics' of difference discussed above which has been very central to recent western feminism. In such 'iden-tity politics' individual identity has become equated with collective identity, whereas differences, rather than being acknowledged, have been interpreted by those holding the hegemonic power within the movement as mainly reflec-tions of different stages of raised consciousness, while the difference between groups is perceived to be the authentic and important one. As Linda Gordon points out, such essentialist notions of difference are necessarily exclusive:

> We are in danger of losing any ability to offer any interpretation that reaches beyond the particular groups . . . it does not capture the experience of all . . . women. (1991: 103)

Even more importantly, as Bonnie Thornton Dill points out,

> As an organizing principle, difference obliterates relation . . . Difference often implies separation, but these relationships frequently involve proximity, involve-ment. (1988: 106)

An attempt at a more sophisticated type of identity politics was theorized by Rosalind Brunt who wrote in the influential collection *New Times*. Brunt argued that:

> Unless the question of identity is at the heart of any transformatory project, then
> not only will the political agenda be inadequately 'rethought' but more to the
> point, our politics aren't going to make much headway beyond the Left's own cir-
> cles. (1989: 150)

Reflecting upon one's own identity, the return to the 'subjective', does not
imply for Brunt withdrawal from politics, but rather the opposite: locating
grids of power and resistance in the Foucauldian way, which are horizontal
and not just vertical, while keeping political frameworks of action heterogeneous and floating. She rejects the logic of 'broad democratic alliances' and
'rainbow coalitions' because, she argues, political action should be based on
'unity in diversity', which should be founded not on common denominators
but on

> a whole variety of heterogeneous, possibly antagonistic, maybe magnificently
> diverse, identities and circumstances . . . the politics of identity recognizes that
> there will be many struggles, and perhaps a few celebrations, and writes into all of
> them a welcome to contradiction and complexity. (1989: 158)

As a positive example of this type of political struggle Brunt points to the
support activities which surrounded the UK miners' strike in 1984–5. This is,
however, an unfortunate example, because, with all its positive features, the
strike ended up in a crushing defeat, not only of the miners and the trade
union movement, but of the anti-Thatcherite movement as a whole.

Defeats and real politics aside, Brunt's model of politics could be seen as
seductive: it incorporates theoretical insights of highly sophisticated social
analysis, is flexible, is dynamic and is totally inclusive. However, it is in this
last point that the danger lies. What ultimately lies behind Brunt's approach
is a naive populist assumption that in spite of contradictions and conflicts,
in the last instance all popular struggles are inherently progressive. She
shares with other multi-culturalists a belief in the inherent reconcilability
and limited boundaries of interest and political difference among those
who are disadvantaged and discriminated against. Such a belief, as discussed above, has created a space for fundamentalist leaderships to rise, and
ultimately has caused Jesse Jackson, a main promoter of 'rainbow coalitions' in the 1980s (as well as many other progressive black activists,
including Tony Morison), to join the 'Million Men March' to Washington,
DC organized by the fundamentalist, racist and sexist 'Nation of Islam' in
the 1990s.

The next example I want to discuss is of feminist politics which has pro-
gressed beyond such assumptions. It is that of Women Against
Fundamentalism (WAF), which was organized in London in the wake of the
Rushdie affair to struggle exactly against such fundamentalist leaderships of
all religions as well as against expressions of racism which masqueraded
themselves as anti-fundamentalism.

WAF includes women from a variety of religious and ethnic origins
(Christians, Jews, Muslims, Sikhs, Hindus and so on). Many of the members
also belong to other campaigning organizations, often with a more specific

ethnic affiliation – such as the Southall Black Sisters (SBS), the Jewish Socialist Group, and the Irish Abortion Support Group. However, except for SBS which has had an organizational and ideological initiatory role in establishing WAF, women come there as individuals rather than as representatives of any group or ethnic category. On the other hand, there is no attempt to 'assimilate' the women who come from the different backgrounds. Differences in ethnicity and points of view – and the resulting different agendas – are recognized and respected. But what is celebrated is the common political stance of WAF members, as advocating 'the third way' against fundamentalism and against racism.

This 'third way' corresponds to some of the ideas expressed by Patricia Hill-Collins in her book *Black Feminist Thought* (1990). In this book she discusses the importance of recognizing the different positionings from which different groupings view reality. Her analysis (which follows to a great extent the feminist epistemological perspective of 'standpoint theory' elaborated by Donna Haraway, 1988) echoes exactly the agenda which has been guiding the members of WAF:

> Each group speaks from its own standpoint and shares its own partial, situated knowledge. But because each group perceives its own truth as partial, its knowledge is *unfinished* [to differentiate from invalid] . . . Partiality and not universality is the condition of being heard; individuals and groups forwarding knowledge claims without owning their position are deemed less credible than those who do . . . Dialogue is critical to the success of this epistemological approach. (1990: 236)

In this Hill-Collins side-steps the trap that Marxists and many sociologists of knowledge have been caught in – of relativism on the one hand, and locating specific social groupings as the epistemological 'bearers of the truth' on the other hand. Dialogue, rather than fixity of location, becomes the basis of empowered knowledge. The campaigns of WAF on, for instance, state religious education or women's reproductive rights have been informed by the differential experiences of the women of different positionings and backgrounds in the group. Similar ways of organizing around the San Francisco Bay area are discussed by Inderpal Grewal and Caren Kaplan in the introduction to their 1994 book (Grewal and Kaplan, 1994).

The last example I want to discuss is also based on dialogue – a dialogue which has been developed by Italian feminists (from the movement Women In Black – especially the women from the Bologna and Torino Women's Centres) working with feminists who are members of conflicting national groups, like the Serbs and the Croats, but especially Palestinian and Israeli Jewish women. On the face of it, such a dialogue does not seem very different from the more common 'identity politics' type of dialogue such as was described by Gail Pheterson. However, several important differences exist.

The boundaries of the groupings were determined not by an essentialist notion of difference, but by a concrete and material political reality. Also, the women involved in the different groups were not perceived simplistically as representatives of their groupings. While their different positioning and background were recognized and respected – including the differential power relations inherent in their corresponding affiliations as members of the occupier and the occupied collectivities – all the women who were sought and invited to participate in the dialogue were committed to 'refuse to participate unconsciously in the reproduction of the existing power relations' and were 'committed to finding a fair solution to the conflict' (Italian initial letter of invitation, December 1990).

The basic perspective of the dialogue was very similar to that of Patricia Hill-Collins. The terminology is somewhat different. The Italian women used as key words 'rooting' and 'shifting'. The idea is that each participant in the dialogue brings with her the rooting in her own membership and identity, but at the same time tries to shift in order to put herself in a situation of exchange with women who have different membership and identity. They called this form of dialogue 'transversalism' – to differentiate from 'universalism' which, by assuming a homogeneous point of departure, ends up being exclusive instead of inclusive, and 'relativism' which assumes that, because of the differential points of departure, no common understanding and genuine dialogue are possible at all.

Two things are vital in developing the transversal perspective. Firstly, the process of shifting should not involve self-decentring, that is losing one's own rooting and set of values. There is no need for it, as Elsa Barkley Brown claims:

> All people can learn to center in another experience, validate it and judge it by its own standards without need of comparison or need to adopt that framework as their own . . . one has no need to 'decenter' anyone in order to center someone else; one has only to constantly pivot the centre. (1989: 922)

It is vital in any form of coalition and solidarity politics to keep one's own perspective on things while empathizing and respecting others. In multiculturalist types of solidarity politics there can be a risk of uncritical solidarity. This was very prevalent, for instance, in the politics of some sections of the left around the Iranian Revolution or the Rushdie affair. They saw it as 'imperialist' and 'racist' to intervene in 'internal community matters'. Women are often the victims of such a perspective which allows the so-called representatives and leaders of 'the community' to determine policies concerning women.

Secondly, and following from the first point, the process of shifting should not homogenize the 'other'. As there are diverse positions and points of view among people who are similarly rooted, so there are among the members of the other group. The transversal coming together should be not with the members of the other group *en bloc*, but with those who, in their different rooting, share values and goals compatible with one's own.

A word of caution, however, is required here. Transversal politics are not always possible, as conflicting interests of people who are situated in specific positionings are *not* always reconcilable. However, when solidarity *is* possible, it is important that it is based on transversalist principles so as not to fall into the pitfalls of 'identity politics' of the feminist, nationalist or anti-racist kinds.

Empowerment of the oppressed, whether one fights for it for it for one's own – individual or group – sake or that of others, cannot by itself be the goal for feminist and other anti-oppression politics. During the last few years, for instance, memoirs by former members, especially Elaine Brown, have brought to light the 'disciplinary' practices of brutality and violence which became part of the daily reality of the American Black Panthers (Walker, 1993); and the murder of a teenager, to which Winnie Mandela has allegedly been party, has been just one dreadful demonstration of the old truism that 'power corrupts'. And this also applies to the power of previously disempowered people, and to power which is only relative and confined to specific contingencies.

The ideology of 'empowerment' has sought to escape this dilemma by confining 'positive' power to 'power of' rather than 'power over' (Bystydzienski, 1992: 3). However, in doing that, empowerment has been constructed as a process which breaks the boundaries between the individual and the communal. As Bookman and Morgan point out, the notion of empowerment connotes

> a spectrum of political activity ranging from acts of individual resistance to mass
> political mobilizations that challenge the basic power relations in our society.
> (1988: 4)

Such constructions assume a specific 'identity politics' which, as we discussed above, homogenizes and naturalizes social categories and groupings, denying shifting boundaries and internal power differences and conflicts of interest. Also in such an approach cultures and traditions are transformed from heterogeneous, sometimes conflicting reservoirs of resources into unified, ahistorical and unchanging essence.

As an alternative to this kind of 'identity politics' the book suggests that the idea of 'transversal politics' provides the way forward. In 'transversal politics', perceived unity and homogeneity are replaced by dialogues which give recognition to the specific positionings of those who participate in them as well as to the 'unfinished knowledge' that each such situated positioning can offer. Transversal politics, nevertheless, does not assume that the dialogue is boundary free, and that each conflict of interest is reconcilable – although, as Jindi Pettman points out, 'there are almost always possibilities for congenial or at least tolerable personal, social and political engagements' (1992: 157). The boundaries of a transversal dialogue are determined by the message, rather than the messenger. In other words, transversal politics differentiates between social identities and social values, and assumes that what Alison Assiter calls 'epistemological communities' (1996: Chapter 5), which share common value systems, can exist across differential positionings and identities. The struggle against oppression and discrimination might (and mostly does) have a specific categorical focus but is never confined just to that category.

It is a difficult question what the boundaries of the feminist 'epistemo-logical community' and coalition politics should be, not only because the specific historical conditions in which any specific feminist campaign might be carried out can vary so much, but also because there are so many strands among self-identified feminists, among whom there may be very serious divisions of opinion. Moreover, as Angela Davis has pointed out (Davis and Martinez, 1994: 47), if the struggle against her imprisonment in the 1970s had been limited only to those who shared her politics, the campaign would never have been successful. Also, not all political campaigns are the same. There are different levels of overlapping value systems and different levels of common political work, from a tight formal organization to a loose informal network, from ideological alliance to single-issue coalition. However, this multiplicity of forms and intensities of coalition politics should not make us all into postmodern 'free floating signifiers' (Wexler, 1990) for whom 'any-thing goes'. Transversal politics stop where the proposed aims of the struggle are the conserving or promoting of unequal relations of power, and where essentialized notions of identity and difference naturalize forms of social, political and economic exclusion. The processes of 'shifting' and 'rooting' can help to distinguish between differences of context and terminology and differences of values and goals. This can have very little to do with labels and stereotypes of 'otherness'.

If empowerment of women is to transcend some of the pitfalls discussed in this book, it is perhaps wise to adhere to Gill Bottomley's warning:

> The dualistic approach of a unitary Us vs a unitary Them continues to mystify the interpenetration and intermeshing of the powerful constructs as race, class and gender and to weaken attempts at reflexivity . . . Both the subjective and the objec-tive dimensions of experience need to be addressed as well as the thorny issue of the extent to which observers remain within the discourses they seek to criticise. (1991: 309)

The transversal pathway might be full of thorns, but at least it leads in the right direction.

An Endnote

There is no 'end of history', nor is there an 'end goal' for political struggles. Transversal politics might offer us, however, a way for mutual support and probably greater effectiveness in the continuous struggle towards a less sexist, less racist and more democratic society, an agency within the continuously changing political, economic and environmental contexts in which we live and act.

As we can never accomplish, by definition, what we set out to do, one of the important tasks we have to think about is how to sustain and sometimes even celebrate our lives while struggling, including how to have fun! As Emma Goldman has said, 'If I can't dance to it, it's not my revolution.' Granted, in situations of acute racisms, imposed identities, ethnic cleansings and national conflicts and wars, this sentiment might seem sometimes to be too shallow and flimsy. And yet, maybe this is not completely so. As expressed in a saying from Zimbabwe, quoted on a postcard sent to me by one of my 'transversal' friends, 'If you can talk, you can sing; if you can walk, you can dance!'

(I dedicate this endnote to the lovers of 'Barefoot Boogie'.)

REFERENCES

Abdo, Nahla and Yuval-Davis, Nira (1995) 'Palestine, Israel and the Zionist settler project', in D. Stasiulis and N. Yuval-Davis (eds), *Unsettling Settler Societies*. London: Sage. pp. 291–322.

Abeyesekera, Sunila (1994) 'Organizing for peace in the midst of war: experiences of women in Sri-Lanka'. Paper presented for a course *Gender and Nation*, Institute of Social Studies, The Hague.

Accad, Evelyne (1990) *Sexuality and War: Literary Mask of the Middle East*. New York: New York University Press.

Ackelsberg, Martha (forthcoming) 'Liberalism' and 'Community politics'. Draft entries for the *Encyclopedia of Women's Studies*. New York: Simon and Schuster.

Addis, Elizabetta (1994) 'Women and the economic consequences of being a soldier', in Elizabetta Addis, Valeria E. Russo and Lorenza Sebesta (eds), *Women Soldiers: Images and Realities*. London: Macmillan/St Martin's Press.

Afshar, Haleh (1994) 'Women and the politics of fundamentalism in Iran', *WAF (Women Against Fundamentalism) Journal*, no. 5: 15–21.

Afshar, Haleh and Dennis, Carolynne (eds) (1992) *Women and Adjustment in the Third World*. London: Macmillan.

Ali, Yasmin (1992) 'Muslim women and the politics of ethnicity and culture in northern England', in G. Sahgal and N. Yuval-Davis (eds), *Refusing Holy Orders: Women and Fundamentalism in Britain*. London: Verso, pp. 101–23.

Allen, Sheila and Macey, Marie (1990) 'At the cutting edge of citizenship: race and ethnicity in Europe 1992'. Paper presented at the conference *New Issues in Black Politics*, University of Warwick, May.

Althusser, L. (1971) 'Ideology and state ideological apparatuses', in *Lenin and Philosophy and Other Essays*. London: New Left Books.

Ålund, Aleksandra (1995) 'Alterity in modernity', *Acta Sociologica*, 38: 311–22.

Amin, Samir (1978) *The Arab Nation*. London: Zed Books.

Amnesty International (1995) *Human Rights Are Women's Rights*. London: Amnesty International.

Amos, Valerie and Parmar, Pratiba (1984) 'Challenging imperial feminism', *Feminist Review*, 17 (Autumn): 3–20.

ANC (1987) *ANC Calls for Advance to People's Power*. Lusaka/London: ANC.

Anderson, Ben (1983) *Imagined Communities*. London: Verso.

Anderson, Ben (1991) *Imagined Communities* (revised edn). London: Verso.

Anderson, Ben (1995) 'Ice empire and ice hockey: two *fin de siècle* dreams', *New Left Review*, 214: 146–50.

Anthias, Floya (1991) 'Parameters of difference and identity and the problem of connections – gender, ethnicity and class', *Revue Internationale de Sociologie*, no. 2: 29–52.

Anthias, Floya (1993) 'Rethinking categories and struggles: racism, anti-racisms and multi-culturalism'. Paper presented at the European workshop *Racism and Anti-Racist Movements*, University of Greenwich, September.

Anthias, Floya and Yuval-Davis, Nira (1983) 'Contextualizing feminism: gender, ethnic and class divisions', *Feminist Review*, no. 14: 62–75.

Anthias, Floya and Yuval-Davis, Nira (1989) 'Introduction', in Nira Yuval-Davis and Floya Anthias (eds), *Woman–Nation–State*. London: Macmillan.

Anthias, Floya and Yuval-Davis, Nira (1992) *Racialized Boundaries: Race, Nation, Gender, Colour and Class and the Anti-Racist Struggle*. London: Routledge.

Anzaldua, Gloria (1987) *Borderlines/La Frontera*. San Francisco: Spinsters/Aunt Lute Books.

Arendt, Hannah (1975) *The Origins of Totalitarianism* (1951). New York: Harcourt Brace Jovanovitch.

Armstrong, John (1982) *Nations before Nationalism*. Chapel Hill, NC: University of North Carolina Press.

Ashworth, Georgina (ed.) (1995) *The Diplomacy of the Oppressed: New Directions in International Feminism*. London: Zed Books.

Assad, Talal (1993) *Genealogies of Religion*. Baltimore: Johns Hopkins University Press.

Assiter, Alison (1996) *Enlightened Women: Modernist Feminism in a Postmodern Age*. London: Routledge.

Avineri, S. and Shalit, A. (eds) (1992) *Communitarianism and Individualism*. Oxford: Oxford University Press.

Bakan, Abigail B. and Stasiulis, Daiva (1994) 'Foreign domestic worker policy in Canada and the social boundaries of modern citizenship', *Science and Society*, 58(1): 7–33.

Balibar, Etienne (1990a) 'The nation form – history and ideology', *New Left Review*, XIII (3, summer): 329–61.

Balibar, Etienne (1990b) 'Paradoxes of universality', in D.T. Goldberg (ed.), *Anatomy of Racism*. Minneapolis, MN: University of Minnesota Press.

Bang, Rani and Bang, Abhay (1992) 'Contraceptive technologies – experience of rural Indian women', *Manushi*, no. 70: 26–31.

Barker, Martin (1981) *The New Racism*. Brighton: Junction.

Barkley Brown, Elsa (1989) 'African-American women's quilting: a framework for conceptualizing and teaching African-American women's history', *Signs*, 14(4): 921–9.

Barrett, Michelle (1987) 'The concept of difference', *Feminist Review*, no. 26.

Barrett, Michelle and McIntosh, Mary (1985) 'Ethnocentrism in socialist feminist theory', *Feminist Review*, no. 20.

Barrett, Michelle and Phillips, Anne (eds) (1992) *Destabilizing Theory: Contemporary Feminist Debates*. Cambridge: Polity Press.

Bauer, Otto (1940) *The National Question* (in Hebrew). Hakibutz Haartzi.

Bauman, Gerd (1994) 'Dominant and demotic discourses of culture'. Paper presented at the conference *Culture, Communication and Discourse: Negotiating Difference in Multi-Ethnic Alliances*, University of Manchester, December.

Bauman, Zygmunt (1988) 'Sociology and post-modernity', *Sociological Review*, 36: 790–813.

Bauman, Zygmunt (1995) *Life in Fragments*. Cambridge: Polity Press.

Bennett, Olivia, Bexley, Jo and Warnock, Kitty (eds) (1995) *Arms to Fight, Arms to Protect: Women Speak Out about Conflict*. London: Panos.

Berer, Marge (1995) 'The Quinacrine controversy continues', *Reproductive Health Matters*, no. 6 (November): 142–61.

Beth-Halakhmi, Benjamin (1996) 'Interview with Nira Yuval-Davis', *WAF (Women Against Fundamentalism) Journal*, no. 8: 32–4.

Beveridge, William (1942) *Report on Social Insurance and Allied Services*. London: HMSO.

Beyer, Peter (1994) *Religion and Globalization*. London: Sage.

Bhabha, Homi (ed.) (1990) *Nation and Narration*. London: Routledge.

Bhabha, Homi (1994a) *The Location of Culture*. London: Routledge.

Bhabha, Homi (1994b) 'Subaltern secularism', *WAF (Women Against Fundamentalism) Journal*, no. 6: 5–8.

Bhabha, Jacqueline and Shutter, Sue (1994) *Women's Movement: Women under Immigration, Nationality and Refugee Law*. Stoke-on-Trent: Trentham Books.

Biehl, Amy (1994) 'Custom and religion in a non-racial, non-sexist South Africa', *WAF (Women Against Fundamentalism) Journal*, no. 5: 51–4.

Bonnet, Catherine (1995) 'Rape as a weapon of war in Rwanda', *European Forum of Left Feminists Newsletter*, July.

Bookman, Ann and Morgan, Sancha (eds) (1988) *Women and the Politics of Empowerment*. Philadelphia: Temple University Press.

Boose, Lynda E. (1993) 'Techno-muscularity and the "Boy Eternal": from the quagmire to the Gulf', in Miriam Cooke and Angela Woollacott (eds), *Gendering War Talk*. Princeton, NJ: Princeton University Press.

Bottomley, Gill (1991) 'Culture, ethnicity and the politics/poetics of representation', *Diaspora*, 1(3): 303–20.

Bottomley, Gill (1992) *From Another Place: Migration and the Politics of Culture*. Cambridge: Cambridge University Press.

Bottomley, Gill (1993) 'Post-multiculturalism? The theory and practice of heterogeneity'. Paper presented at the conference *Post-colonial Formations: Nations, Culture, Policy*, Griffith University, Queensland (June).

Bourdieu, P. (1977) *Outline of a Theory of Practice*. Cambridge: Cambridge University Press.

Bourne, J. and Sivanandan, A. (1980) 'Cheerleaders and ombudsmen: the sociology of race relations in Britain', *Race and Class*, 21(4).

Bowman, Glenn (1989) 'Fucking tourists: sexual relations and tourism in Jerusalem's Old City', *Critique of Anthropology*, ix, 2: 77–93.

Bradiotti, Rosi, Chazkiewlez, Ewa, Hausler, Sabine and Wieringa, Saskia (1994) *Women, the Environment and Sustainable Development: Towards a Theoretical Synthesis*. London: Zed.

Brah, Avtar (1992) 'Difference, diversity and differentiation', in J. Donald and A. Rattansi (eds), *Race, Culture and Difference*. London: Sage.

Brah, Avtar (1996) *Cartographies of Diaspora: Contested Identities*. London: Routledge.

Brunt, Rosalind (1989) 'The politics of identity', in S. Hall and M. Jacques (eds), *New Times*. London: Lawrence and Wishart.

Burney, Elizabeth (1988) *Steps to Social Equality: Positive Action in a Negative Climate*. London: Runnymede Trust.

Butler, J. (1990) *Gender Trouble: Feminism and the Subversion of Identity*. New York: Routledge.

Bystydzienski, Jill M. (ed.) (1992) *Women Transforming Politics: Worldwide Strategies for Empowerment*. Bloomington, IN: Indiana University Press

Cain, Harriet and Yuval-Davis, Nira (1990) '"The equal opportunities community" and the anti-racist struggle', *Critical Social Policy*, no. 29 (Autumn): 5–26.

Chapkis, Wendy (1981) *Loaded Questions: Women in the Military*. Amsterdam: Transnational Institute.

Chatterjee, Partha (1986) *Nationalist Thought and the Colonial World: a Derivative Discourse*. London: Zed.

Chatterjee, Partha (1990) 'The nationalist resolution of the women's question', in K. Sangari and S. Vaid (eds), *Recasting Women: Essays in Colonial History*. New Brunswick, NJ: Rutgers University Press.

Chhachhi, Amrita (1991) 'Forced identities: the state, communalism, fundamentalism and women in India', in D. Kandiyoti (ed.), *Women, Islam and the State*. London: Macmillan. pp. 144–75.

Clifford, James (1988) *The Predicament of Culture*. Cambridge, MA: Harvard University Press.

Cock, Jacklyn (1992) *Women in War in South Africa*. London: Open Letters.

Cohen, Eric (1971) 'Arab boys and tourist girls in a mixed Jewish-Arab city', *International Journal of Comparative Sociology*, 12(4): 217–33.

Cohen, J. (1982) *Class and Civil Society: the Limits of Marxian Critical Theory*. Amhurst, MA: University of Massachusetts Press.

Cohen, Phil (1988) 'The perversions of inheritance', in P. Cohen and H.S. Bains (eds), *Multi-Racist Britain*. London: Macmillan.

Cohen, Phil (1995) 'Out of the melting pot into the fire next time: local/global cities, bodies, texts'. Paper presented at the BSA conference *Contested Cities*, Essex University, 11–13 April.

Cohn, Caroline (1993) 'Wars, wimps and women: talking gender and thinking war', in Miriam Cooke and Angela Woollacott (eds), *Gendering War Talk*. Princeton, NJ: Princeton University Press.

Connell, R.W. (1987) *Gender and Power*. Cambridge: Polity Press.

Contention (1995) Special issue *Comparative Fundamentalisms*, no. 2 (Winter).

Cooke, Miriam (1993) 'WO-man, retelling the war myth', in Miriam Cooke and Angela Woollacott (eds), *Gendering War Talk*. Princeton, NJ: Princeton University Press.

Correa, Sonia (1994) *Population and Reproductive Rights: Feminist Perspectives from the South.* London: Zed in association with DAWN.

Correa, Sonia and Petchesky, Rosalind (1994) 'Reproductive and social rights: a feminist perspective', in G. Sen, A. Germain and L.C. Cohen (eds), *Population Policies Considered.* Cambridge, MA: Harvard University Press. pp. 107–26.

Cox, Robert W. (1995) 'Civilizations: encounters and transformations', *Studies in Political Economy*, no. 7: 7–32.

Dahl, R. (1971) *Polyarchy*. New Haven, CT: Yale University Press.

Daly, Markate (1993) *Communitarianism: Belonging and Commitment in a Pluralist Democracy*.Wadsworth.

Davis, Angela (1993) 'Racism, birth control and reproductive rights', in L. Richardson and V. Taylor (eds), *Feminist Frontiers II*. New York: McGraw-Hill.

Davis, Angela and Martinez, Elizabeth (1994) 'Coalition building among people of color', in M. Ochoa and T. Teaiwa (eds), *Enunciating Our Terms: Women of Color in Collaboration and Conflict*. Inscriptions 7. Santa Cruz, CA: Center for Cultural Studies, University of California.

Davis, F. James (1993) *Who Is Black? One Nation's Definition*. Pennsylvania State University Press.

de la Campagne, C. (1983) *L'Invention du racisms – antique et moyen âge*. Paris: University of Paris Press.

deLepervanche, Marie (1980) 'From race to ethnicity', *Australian and New Zealand Journal of Sociology*, 16(1).

deLepervanche, Marie (1989) 'Women, nation and the state in Australia', in N. Yuval-Davis and F. Anthias (eds), *Woman–Nation–State*. London: Macmillan. pp. 36–57.

Delphy, C. (1993) 'Rethinking sex and gender', *Women Studies International Forum*, 16(1): 1–9.

Deutch, K.W. (1966) *Nationalism and Social Communications: an Enquiry into the Foundations of Nationality*. Cambridge, MA: MIT Press.

Dickanson, Olive P. (1992) *Canada's First Nations*. Toronto: McClelland and Stanley.

Dietz, Mary G. (1987) 'Context is all: feminism and theories of citizenship', *Daedalus*, 116: 4.

Donald, James (1993) 'How English is it? Popular literature and national culture', in Erica Carter, Donald James and Judith Squires (eds), *Space and Place: Theories of Identity and Location*. London: Lawrence and Wishart in association with New Formations.

Dransart, Penny (1987) 'Women and ritual conflict in Inka society', in Sharon Macdonald, Pat Holden and Shirley Ardener (eds), *Images of Women in Peace and War*. London: Macmillan.

Durkheim, Emile (1965) *Elementary Forms of Religious Life*. New York: Free Press.

Edwards, J. (1988) 'Justice and the bounds of welfare', *Journal of Social Policy*, no. 18.

Ehrlich, Avishai (1987) 'Israel: conflict, war and social change', in Colin Creighton and Martin Shaw (eds), *The Sociology of War and Peace*. London: Macmillan.

Ehrlich, Paul (1968) *The Population Bomb*. Stanford, CA: Stanford University Press.

Eisenstein, Zillah (ed.) (1979) *Capitalist Patriarchy*. New York: Monthly Review Press.

Eisenstein, Zillah (1989) *The Female Body and the Law*. Berkeley, CA: University of California Press.

Eisenstein, Zillah (1993) *The Color of Gender – Reimaging Democracy*. Berkeley, CA: University of California Press.

Enloe, Cynthia (1980) *Ethnic Soldiers: State Security in Divided Societies*. Harmondsworth: Penguin.

Enloe, Cynthia (1983) *Does Khaki Become You?* London: Pluto Press.

Enloe, Cynthia (1989) *Bananas, Beaches, Bases: Making Feminist Sense of International Politics*. London: Pandora.

Enloe, Cynthia (1990) 'Womenandchildren: making feminist sense of the Persian Gulf Crisis', *The Village Voice*, 25 September.

Enloe, Cynthia (1993) *The Morning After: Sexual Politics at the End of the Cold War*. Berkeley, CA: University of California Press.

Esping-Andersen, Gosta (1990) *The Three Worlds of Welfare Capitalism*. Cambridge: Polity Press.

Evans, David T. (1993) *Sexual Citizenship: the Material Construction of Sexualities*. London: Routledge.

Faludi, Susan (1992) *Backlash: the Undeclared War against Women*. London: Chatto and Windus.

Fanon, Franz (1986) *Black Skin, White Masks* (1952). London: Pluto.

Feminism and Nonviolence Study Group (1983) *Piecing It Together: Feminism and Nonviolence*. London: Calvert.

Feminist Review (1984) Special issue *Many Voices, One Chant: Black Feminist Perspectives*, no. 17 (Autumn).

Fine, Robert (1994) 'The "new nationalism" and democracy: a critique of *pro patria*', *Democratization*, 1(3): 423–43.

Fisher, Jo (1989) *Mothers of the Disappeared*. London: Zed.

Focus on Gender (1994) Special issue *Population and Reproductive Rights*, 2 (2, June), Oxfam.

Forbes Martin, Susan (ed.) (1992) *Refugee Women*. London: Zed.

Foster, Elaine (1992) 'Women and the inverted pyramid of the Black Churches in Britain', in G. Sahgal and N. Yuval-Davis (eds), *Refusing Holy Orders: Women and Fundamentalism in Britain*. London: Verso. pp. 45–68.

Foucault, M. (1980a) *Herculine Barbin*. New York: Colophon.

Foucault, M. (1980b) *Power/Knowledge: Selected Interviews 1972–77* (ed. C. Gordon). Brighton: Harvester.

Friedman, Jonathan (1994) *Cultural Identity and Global Process*. London: Sage.

Fuszara, Malgorzata (1993) 'Abortion and the formation of the public sphere in Poland', in N. Funk and M. Mueller (eds), *Gender, Politics and Post-Communism*. London: Routledge.

Gaitskell, Deborah and Unterhalter, Elaine (1989) 'Mothers of the nation: a comparative analysis of nation, race and motherhood in Afrikaner nationalism and the African National Congress', in N. Yuval-Davis and F. Anthias (eds), *Woman–Nation–State*. London: Macmillan.

Gans, H.J. (1979) 'Symbolic ethnicity: the future of ethnic groups and cultures in America', *Ethnic and Racial Studies*, 2(2).

Gatens, M. (1991) 'A critique of the sex/gender distinction', in S. Gunew (ed.), *A Reader in Feminist Knowledge*. London: Routledge. pp. 139–57.

Geertz, Clifford (ed.) (1963) *Old Societies and New States*. New York: Free Press.

Geertz, Clifford (1966) 'Religion as a cultural system', in M. Bainton (ed.), *Anthropological Approaches to the Study of Religion*. London: Tavistock.

Gellner, E. (1983) *Nations and Nationalism*. Oxford: Basil Blackwell.

Giddens, Anthony (1989) *Sociology*. Cambridge: Polity.

Gilbert, Sandra (1983) 'Soldiers' heart: literary men, literary women and the Great War', in *Signs Special Issue on Women and Violence*, 8(3): 422–50.

Gilligan, Carol (1982) *In a Different Voice: Psychological Theory and Women's Development*. Cambridge: Cambridge University Press.

Gilman, Sander L. (1985) *Difference and Pathology: Stereotypes of Sexuality, Race and Madness*. Ithaca, NY: Cornell University Press.

Gilman, Sander L. (1991) *The Jew's Body*. New York: Routledge.

Gilroy, Paul (1987) *There Ain't No Black in the Union Jack*. London: Hutchinson.

Gilroy, Paul (1994) *The Black Atlantic, Modernity and Double Consciousness*. London: Verso.

Gilroy, Paul (1996) 'Revolutionary conservatism and the tyrannies of unanimism', *New Formations*, no. 28: 65–84.

Goodale, J. (1980) 'Gender, sexuality and marriage', in C. MacCormac and M. Strathern (eds), *Nature, Culture and Gender*. Cambridge: Cambridge University Press.

Gordon, Linda (1991) 'On difference', *Genders*, no. 10 (Spring): 91–111.

Gordon, Paul (1989) *Citizenship for Some? Race and Government Policy 1979–1989*. London: Runnymede Trust.

Grant, Rebecca (1991) 'The sources of gender bias in international relations theory', in R. Grant and K. Newland (eds), *Gender and International Relations*. Bloomington, IN: Indiana University Press. pp. 8–26.

Grant, Rebecca and Newland, Kathleen (eds) (1991) *Gender and International Relations*. Bloomington, IN: Indiana University Press.

Greenfeld, Liah (1992) *Nationalism: Five Roads to Modernity*. Cambridge, MA: Harvard University Press.

Grewal, Inderpal and Kaplan, Caren (eds) (1994) *Scattered Hegemonies; Postmodernity and Transnational Feminist Practices*. Minneapolis, MN: University of Minnesota Press.

Gutierrez, Natividad (1995) 'Mixing races for nation building: Indian and immigrant women in Mexico', in D. Stasiulis and N. Yuval-Davis (eds), *Unsettling Settler Societies: Articulations of Gender, Ethnicity, Race and Class*. London: Sage.

Habermas, J. (1992) 'Citizenship and national identity: some reflections on the future of Europe', *Praxis International*, 12(1).

Hall, Catherine (1994) 'Rethinking imperial histories: the Reform Act of 1867', *New Left Review*, no. 208: 3–29.

Hall, Stuart (1984) 'The state in question', in D. McLennan, D. Held and S. Hall (eds), *The Idea of the Modern State*. Milton Keynes: Open University Press.

Hall, Stuart (1987) 'Minimal selves', in *Identity, the Real Me*, ICA Document 6. London: ICA. pp. 44–6.

Hall, Stuart (1992) 'New ethnicities', in J. Donald and A. Rattansi (eds), *'Race', Culture and Difference*. London: Sage.

Hall, Stuart (1996) 'Who needs "identity?"', introduction to S. Hall and P. du Gay (eds), *Questions of Cultural Identity*. London: Sage.

Hall, Stuart and Held, David (1989) 'Citizens and citizenship', in Stuart Hall and Martin Jacques (eds), *New Times*. London: Lawrence and Wishart.

Haraway, Donna (1988) 'Situated knowledge: the science question in feminism and the privilege of partial perspective', *Feminist Studies*, 14(3): 575–99.

Haraway, Donna (1990) *Simians, Cyborgs and Women: the Reinvention of Women*. London: Free Association Books.

Harding, S. (1986) *The Science Question in Feminism*. Ithaca, NY: Cornell University Press.

Harris, D. (1987) *Justifying State Welfare: the New Right v. the Old Left*. Oxford: Basil Blackwell.

Hartman, Betsy (1987) *Reproductive Rights and Wrongs: the Global Politics of Population Control and Contraceptive Choice*. New York: Harper and Row.

Hartman, Heidi I. (1981) 'The unhappy marriage of Marxism and feminism: towards a more progressive union', in L. Sargent (ed.), *Women and Revolution*. London: Pluto.

Hartman, Heinz (1995) 'Clash of cultures, when and where: critical comments on a new theory of conflict – and its translation into German', *International Sociology*, 10(2): 115–25.

Hasan, Manar (1994) 'The murder of Palestinian women for family "honour" in Israel'. MA dissertation, Gender and Ethnic Studies, University of Greenwich.

Hassan, Riffat (1993) 'The issue of women's and men's equality in the Islamic tradition', in L. Grob, R. Hassan and H. Gordon (eds), *Women's and Men's Liberation Testimonies of Spirit*. Greenwood.

Held, D. (1984) 'Central perspectives on the modern state', in D. McLennan, D. Held and S. Hall (eds), *The Idea of the Modern State*. Milton Keynes: Open University Press.

Helie-Lucas, Marieme (1987) 'The role of women during the Algerian liberation struggle and after'. Paper presented at the conference *Women and the Military System*, Siunto Baths, Finland, January.

Helie-Lucas, Marieme (1993) 'Women living under Muslim laws', in J. Kerr (ed.), *Ours by Rights: Women's Rights as Women's Rights*. London: Zed.

Heng, Geraldine and Devan, Janadas (1992) 'State fatherhood: the politics of nationalism, sexuality and race in Singapore', in Andrew Parker, Mary Russo, Doris Somner and Patricia Yaeger (eds), *Nationalisms and Sexualities*. New York: Routledge. pp. 343–64.

Hernes, Helga Maria (1987) 'Women and the welfare state: the transition from private to public dependence', in A. Showstack Sassoon (ed.), *Women and the State*. London: Hutchinson. pp. 72–92.

Herrnstein, Richard and Murray, Charles A. (1994) *The Bell Curve: Intelligence and Class Structure in American Life*. New York: Free Press.

Hill-Collins, Patricia (1990) *Black Feminist Thought: Knowledge, Consciousness and the Politics of Empowerment*. London: HarperCollins.

Hobsbawm, Eric (1990) *Nations and Nationalism since 1780*. Cambridge: Cambridge University Press.

Hobsbawm, Eric and Ranger, Terance (eds) (1983) *The Invention of Traditions*. Cambridge: Cambridge University Press.

Hood-Williams, John (1996) 'Goodbye to sex and gender', *Sociological Review*, 44(1): 1–16.

hooks, bell (1981) *Ain't I a Woman: Black Women and Feminism*. London: South End Press.

hooks, bell (1991) *Yearning: Race, Gender and Cultural Politics*. London: Turnaround.

Hutchinson, John and Smith, Anthony D. (eds) (1994) *Nationalism – the Reader*. Oxford: Oxford University Press.

Hyman, A. (1985) *Muslim Fundamentalism*. Institute for the Study of Culture, no. 174.

Ignatieff, M. (1993) *Blood and Belonging: Journeys into the New Nationalisms*. London: BBC Books/Chatto and Windus.

Jakubowicz, Andrew (1984) 'State and ethnicity: multiculturalism as an ideology', *Australia and New Zealand Journal of Sociology*, 17(3).

Janowitz, Morris (1991) *The Professional Soldiers: a Social and Political Portrait*. New York.

Jayasuriya, L. (1990) 'Multiculturalism, citizenship and welfare: new directions for the 1990s'. Paper presented at the 50th Anniversary Lecture Series, Department of Social Work and Social Policy, University of Sydney.

Jayawardena, Kumari (1986) *Feminism and Nationalism in the Third World*. London: Zed.

Jayawardena, Kumari (1995) *The White Woman's Other Burden: Western Women and South Asia during British Rule*. London: Routledge.

Jones, Adam (1994) 'Gender and ethnic conflict in ex-Yugoslavia', *Ethnic and Racial Studies*, 17(1): 115–29.

Jones, Kathleen B. (1990) 'Citizenship in a woman-friendly polity', *Signs*, 15: 4.

Jordan, W.D. (1974) *The White Man's Burden: Historical Origins of Racism in the United States*. Oxford: Oxford University Press.

Joseph, Suad (1993) 'Gender and civil society', *Middle East Report*, no. 183: 22–6.

Kandiyoti, Deniz (1988) 'Bargaining with patriarchy', *Gender and Society*, 2(3): 274–90.

Kandiyoti, Deniz (1991a) 'Identity and its discontents: women and the nation', *Millennium*, 20(3): 429–44.

Kandiyoti, Deniz (ed.) (1991b) *Women, Islam and the State*. London: Macmillan.

Kazi, Seema (1993) 'Women and militarization: a gender perspective'. MA dissertation, ISS, The Hague.

Keane, John (ed.) (1988) *Civil Society and the State: New European Perspectives*. London: Verso.

Kedourie, Elie (1993) *Nationalism* (1960). Cambridge: Blackwell.

Kimble, Judith and Unterhalter, Elaine (1982) '"We opened the road for you, you must go forward": ANC Women's Struggles, 1912–1982', *Feminist Review*, no. 12: 11–36.

King, Ursula (ed.) (1995) *Religion and Gender*. Oxford: Blackwell.

Kitching, Gavin (1985) 'Nationalism: the instrumental passion', *Capital and Class*, 25: 98–116.

Knight, Chris (1991) *Blood Relations: Menstruation and the Origins of Culture*. New Haven, CT: Yale University Press.

Knopfelmacher, Professor (1984) 'Anglomorphism in Australia', *The Age*, Melbourne, 31 March.

Koontz, Claudia (1986) *Mothers in the Fatherland: Women, the Family and Nazi Politics*. London: Cape.

Kosmarskaya, Natalya (1995) 'Women and ethnicity in former day Russia – thoughts on a given theme', in H. Lutz, A. Phoenix and N. Yuval-Davis (eds), *Crossfires: Nationalism, Racism and Gender in Europe*. London: Pluto.

Kosofsky Sedgwick, Eve (1992) 'Nationalisms and sexualities in the age of Wilde', in A. Parker, M. Russo, D. Sommer and P. Yaegger (eds), *Nationalities and Sexualities*. London: Routledge.

Kristeva, Julia (1993) *Nations Without Nationalism*. New York: Columbia University Press.

Kymlicka, Will (1995) *Multicultural Citizenship: a Liberal Theory of Minority Rights*. Oxford: Clarendon Press.

Lacan, J. (1982) 'The meaning of the phallus' (1958), in J. Mitchell and J. Rose (eds), *Feminine Sexuality: Jacques Lacan and the Ecole Freudienne*. London: Macmillan.

Laqueur, T. (1990) *Making Sex*. Cambridge, MA: Harvard University Press.

Laszlo, Ervin (ed.) (1993) *The Multi-Cultural Planet*. Oxford: One World.

Lavie, Smadar (1992) 'Blow-ups in the borderzones: 3rd world Israeli authors' groping for home', *New Formations*, special issue on *Hybridity*, no. 18, Winter.

Lavie, Smadar and Swedenburg, Ted (eds) (1996) *Displacement, Diaspora and Geographies of Identity*. Durham, NC: Duke University Press.

Lechte, John (1994) 'Freedom, community and cultural frontiers'. Paper presented to the conference *Citizenship and Cultural Frontiers*, Staffordshire University, Stoke-on-Trent, 16 September.

Lemelle, S. and Kelly, R. (eds) (1994) *Imagining Home: Class, Culture and Nationalism in the African Diaspora*. London: Verso.

Lenin, V. (1977) *The State and Revolution* (1917). Moscow: Progress.

Lentin, Ronit (1995) 'Woman – the peace activist who isn't there: Israeli and Palestinian women working for peace'. Paper written for the Irish Peace Institute Research Centre, University of Limerick.

Lentin, Ronit (forthcoming) 'Genocide'. Draft entry for the *Women's Studies Encyclopedia*. New York: Simon and Schuster.

Leonardo, Micaela di (1985) 'Morals, mothers, militarism: antimilitarism and feminist theory', *Feminist Studies*, 11(3, Autumn): 599–618.

Lévi-Strauss, Claude (1969) *The Elementary Structures of Kinship*. Boston.

Lewis, Reina (1996) *Gendering Orientalism*. London: Routledge.

Lister, Ruth (1990) *The Exclusive Society: Citizenship and the Poor*. London: Child Poverty Action Group.

Lloyd, Cathy (1994) 'Universalism and difference: the crisis of anti-racism in the UK and France', in A. Rattansi and S. Westwood (eds), *Racism. Modernity and Difference*. Cambridge: Polity.

Lowenhaupt Tsing, Anna (1993) *In the Realms of the Diamond Queen*. Princeton, NJ: Princeton University Press.

Luckman, Thomas (1967) *The Invisible Religion*. London: Macmillan.

Lutz, Helma (1991) 'The myth of the "Other": western representation and images of migrant women of so-called "Islamic background"', *International Review of Sociology*, New Series, no. 2 (April): 121–38.

Macdonald, Sharon, Holden, Pat and Ardener, Shirley (eds) (1987) *Images of Women in Peace and War*. London: Macmillan.

McTighe Musil, Caryn (1990), Preface, in Lisa Albrecht and Rose M. Brewer (eds), *Bridges of Power: Women's Multi-Cultural Alliances*. New York: New Society.

Maitland, Sara (1992) 'Biblicism: a radical rhetoric?', in G. Sahgal and N. Yuval-Davis (eds), *Refusing Holy Orders: Women and Fundamentalism in Britain*. London: Verso. pp. 26–44.

Makhlouf Obermeyer, Carla (1994) 'Reproductive choice in Islam: gender and the state in Iran and Tunisia', in Women Living Under Muslim Laws (eds), *Women's Reproductive Rights in Muslim Communities and Countries: Issues and Resources*. Dossier prepared for the NGO Forum, UN conference *Population and Development Policies*, Cairo.

Mangan, J.A. (ed.) (1996) *Tribal Identities: Nationalism, Europe, Sport*. London: Frank Cass.

Mani, Lata (1989) 'Contentious traditions: the debate on Sati in colonial India', in K. Sangari and S. Vaid (eds), *Recasting Women: Essays in Colonial History*. New Delhi: Kali for Women.

Marsden, G. (1980) *Fundamentalism and American Culture*. Oxford: Oxford University Press.

Marshall, T.H. (1950) *Citizenship and Social Class*. Cambridge: Cambridge University Press.

Marshall, T.H. (1975) *Social Policy in the Twentieth Century* (1965). London: Hutchinson.

Marshall, T.H. (1981) *The Right to Welfare and Other Essays*. London: Heinemann.

Martin, Denis-Constant (1995) 'The choices of identity', *Social Identities*, 1(1): 5–16.

Martin, Jeannie (1991) 'Multiculturalism and feminism', in G. Bottomley, M. deLepervanche and J. Martin (eds), *Intersexions*. Sydney: Allen and Unwin.

Marx, Karl (1975) 'On the Jewish question', in *Early Writings*. Harmondsworth: Penguin. pp. 211–42.

Massey, Doreen (1994) *Space, Place and Gender*. Cambridge: Polity.

Meaney, Geraldine (1993) 'Sex and nation: women in Irish culture and politics', in E. Smyth (ed.), *Irish Women's Studies*. Dublin: Attic Press. pp. 230–44.

Meekosha, Helen and Dowse, Leanne (1996) 'Enabling citizenship: gender, disability and citizenship'. Paper presented at the conference *Women, Citizenship and Difference*, University of Greenwich, July.

Melucci, A. (1989) *Nomads of the Present: Social Movements and Individual Needs in Contemporary Society*. London: Verso.

Mercer, Kubena (1990) 'Welcome to the jungle: identity and diversity in postmodern politics', in J. Rutherford (ed.), *Identity, Community, Culture, Difference*. London: Lawrence and Wishart.

Meyer, John W. (1980) 'The world polity and the authority of the nation-state', in A. Bergesen (ed.), *Studies of the Modern World System*. New York: Academic.

Meznaric, Silva (1995) 'The discourse of endangered nation: ethnicity, gender and reproductive policies in Croatia'. Paper presented at the ESRC seminar series, *Gender, Class and Ethnicity in Post Communist States*, organized by Maxine Molineux, University of London.

Minh-ha, Trinh T. (1989) *Woman, Native, Other*. Bloomington, IN: Indiana University Press.

Modood, Tariq (1988) '"Black": racial equality and Asian identity', *New Community*, 14(3).

Modood, Tariq (1994) 'Political blackness and British Asians', *Sociology*, 28 (November): 859–76.

Moghadam, Valentine (1994) *Gender and National Identity: Women and Politics in Muslim Societies*. London: Zed.

Moghadam, Valentine (forthcoming) 'Revolution'. Draft entry for the *Women's Studies Encyclopedia*. New York: Simon and Schuster.

Mohanty, Chandra Talpade (1991) 'Under western eyes: feminist scholarship and colonial discourses', in C.T. Mohanty, A. Russo and L. Torres (eds), *Third World Women and the Politics of Feminism*. Bloomington, IN: Indiana University Press.

Mohanty, Chandra Talpade, Russo, Ann and Torres, Lourdes (eds) (1991) *Third World Women and the Politics of Feminism*. Bloomington, IN: Indiana University Press.

Molineux, Maxine (1994) 'Women's rights and the international context: some reflections on the post-communist states', *Millennium*, 23(2): 287–314.

Moore, H. (1988) *Feminism and Anthropology*. Oxford: Polity.

Morgan, Robyn (1989) *The Demon Lover: on the Sexuality of Terrorism*. London: Methuen.

Morris, Lydia (1994) *Dangerous Classes: the Underclass and Social Citizenship*. London: Routledge.

Mosse, George L. (1985) *Nationalism and Sexuality: Middle Class Morality and Sexual Norms in Modern Europe*. Madison, WI: University of Wisconsin Press.

Mouffe, Chantal (1993) 'Liberal socialism and pluralism: which citizenship?', in J. Squires (ed.), *Principled Positions*. London: Lawrence and Wishart.

Mullard, Chris (1980) *Racism in Society and Schools*. London: Institute of Education, London University.

Nairn, T. (1977) *The Break-Up of Britain*. London: Verso.

Najmabadi, Afsane (1995) 'Feminisms in an Islamic republic: "years of hardship, years of growth"'. Paper presented at the School of Oriental and African Studies, University of London.

Nandy, Ashis (1983) *The Intimate Enemy: Loss and Recovery of Self under Colonialism*. Oxford: Oxford University Press.

National Peace Council (1995) 'Peace action in Russia and Chechnya' (leaflet). London: NPC.

Nederveen Pieterse, Jan (1994) 'Globalization as hybridization'. Working paper no. 152, Institute of Social Studies, The Hague.

Neuberger, Benjamin (1986) *National Self-Determination in Post-Colonial Africa*. Boulder, CO: Lynne Rienner.

Nicholson, Linda J. (ed.) (1990) *Feminism/Postmodernism*. London: Routledge.

Nimni, Ephraim (1991) *Marxism and Nationalism*. London: Pluto.

Nimni, Ephraim (1996) 'The limits to liberal democracy'. Unpublished paper given at the departmental seminar of the Sociology Subject Groups at the University of Greenwich, London.

Oakley, Ann (1985) *Sex, Gender and Society* (1972). London: Temple Smith.

Oakley, Ann and Mitchell, Juliet (eds) (1997) *Who's Afraid of Feminism*. Harmondsworth: Penguin.

O'Connor, Julia S. (1993) 'Gender, class and citizenship in the comparative analysis of welfare state regimes: theoretical and methodological issues', *British Journal of Sociology*, 44(3): 501–18.

Office of Multi-Cultural Affairs (1989) *National Agenda for a Multi-cultural Australia*. Canberra: Australian Government Printing Service.

Oldfield, Adrian (1990) *Citizenship and Community: Civic Republicanism and the Modern World*. London: Routledge.

Oliver, Michael (1995) *Understanding Disability: from Theory to Practice*. Basingstoke: Macmillan.

Orloff, Ann Shola (1993) 'Gender and the social rights of citizenship: the comparative analysis of gender relations and welfare states', *American Sociological Review*, 58 (June): 303–28.

Ortner, S. (1974) 'Is female to male as nature is to culture?', in M. Rosaldo and L. Lamphere (eds), *Women, Culture and Society*. Stanford, CA: Stanford University Press.

Parekh, Bhiku (1990) 'The Rushdie affair and the British press: some salutary lessons', in *Free Speech*. Report of a seminar by the CRE, London.

Parker, Andrew, Russo, Mary, Sommer, Doris and Yaeger, Patricia (eds) (1992) *Nationalisms and Sexualities*. New York: Routledge.

Pateman, Carole (1988) *The Sexual Contract*. Cambridge: Polity.

Pateman, Carole (1989) *The Disorder of Women*. Cambridge: Polity.

Peled, Alon (1994) 'Force, ideology and contract: the history of ethnic conscription', *Ethnic and Racial Studies*, 17(1): 61–78.

Peled, Yoav (1992) 'Ethnic democracy and the legal construction of citizenship: Arab citizens of the Jewish state', *American Political Science Review*, 86(2): 432–42.

Petchesky, Rosalind and Weiner, Jennifer (1990) *Global Feminist Perspectives on Reproductive Rights and Reproductive Health*. Conference report, Hunter College, New York.

Peterson, V.S. (ed.) (1992) *Gendered States: Feminist (Re)Visions of International Relations Theory*. Boulder, CO: Lynne Rienner.

Petrova, Dimitrina (1993) 'The winding road to emancipation in Bulgaria', in N. Funk and M. Mueller (eds), *Gender, Politics and Post-Communism*. London: Routledge.

Pettman, Jan Jindi (1992) *Living in the Margins: Racism, Sexism and Feminism in Australia*. Sydney: Allen and Unwin.

Pettman, Jan Jindi (1995) 'Race, ethnicity and gender in Australia', in D. Stasiulis and N. Yuval-Davis (eds), *Unsettling Settler Societies*. London: Sage.

Pettman, Jan Jindi (1996) *Worlding Women: a Feminist International Politics*. London: Routledge.

Pheterson, Gail (1990) 'Alliances between women – overcoming internalized oppression and internalized domination', in L. Albrecht and R. Brewer (eds), *Bridges of Power: Women's Multi-Cultural Alliances*. New Society.

Phillips, Anne (1993) *Democracy and Difference*. Cambridge: Polity.

Phillips, Derek (1993) *Communitarian Thought*. Princeton, NJ: Princeton University Press.

Phillips, Melanie (1990) 'Citizenship sham in our secret society', *The Guardian*, 14 September.

Portuguese, Jackie (1996) 'The gendered politics of fertility policies in Israel'. Unpublished PhD dissertation draft, University of Exeter.

Ramazanoglu, Caroline (1989) *Feminism and the Contradictions of Oppression*. London: Routledge.

Rattanzi, Ali (1992) 'Changing the subject? Racism, culture and education', in J. Donald and A. Rattanzi (eds), *Race, Culture, Difference*. London: Sage.

Rattansi, Ali (1994) '"Western" racisms, ethnicities and identities in a "postmodern" frame' in Ali Rattansi and Sally Westwood (eds), *Racism, Modernity and Identity: on the Western Front*. Cambridge: Polity. pp. 15–86.

Rätzel, Nora (1994) 'Harmonious "Heimat" and disturbing "Auslander"', *Feminism and Psychology*, special issue *Shifting Identities, Shifting Racisms* (ed. K. Bhavnani and A. Phoenix), 4(1): 81–98.

Raymond, Janice G. (1993) *Women as Wombs*. San Francisco: Harper.

Rex, John (1995) 'Ethnic identity and the nation state: the political sociology of multi-cultural societies', *Social Identities*, 1(1): 21.

Riley, Denise (1987) 'Does sex have a history? Women and feminism', *New Formations*, no. 1 (Spring).

Riley, Denise (1981a) 'The free mothers', *History Workshop Journal*: 59–119.

Riley, Denise (1981b) 'Feminist thought and reproductive control: the state and the "right to choose", in Cambridge Women Studies Group (eds), *Women in Society: Interdisciplinary Essays*. London: Virago.

Robertson, Roland (1992) *Globalization: Social Theory and Global Culture*. London: Sage.

Roche, Maurice (1987) 'Citizenship, social theory and social change', *Theory and Society*, no. 16: 363–99.

Rosaldo, Renate (1991) 'Reimagining national communities'. Paper presented at the symposium *Colonial Discourses: Postcolonial Theory*, University of Essex, 7–10 July.

Roseneil, Sasha (1995) *Disarming Patriarchy: Feminism and Political Action at Greenham*. Buckingham: Open University Press.

Rowbotham, Sheila (1973) *Hidden from History*. London: Pluto.

Rowbotham, Sheila (1992) *Women in Movement: Feminism and Social Action*. London: Routledge.

Rozario, Santi (1991) 'Ethno-religious communities and gender divisions in Bangladesh: women as boundary markers', in G. Bottomley, M. deLepervanche and J. Martin (eds) (1991) *Intersexions: Gender/Class/Culture/Ethnicity*. Sydney: Allen and Unwin.

Rubin, Gayle (1975) 'The traffic in women: notes on the "political economy" of sex', in Rayner Rapp-Reiter, *Towards an Anthropology of Women*. New York: Monthly Review Press.

Ruddick, Sara (1983) 'Pacifying the forces: drafting women in the interests of peace', *Signs*, 8(3): 490–531.

Ruddick, Sara (1989) *Maternal Thinking: towards a Politics of Peace*. London: The Women's Press.

Sahgal, Gita (1992) 'Secular spaces: the experience of Asian women organizing', in G. Sahgal and N. Yuval-Davis (eds), *Refusing Holy Orders: Women and Fundamentalism in Britain*. London: Virago.

Sahgal, Gita and Yuval-Davis, Nira (eds) (1992) *Refusing Holy Orders: Women and Fundamentalism in Britain*. London: Virago.

Said, Edward (1978) *Orientalism*. London: Routledge.

Sandel, Michael J. (1982) *Liberalism and the Limits of Justice*. Cambridge: Cambridge University Press.

Sartre, Jean-Paul (1948) *Anti-Semite and Jew*. New York: Schoken.

Scales-Trent, Judy (1995) *Notes of a White Black Woman: Race, Colour, Community*. Pennsylvania University Press.

Schierup, Carl-Ulrik (1995) 'Multiculturalism and universalism in the USA and EU Europe'. Paper for the workshop *Nationalism and Ethnicity*, Berne, March.

Schlesinger, Arthur M., Jr. (1992) *The Disuniting of America: Reflections on a Multicultural Society*. New York: Norton.

Schlesinger, Philip (1987) 'On national identity: some conceptions and misconceptions criticized', *Social Science Information*, 26(2).

Schutz, Alfred (1976) 'The stranger: an essay in social psychology'(1944), in A. Brodersen (ed.), *Alfred Schutz: Studies in Social Theory; Collected Papers II*. The Hague: Martinus Nijhoff. pp. 91–106.

Seifert, Ruth (1995) 'Destructive constructions: the military, the nation and gender dualism', in Erika Haas (ed.), *Feminismus und Dekonstruktion*. Munich: Profil Verlag.

Shahak, Israel (1994) *Jewish Religion: the Burden of 3000 Years*. London: Pluto.

Shanin, Theodor (1986) 'Soviet concepts of ethnicity: the case of a missing term', *New Left Review*, no. 158: 113–22.

Shils, Edward (1957) 'Primordial, personal, sacred and civil ties', *British Journal of Sociology*, 7: 113–45.

Showstack Sassoon, Anne (ed.) (1987) *Women and the State: the Shifting Boundaries of Public and Private*. London: Hutchinson.

Siboni, Daniel (1974) *Le nom et le corps*. Paris: University of Paris Press.

Siboni, Daniel (1983) *La juive – une transmission inconscient*. Paris: University of Paris Press.

Signs (1983) Special issue *Women and Violence*, 8(3).

Simmel, George (1950) 'The Stranger', in H.K. Wolff (ed.), *The Sociology of George Simmel*. New York: Free Press of Glencoe. pp. 402–9.

Smith, Anthony (1971) *Theories of Nationalism*. London: Duckworth.

Smith, Anthony (1986) *The Ethnic Origin of Nations*. Oxford: Basil Blackwell.

Smith, Anthony (1995) *Nations and Nationalism in a Global Era*. Cambridge: Polity.

Snyder, L.L. (1968) *The New Nationalism*. Ithaca, NY: Cornell University Press.

Sociology (1989) Special issue *Patriarchy*, 23(2).

Southall Black Sisters (1990) *Against the Grain: a Celebration of Survival and Struggle*. London: SBS.

Soysal, Yasemin (1994) *Limits of Citizenship: Migrants and Postnational Membership in Europe*. Chicago: University of Chicago Press.

Spelman, Elizabeth (1988) *Inessential Woman: Problems of Exclusion in Feminist Thought*. London: The Women's Press.

Spivak, Gayatri Chakravorty (1991) 'Reflections on cultural studies in the post-colonial conjuncture', *Critical Studies*, special issue *Cultural Studies Crossing Borders*, 3(1): 63–78.

Spivak, Gayatri Chakravorty (1993) *Outside in the Teaching Machine*. London: Routledge.

Staffulah Khan, Verity (ed.) (1979) *Minority Families in Britain: Support and Stress*. London: Macmillan.

Stalin, J.C. (1972) *The National Question and Leninism* (1929). Calcutta: Mass Publications.

Stasiulis, Daiva and Yuval-Davis, Nira (eds) (1995) *Unsettling Settler Societies: Articulations of Gender, Race, Ethnicity and Class*. London: Sage.

Stiehm, Judith Hicks (1989) *Arms and the Enlisted Woman*. Philadelphia: Temple University Press.

Stolcke, Verena (1987) 'The nature of nationality'. Paper presented at the conference *Women and the State*, Wissenschaftsinstitut, Berlin.

Stolcke, Verena (1995) 'Talking culture: new boundaries, new rhetorics of exclusion in Europe', *Current Anthropology*, 16(1): 1–23.

Strathern, Marilyn (1996a) 'Enabling identity? Biology, choice and the new reproductive technologies', in S. Hall and P. du Gay (eds), *Questions of Cultural Identity*. London: Sage. pp. 37–52.

Strathern, Marilyn (1996b) 'Kinship knowledge'. Paper presented at the international symposium *Governing Medically Assisted Human Reproduction*, University of Toronto, February.

Tabet, Paola (1996) 'Natural fertility, forced reproduction', in D. Leonard and L. Atkins (eds), *Sex in Question: French Materialist Feminism*. London: Taylor and Francis.

Tajfel, H. (1965) 'Some psychological aspects of the colour problem', in R. Hooper (ed.), *Colour in Britain*. London: BBC.

Thornton Dill, Bonnie (1988) 'The dialectics of black womanhood', in Sandra Harding (ed.), *Feminism and Methodology*. Bloomington, IN: Indiana University Press.

Tillich, Paul (1957) *The Dynamics of Faith*. New York: Harper and Row.

Tsagarousianou, Roza (1995) '"God, patria and home": "reproductive politics" and nationalist (re)definitions of women in East/Central Europe', *Social Identities*, 1(2): 283–313.

Turner, Bryan (1990) 'Outline of a theory on citizenship', *Sociology*, 24(2): 189–218.

Turner, Bryan (1994) *Orientalism, Postmodernism and Globalism*. London: Routledge.

Urdang, Stephanie (1989) *And Still They Dance: Women, War and the Struggle for Change in Mozambique*. New York: Monthly Review Press.

Van den Berghe, P. (1979) *The Ethnic Phenomenon*. New York: Elsevier.

Vargas, Virginia (1995) 'Women's movement in Peru: rebellion into action', in S. Wieringa (ed.), *Subversive Women*. London: Zed.

Vogel, Ursula (1989) 'Is citizenship gender specific?'. Paper presented at PSA Annual Conference, April.

Voronina, Olga A. (1994) 'Soviet women and politics: on the brink of change', in B.J. Nelson and N. Chowdhury (eds), *Women and Politics Worldwide*. New Haven, CT: Yale University Press. pp. 722–36.

Walby, Sylvia (1990) *Theorizing Patriarchy*. Oxford: Blackwell.

Walby, Sylvia (1994) 'Is citizenship gendered?', *Sociology*, 28(2): 379–95.

Walker, Martin (1993) 'Sisters take the wraps off the brothers', *The Guardian*, 6 May.

Wallerstein, Immanuel (1974) *The Modern World System: Capitalist Agriculture and the Origins of the European World Economy in the 16th Century*. New York: Academic.

Wallerstein, Immanuel (1980) *The Modern World System II: Mercantilism and the Consolidation of the World Economy 1650–1750*. New York: Academic.

Wallerstein, Immanuel (1989) *The Modern World System III: the Second Era of Great Expansion of the Capitalist World Economy 1730–1840*. New York: Cambridge University Press.

Warring, Annette (1996) 'National bodies: collaboration and resistance in a gender perspective'. Paper presented at the session *Women and War* at the conference *European Social Science History*, the Netherlands, May.

Weed, Elizabeth (1989) *Coming to Terms: Feminism, Theory, Politics.* London: Routledge.

Werbner, Pnina and Yuval-Davis, Nira (eds) (1988) *Women, Citizenship and Difference*. London: Zed Books.

Wexler, Philip (1990) 'Citizenship in a semiotic society', in BryanTurner (ed.), *Theories of Modernity and Postmodernity*. London: Sage.

WGNRR (1991) Women's Global Network for Reproductive Rights, *Newsletter*, no. 35 April–June.

Wheelwright, Julie (1991) 'Women at war', *The Guardian*, 24 January.

Wieringa, Saskia (ed.) (1995) *Subversive Women: Women's Movements in Africa, Asia, Latin America and the Caribbean*. London: Zed.

Wieviorka, Michel (1994) 'Racism in Europe: unity and diversity', in A. Rattansi and Sallie Westwood (eds), *Racism, Modernity and Identity*. Cambridge: Polity.

Williams, Raymond (1983) *Keywords*. London: Fontana.

Wilson, William J. (1987) *The Truly Disadvantaged*. Chicago: University of Chicago Press.

WING (1985) *Worlds Apart: Women under Immigration and Nationality Laws*, Women, Immigration and Nationality Group. London: Pluto.

Wobbe, Theresa (1995) 'The boundaries of community: gender relations and racial violence', in H. Lutz, A. Phoenix and N. Yuval-Davis (eds), *Crossfires: Nationalism, Racism and Gender in Europe*. London: Pluto.

Woollacott, Angela (1993) 'Sisters and brothers in arms: family, class and gendering in World War I Britain' in M. Cooke and A. Woollacott (eds), *Gendering War Talk*. Princeton, NJ: Princeton University Press.

WREI (1992) *Women in the Military: International Perspectives*, Women Research and Education Institute. Proceedings of the conference, Washington, DC, 30 April.

Yeatman, Anna (1992) 'Minorities and the politics of difference', *Political Theory Newsletter*, 4(1): 1–11.

Young, Iris Marion (1989) 'Polity and group difference: a critique of the ideal of universal citizenship', *Ethics*, 99.

Yuval-Davis, Nira (1980) 'The bearers of the collective: women and religious legislation in Israel', *Feminist Review*, no. 4: 15–27.

Yuval-Davis, Nira (1984) 'Anti-semitism, anti-Zionism and the struggle against racism', *Spare Rib*, April.

Yuval-Davis, Nira (1985) 'Front and rear: the sexual division of labour in the Israeli army', *Feminist Studies*, 11(3): 649–76.

Yuval-Davis, Nira (1987a) 'Marxism and Jewish nationalism', *History Workshop Journal*, no. 24 (Autumn).

Yuval-Davis, Nira (1987b) 'The Jewish collectivity and national reproduction in Israel', in Khamsin (ed.), *Women in the Middle East*. London: Zed.

Yuval-Davis, Nira (1989) 'National reproduction and the "demographic race" in Israel', in

N. Yuval-Davis and F. Anthias (eds), *Woman–Nation–State*. London: Macmillan. pp. 92–109.

Yuval-Davis, Nira (1991a) 'The gendered Gulf War: women's citizenship and modern warfare', in Haim Bresheeth and Nira Yuval-Davis (eds), *The Gulf War and the New World Order*. London: Zed.

Yuval-Davis, Nira (1991b) 'The citizenship debate: women, the state and ethnic processes', *Feminist Review*, no. 39: 58–68.

Yuval-Davis, Nira (1991c) 'Anglomorphism and the construction of ethnic and racial divisions in Australia and Britain', in R. Nile (ed.), *Immigration and the Politics of Ethnicity and Race in Australia and Britain*. Canberra: Bureau of Immigration.

Yuval-Davis, Nira (1992a) 'Jewish fundamentalism and women's empowerment', in G. Sahgal and N. Yuval-Davis (eds), *Refusing Holy Orders: Women and Fundamentalism in Britain*. London: Verso. pp. 198–226.

Yuval-Davis, Nira (1992b) 'Multi-culturalism, fundamentalism and women', in J. Donald and A. Rattansi (eds), *Race, Culture and Difference*. London: Sage.

Yuval-Davis, Nira (1993) 'Gender and nation', *Ethnic and Racial Studies*, 16(4): 621–32.

Yuval-Davis, Nira (1994a) 'Identity politics and women's ethnicity', in V.M. Moghadam (ed.), *Identity Politics and Women*. Boulder, CO: Westview Press.

Yuval-Davis, Nira (1994b) 'Women, ethnicity and empowerment', in K. Bhavnani and A. Phoenix (eds), *Shifting Identities, Shifting Racisms*, special issue of *Feminism and Psychology*, 4(1): 179–98.

Yuval-Davis, Nira and Anthias, Floya (eds) (1989) *Woman–Nation–State*. London: Macmillan.

Zajovic, Stasa (ed.) (1994) *Women for Peace*. Belgrade: Women In Black.

Zerai, Worku (1994) 'Women in the Eritrean military'. Unpublished project for a course *Gender and Nation*, Institute of Social Studies, The Hague.

Zubaida, S. (1989) 'Nations: old and new. Comments on Anthony D. Smith's "The myth of the 'modern nation' and the myths of nations"'. Paper presented at the *Anthropology Seminar Series*, University College, London.

INDEX